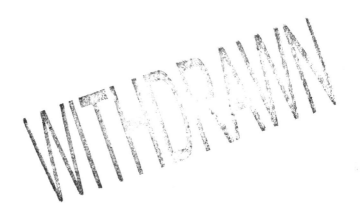

Kidding Around

Kidding Around

The Child in Film and Media

Edited by Alexander N. Howe and Wynn Yarbrough

B L O O M S B U R Y

NEW YORK • LONDON • NEW DELHI • SYDNEY

Bloomsbury Academic

An imprint of Bloomsbury Publishing Inc

1385 Broadway	50 Bedford Square
New York	London
NY 10018	WC1B 3DP
USA	UK

www.bloomsbury.com

Bloomsbury is a registered trade mark of Bloomsbury Publishing Plc

First published 2014

Library of Congress Cataloging-in-Publication Data

Kidding around : the child in film and media / edited by Alexander N. Howe and Wynn Yarbrough.

pages cm

Papers presented at a conference held at the University of the District of Columbia, September, 2008.

Includes bibliographical references and index.

ISBN 978-1-62356-056-0 (hardback : alk. paper) 1. Children in motion pictures–Congresses. 2. Children in mass media–Congresses. 3. Mass media and children–Congresses. I. Howe, Alexander N., 1973- editor of compilation. II. Yarbrough, Wynn William, editor of compilation.

PN1995.9.C45K465 2014

791.43′6523–dc23

2013035150

ISBN: HB: 978-1-6235-6056-0
ePDF: 978-1-6235-6054-6
ePub: 978-1-6235-6120-8

Typeset by Fakenham Prepress Solutions, Fakenham, Norfolk NR21 8NN
Printed and bound in the United States of America

Contents

Acknowledgments   vii

Introduction: Representations and Renegotiations: Childhood and Its
Uses *Wynn Yarbrough and Alexander N. Howe*   1

Part 1   Rites of Passage and Impasse

1   Betwixt and Between: The Child in M. Night Shyamalan's Films
   Kevin A. Wisniewski   11

2   The Monstrous Masculine: Abjection and Todd Solondz's
   Happiness *Adam P. Wadenius*   33

3   Only a Child: Spectacles of Innocence in the *Lolita* Films *Brian Walter*   51

Part 2   Childhood as Text

4   The "Rubbing Off" of "Art and Beauty": Child Citizenship, Literary
   Engagement, and the Anglo-American Playground and Play Center
   Movement *Michelle Beissel Heath*   71

5   "The Studio World Surprised and Disturbed Ruth": The Diffident
   Stage Mother and the Difficult Child in a Post-War Novel by Noel
   Streatfeild *Sally Sims Stokes*   95

6   Building a Mystery: *Relative Fear* and the 1990s Autistic
   Thriller *Chris Foss*   119

7   Pundit Knows Best: The Self-Help Boom, Brand Marketing, and
   The O'Reilly Factor for Kids *Michelle Ann Abate*   139

Part 3   Disney and Its Progeny

8   Power to the Princess: Disney and the Creation of the Twentieth-
   Century Princess Narrative *Bridget Whelan*   167

9   Surreal Estate: Building Self-Identity in *Monster House*
    Michael Howarth   193

10 The Wild and the Cute: Disney Animation and Environmental
    Awareness *David Whitley*   211

Conclusion: Criticism and Multicultural Children's Films *Iris Shepard
and Ian Wojcik-Andrews*   223

Notes on Contributors   233
Index   237

Acknowledgments

The editors would like to thank the Provost's Office at the University of the District of Columbia for generously supporting the conference that generated the essays collected in this volume. A special thanks is also due to Deirdre Evans-Pritchard for her tireless efforts organizing the film festival that accompanied the original conference.

We are grateful to the following publishers for granting permission to reprint these essays in the current volume:

Chapter 2, "The Monstrous Masculine: Abjection and Todd Solondz's *Happiness*," by Adam Wadenius, originally appeared in *Widescreen* 1, no. 1 2009.

Chapter 7, "Pundit Knows Best: The Self-Help Book, Brand Marketing and *The O'Reilly Factor for Kids*," first appeared in Michelle Ann Abate's *Raising Your Kids Right: Children's Literature and American Political Conservativism* (Rutgers, 2010).

A prior version of Chapter 8, "Power to the Princess: Disney and the Creation of the 20th Century Princess Narrative," by Bridget Whelan, appeared in the journal *Interdisciplinary Humanities* in the Spring of 2012.

Introduction: Representations and Renegotiations: Childhood and Its Uses

Wynn Yarbrough and Alexander N. Howe

University of the District of Columbia

As scholarship of media evolves in the second decade of this new millennium, intersections with traditional modes of criticism have produced rich and often divided conversations. Contemporary media theory has left the "high" Humanist binaries of "natural" and "commercial" art far behind, and inquiries that combine cultural theory and discussions of consumption and marketing have become de rigueur. And yet academic analysis of children and media, particularly in the US, remains in the initial stages of reconciling the interactions of audience, message, and marketing.

A necessary point of intersection to open the examination of children's media is the field of children's literature. Here, scholars have been studying children's works from the perspectives of gender and thematic criticism, semiotics, cultural studies, new historicism, commercial marketing, and a host of other avenues of inquiry. Journals like *The Lion and the Unicorn* and the *Children's Literature Association Quarterly* have offered a platform for analyzing the sociological, cultural, and political mechanisms driving a vast array of media (e.g. fiction, film, TV programs, poetry, illustrations, and new media) designated for children. In many ways, these journals, and organizations like the Children's Literature Association, have "legitimized" the field of scholarship known as "children's literature," even though the organization and the conferences, journals, and books it produces examine all sorts of children's media. The chapters collected in this volume continue these ongoing discussions surrounding children's media.

The study of children and media is not without its pitfalls, and we are wise to remember Marcia Kinder's comments in her *Kids' Media Culture*—a work that discusses toys, games, TV shows, film, and other child-targeted media alike—regarding the ethical entanglements that await any critical discussion of children's media:

Those who see kids primarily as passive victims tend to focus on a single element of media culture (such as violence or pornography), which can readily be isolated for study or censorship, and whose representations and dangers are presumed to affect all children in the same way. Thus, it is hardly surprising that this camp tends to rely on monolithic depictions not only of the texts, but also of the children they affect, the media through which they are transmitted, and the eras in which they are produced and consumed.[1]

Kinder positions critical studies of children's media next to popular commentary acknowledging political pressures that studying children and their media can produce—often to extremely misguided and damaging purposes. For instance, social scientists are "certain" that violence found in games is to blame for children committing actual violence, and many specialists have gone so far as to lend their expertise to lawsuits to ban or censor such games. In so doing, they have categorized children in a monolithic manner, too hurried to examine the social contexts of textual consumption and production; likewise they ignore the history of children and their representations in media, as well as the increasingly sophisticated consumption of media by children.

This volume responds to such issues, while also casting a wide net to include investigations into how children are represented, recycled, transformed, used, and misused by adults in both media targeted at children and media that represents children for a broader (i.e. adult) audience. This anthology was produced from the conference "Kidding Around: The Child in Film and Media" held at the University of the District of Columbia in September 2008. The conference was composed of engaging interdisciplinary panel sessions on topics as various as cartoons, Hannah Montana, horror films, and autism, culminating in a memorable keynote address given by Linda Simensky, Vice President of PBSKIDS. Screenings of films from all over the globe ran concurrently throughout the weekend, demonstrating the great variety of culturally determined ways in which children are integrated into the world—from the mythic African village in *Kirikou*, directed by Michel Ocelot, to Peter Jackson's 1950s New Zealand depicted from the imaginative perspective of two girls in *Heavenly Creatures*. Culled from the most engaging presentations, this collection addresses a variety of issues and themes discussed at the sessions along with the "larger ecology" of children's literature and its relationship with media.[2]

While this collection has its largest concentration in US-based media—particularly film—we believe that the theoretical models employed in these essays possess the sophistication necessary to be imported into other critical contexts to analyze primary works from other nations and cultures. Because media companies and their distribution continue to grow as an international enterprise, media scholarship increasingly becomes a global exercise with exciting results. The bias toward film in the anthology reflects the ever-growing interest in children's film in the academy, but at the same time we are hopeful that the essays included on children's literature, playgrounds, and teen self-help manuals offer scholars insight into other avenues of study in children's media.

In the first section of this anthology, entitled "Rites of Passage and Impasse," scholars explore representations of children in a variety of films and examine the ways in which children are transformed by forces such as trauma and environment. Kevin Wisniewski argues, in "Betwixt and Between: Reading the Child in M. Night Shyamalan's Films," that the child characters in M. Night Shyamalan's films inhabit spaces where normalcy and reality give way to fantasy or what Victor Turner has labeled a "liminal space." Incorporating a Foucauldian approach to pertinent representations of children in modern history, Wisniewski explores Shyamalan's use of lighting, mise-en-scène, and narrative structure, as well as the director's reworking of horror conventions to position children as "others" in his work. The second essay of this section, "The Monstrous Masculine: Abjection and Todd Solondz's *Happiness*," by Adam Wadenius, explores abjection and deviant masculinity in Todd Solondz's *Happiness*. Beginning with Julia Kristeva's theorization of the abject—a category more typically represented as feminine in horror films—Wadenius analyzes the monstrous portrayal of male maturation in Solondz's film as crucial to understanding the perverse underpinnings of the patriarchal family structure in today's social climate. Like Shyamalan, Solondz uses the conventions of the horror film as artistic tools to manipulate audience expectations about children and their development, albeit in a much more sinister fashion that explores, as Wadenius argues, the contemporary crisis of masculinity. In the final essay of this section, "Only a Child: Spectacles of Innocence in the Lolita films," Brian Walter compares the film versions of *Lolita* directed by Stanley Kubrick and Adrian Lyne. Walter argues that Kubrick incorporates a disruptive visual space for childhood apart from Humbert's manipulations—a complicated independence, to be sure—while Lyne uses childhood to reinforce the self-serving perspective of Humbert's narration. In the midst of this discussion, Walter critically engages scholarship on spectatorship theory in cinema, and considers a question central to both Kubrick and Lyne's projects: how is childhood perversely consumed within the media?

In "Childhood as Text," the second section of the anthology, scholars examine how childhood can be "read" and then subsequently made politically or commercially "useful." In her essay, "The 'Rubbing Off' of 'Art and Beauty': Child Citizenship, Literary Engagement, and the Anglo-American Playground Movement," Michelle Beissel Heath plots the curious relationship between the spaces of playgrounds and parks and the ideological notions of child citizenship. This expansive historical analysis broadens to engage literary analysis, as the author links public policy and adult fears evident in the Anglo-American playground movement, while examining the representation of playgrounds in children's works by authors such as Charles Dickens and J. M. Barrie. In the next chapter, "The Studio World Surprised and Disturbed Ruth: The Diffident Stage Mother and the Difficult Child in a Post-War Novel by Noel Streatfeild," Sally Stokes argues that Noel Streatfeild's novel, *Love in a Mist*, critiques the child star system of the mid-twentieth century at the same time as it presciently explores childhood in ways consonant with subsequent child development theories from behavioral psychologists, sociologists, and historians. Drawing upon her own significant research in the Streatfeild archive, Stokes' article demonstrates that while we may consider a novel like *Love in a Mist* as marketed toward adults, the representation of children in such a novel should not be ignored for what it may tell us about an era's constructed notion of childhood. By examining the child stars and stage mothers of the text, Stokes argues that Streatfeild allows the reader insight into the influence of mid-century parenting literature on changing notions of childhood. In the following chapter, Chris Foss critiques the "Autistic Thriller" in his examination of the films *Relative Fear*, *Silent Fall*, and *Mercury Rising*. In his essay "Building a Mystery: The 1990s Autistic Thriller," Foss proposes that these films invoke the autistic child as an object of pity, leaving them to function as little more than a simple plot device. In light of this unapologetic "use" of children with disabilities, the author argues that there is little that is transgressive in these presentations of autism on the screen, contrary to more optimistic critical accounts. Foss' analysis incorporates a variety of methods of disability studies to construct a unique work of autist criticism. Such specificity is all the more urgent, the author argues, given the all too familiar pathologization of Asperger's Syndrome in the media coverage of the tragedy at Sandy Hook Elementary in December 2012. Perhaps the most regressive work examined in this collection of essays is Bill O'Reilly's *The O'Reilly Factor for Kids*. Michelle Abate's essay, "Pundit Knows Best: The Self-Help Boom, Brand Marketing and *The O'Reilly Factor for Kids*," dissects the narrative content, cultural commentary, and commercial success of O'Reilly's work with the marketing of his conservative franchise. O'Reilly's "advice book" comes under close scrutiny as Abate reveals that the ethos of "compassion" and "community" invoked throughout O'Reilly's text in fact requires that race, culture, and ethnicity be marginalized. According to Abate, this is due to the ever-present adult interest in inculcating children with the political attitudes and messages found in O'Reilly's television franchise. As groups and individuals worldwide seek to "normalize" childhood in works aimed at children with a variety of motivations, Abate's criticism of O'Reilly's joining of his brand with children's media serves as a critical touchstone for monitoring the "incorporation" of children's media across the globe. This exploitation, when considered next to innocence, contributes to the overwhelming conclusion running through this book, that is, childhood is a group to be exploited by the "National Entertainment State," particularly by adults.[3]

In Section Three, "Disney and Its Progeny," the authors consider the incredible role of Disney and other animation companies like Pixar—which was purchased by Disney in 2006—have in mediating representations of childhood and the environment. In "Power to the Princess: Disney and the Creation of the 20th Century Princess Narrative," Bridget Whelan examines the phenomenon of Disney Princess culture, a remarkably successful multimedia brand that was launched by the studio in 2000. Whelan analyzes Disney's seemingly monolithic princess narrative as it develops on the screen, beginning with *Snow White and the Seven Dwarves* in 1937 and on to *Brave* in 2012. Read alongside this development is the emergence of the "anti-Disney" princesses found in feminist-inspired children's literature. These more hopeful models of female independence, imagination, and action are used to measure the modicum of change and possibility presented in recent Disney princess films. In the following chapter, Michael Howarth analyzes the externalization of psychological dilemmas via a myriad of cinematographic devices and genre play in Gil Kenan's *Monster House*. Howarth's essay, "Surreal Estate: Building Self-Identity in Monster House," explores, through the lens of psychoanalysis, crises like identity conflict and role confusion in the passage from childhood to adolescence. These teenage years of angst and transition provide productive scaffolding to Kenan's work and Howarth's analysis. In an innovative work of ecocriticism, "The Wild and the Cute: Disney Animation and Environmental Awareness," David Whitley turns his attention to the fascinating portrayal of environmentalism in Disney animation, addressing its uses in films such as *Bambi* and *Finding Nemo*. The impact of Disney's representations of the natural environment is not to be underestimated. Whitley proposes that despite the complex relationship between consumerism, environmentalism, and capitalism in these films, Disney's aesthetic language dramatizes real and lasting notions of what environmentalism can look like in the animated film genre.

In the conclusion to the volume, "Criticism and Multicultural Children's Films," Iris Shepard and Ian Wojcik-Andrews reflect upon the larger issues common to these collected essays and comment upon directions for twenty-first century multicultural children's media criticism. First and foremost, the authors argue, scholarship—and, importantly, teaching beginning as early as elementary school—must expand its purview beyond Hollywood. Opening the discussion to non-Western media is an exceptionally powerful device to illuminate the culturally-determined narratives of childhood, particularly as these narratives relate to history, class, race, gender, ability, and age. Demonstrating what such work might look like, Shepard and Wojcik-Andrews analyze the ending of *Harry Potter and the Deathly Hallows 2* in comparison with an example from Kurdish cinema, Siddiq Barmak's 2003 *Osama*. The stark contrast between these two films clearly demonstrates that culturally determined cinematic tropes—particularly the market demand for a happy ending—all too often leave ideological contradictions neatly displaced. Incorporating "countercultural" children's films like *Osama* into multicultural children's media criticism allows us to reclaim open and progressive readings that are often silenced when Hollywood alone is left to articulate what a child is and might be.

Notes

1　Marsha Kinder (ed.), *Kid's Media Culture (Console-ing Passions)* (Durham and London: Duke University Press, 1999).

2　Annette Wannamaker and Ian Wojcik-Andrews, "Forum: Children's Literature and Media Introduction," *Children's Literature Association Quarterly* 35, no. 4 (Winter 2010): 416.

3　Ibid., 417.

Bibliography

Kinder, Marsha (ed.), *Kid's Media Culture (Console-ing Passions)*. Durham and London: Duke University Press, 1999.

Wannamaker, Annette and Ian Wojcik-Andrews. "Forum: Children's Literature and Media Introduction." *Children's Literature Association Quarterly* 35, no. 4 (Winter 2010): 415–17.

Part One

Rites of Passage and Impasse

Betwixt and Between: The Child in M. Night Shyamalan's Films

Kevin A. Wisniewski

University of Maryland, Baltimore County

At Apartment 16B at the Cove, Cleveland Heap rocks back and forth, loudly chomping down on a chocolate chip cookie and sipping a glass of milk, which leaves a mustache on his upper lip. He leans back on the living room sofa and slowly curls into the fetal position—hands tucked between his knees, one leg innocently flailing loosely in the air like a child ready for bedtime—and sweetly asks his young friend Young-Soon Choi, "Tell her it's a beautiful story. Are there any parts that might be good to hear?"[1] Young Su translates off screen in the background to her mother. After a moment of observing Mr Heap's childlike transformation, the camera cuts to the women who are sitting across the coffee table, giggling. The performance allows Mr Heap full access to the Eastern bedtime story about Narfs, sea nymphs who visit the Earth to inspire their vessel or human counterpart. Days earlier, Mr Heap encountered Story, a young nymph who has been sent to enthuse the work of a young writer who lives in the complex. But, now out of the water, Story is stranded at the complex, unable to return home because of the wolf-like Scrunts who threaten to attack. It is only in accessing this child-like innocence and unquestioning imagination and faith in the legend of Narfs, and in themselves and their identities and roles in this story-turned-reality, that the tenants of the Cove can work together to find resolution in the tale and to safely return Story home to her Blue World.

The significance of youth to Shyamalan's narrative, *Lady in the Water* (2006), quickly takes shape: deriving from Victorian sentiments, the child here may not only be read as innocent victim who fleshes out the gloom, sadness, and violence of the world, but also as a free-spirited, emotional dreamer who is capable of both seeing hope and walking towards it. For Philip Davis, the nineteenth-century child offered "an *un*consciousness at the very root of human existence … [and] gave access to a realm of feeling and imagination prior to both the jadedness of ageing and the skepticism of the times."[2] This also rings true for the child figures in M. Night Shyamalan's films, which are often constructed like fairytales themselves or whose plots are shaped by characters recovering myths and folklore. Within the layers of magic and the journey of his characters unfolds a moral story. Through Mr Heap and his adult company, we encounter both magical and innocent images of the child within Story; her vessel, Vick Ran and his sister; and even the neighborhood boy Joey Dury, who acts as "The Interpreter," a reader of signs via a cupboard full of cereal boxes. We observe the film's adult characters perform childlike mannerisms and activities in an effort to learn and understand the construct of the fairytale in which they are now a part.

Despite their unique insights into the world around them and their often-demure personalities, the child figures here are complicated with their links to evil and danger. For instance, it is clear from her appearance that Story does not belong in this world and is, in fact, the cause of the disruption in these tenants' lives. Moreover, in an intimate conversation in the bathroom between Story and Vick, the audience finds out that Vick's fate ultimately leads to his premature and violent death. Still, the journey of, or perhaps even through, youth as told by Shyamalan may be read as cathartic for some characters. Some become conscious of the flaws in their own relationships and community at large and reconnect to them, and Mr Heap himself is allowed the opportunity to finally grieve the death of his family. But, the larger question remains open at the end of his films: do these characters really gain a new sense of freedom and peace or do the laws and narratives to which these characters are bound only further limit and obstruct?

In his book *Charles Dickens in Cyberspace*, Jay Clayton reveals how contemporary American culture is inherently linked to Romanticism, and nineteenth-century Britain in general. The multimodal, "undisciplined culture" shared by Romanticism and postmodernism is what interests Clayton. While he examines the blurred boundaries of technology, hard sciences, humanities, and popular culture by looking at the past, it may be said that Shyamalan's films blend or blur cinematic genres of science fiction, horror, and suspense and reconceptualize the contemporary from the past. (This may be seen in how Shyamalan's style as a director is shaped by these genres, but also how each film uses past events and memories to shape its narrative arc.) But thematically, the films also address an undisciplined culture in the sense that they reveal breaks or gaps in social order. For Shyamalan, the figure of the child is key in shoring up these gaps and ultimately serves as a vehicle through which constructs are visible and understood by the child's adult counterparts (and his audiences). Here, the image of child is grounded, yet more dynamic than its Victorian precursors. They are ambiguous, no longer tied to archetypes of victim or villain. Elizabeth Tucker traces the evolution of nine archetypes of the child in folklore studies from the nineteenth century to the present—"the savage child," "the secret-keeping child," "the magic-making child," "the cerebral child," "the taboo-breaking child," "the monstrous child," "the bubble-wrapped child," "the creative, conservative child," and "the evolving child."[3] Shyamalan's portraits of the child blend, blur, the characteristics defining each of these categories. Collier extends this by highlighting how the film's narrative itself also blurs genre: "the film, in the process of veering repeatedly from supernatural thriller to period romance to fairy tale to political allegory, thematizes the quite relevant, and contemporary, political question of the ethics of deliberate fictiveness and myth-making in governance."[4] Within the increasingly fragmented and paradoxical cultural logic extent in contemporary culture, the child represents a contagious element in culture, an antinomian impulse that simultaneously leads towards the refusal of law and, with this new awareness, towards the recodification of it. By demonstrating how the social works, Shyamalan's child allows the chance to see how it can also unwork—and an opportunity for each of us to consider how we look at the world and why.

Ideologically, the horror and science fiction genres are oriented towards a description of some otherness, of something beyond that which mainstream society conceives as conventional. This may be seen in terms of the visually realizing of an alternate culture or social order or by depicting images of the grotesque or monstrous and then questioning how this process or image affects the boundaries of past conceptions of what it means to be human. In particular, these genres make existentialist inquiries concerning mortality, ethics, and purpose that aid finding an individual's place in the world. But this introspective journey usually begins with a physical investigation of an unknown or myste-rious force. Alien identities are very much a part of popular culture, and, while their portraits span from angelic and protecting to monstrous and life-threat-ening, fear and angst are often the initial human reactions to the "inhuman."

Aliens—foreigners from beyond this world—are indeed commonplace to M. Night Shyamalan's films, whose cinematographic style and mise-en-scène also owe much to the aforementioned genres. Initially distinguishing themselves as the binary opposite to these "other" creatures, Shyamalan's protagonists and audiences simultaneous explore and reconstruct the uncanny identity of these alien figures together. However, it is not the protagonists' expeditions, but rather the visions of their child protégés that provide access to the awareness and understanding of this otherness. In fact, it is *the child* (and his or her kinship with this Other), not the existence or construction of the otherworldly alien identities, which raise the larger questions concerning the meaning of life and the universe. Without the existence or intervention of these perceptive children, this investigative process might never take place. By depicting the child as contagious sage, Shyamalan reveals the child as a critical component in the construction of ideology.

Children of the Victorian Age, we are the people who fear contagion, restrained by a cultural logic marked by "panic about the social body" and obsessed by purity and danger. Foucault remarks that "in order to see perfect disciplines functioning, rulers dreamt of a state of plague … [T]he image of plague stands for all forms of confusion and disorder."[5] While Foucault sees this plague as an attempt to control the masses, in a different context, Mary Douglas discusses the way that a cultural obsession with pollution ideas makes possible a shoring up of social structures when political or moral authority is weak.[6] Similarly, Julia Kristeva has argued that when paternal structures of social authority are in crisis, a focus upon "abjection" and defilement occurs in a kind of return of fundamental cultural anxieties.[7] It might be said, then, that the topic of contagion offers the possibility of a resolution of vexing questions of law, morality, social order and some revelation to larger universal concepts of authority, power, and knowledge.

Perhaps stemming from a nineteenth-century, Dickensian model, early films depict children in a romantic setting as natural innocents victimized in a harsh and inhumane world. Foucault might then argue that such a figure was a perfect excuse to establish and implement laws designed to "protect" the child. Cinematically, this traditional image was later corrupted, shifting into the cherubic child's converse: a monstrous and demonic creature creating chaos and disorder. In her book *Children Without Childhood*, Marie Winn chronicles the cinematic development of the image of the child:

> In the sixties a new sort of child appeared in motion pictures; from a sweet, idealized Shirley Temple or Margaret O'Brien poppet, the movie child grew into

a monster. First came … a prepubescent killer in *The Bad Seed* in 1956. Then, in *Village of the Damned* (1962), sweet faced children turned out to be malevolent beings from outer space. The trend accelerated in the late sixties and early seventies, culminating in the appearance of a spate of satanic juveniles on movie screens. *Rosemary's Baby* was the first, a mild exercise in horror compared to *The Exorcist*, which featured … a darling little girl transformed just at puberty, into a ravening, sexually rapacious, and murderous creature.[8]

Whether envisioned as angelic or demonic, the child is a compelling motif in cinema capturing the capabilities of human emotion and creativity. In the case of a film like *The Exorcist*, audiences are filled with compassion and sentimentality towards the suffering child and infected with fear of the demons possessing her, a fear that what attacks the child may be transmitted to us all. The popularity of the film also reveals the human fascination with the monstrous, the unknown, and the "spectacle of suffering."[9] While Shyamalan's child certainly descends from both models, the figure remains detached from the antecedent examples of horror and sci-fi, occupying a space that neither qualifies it as the passive victim nor as the monstrous attacker. Whereas Regan in *The Exorcist* transforms from one model to the other, Shyamalan's central child exists in a liminal space between the norm and otherness, the weak and the strong, belonging to neither reality nor the alien world depicted in each film.

It is its indefinable status which allows the child to maneuver from acceptable mainstream culture (or perhaps, in other terms, the adult or patriarchal world) into the uncharted realms occupied by the Other. By entering into the unknown and mysterious and reacting or interacting, however unpleasantly, with the otherworld or the supernatural, the child is identified as an outsider. Within this new construct, the child maintains a unique position in society, potentially capable of assimilation into the norm, and yet still privy to the dealings of the Other and its potential dangers. Regarded as abnormal (by their respective societies and the audience), this curiosity in and perception of the Other forces the child to experience its own sense of alienation as the power temporarily allows the child to escape its predestined role in society. As the monstrous force is defeated, the child, whose position outside the social hierarchy now threatens a power struggle, stands alone as the symbol of evil and must be disciplined and returned to its appropriate place in the world. So to position Shyamalan's child, it becomes necessary to first situate both the Other and the opposing ruling order.

Approaching the figure from this perspective, childhood is a relatively new construct in modern society. Depicting the contemporary sensibility towards the child's welfare, Lloyd deMause introduces *The History of Childhood* by assessing the history of childhood as a "nightmare from which we have only recently begun to awaken. The further back in history one goes, the lower the level of child care, and the more likely children are to be killed, abandoned, beaten, terrorized, and sexually abused."[10] Meanwhile, Philippe Ariès' *Centuries of Childhood* contends that the medieval child lived in a content state of freedom, while its modern counterpart finds itself in an "invented" condition known as childhood under which the child is controlled in a tyrannical concept of the family, thus destroying friendship and sociability. Listing Church, family, and school as systems created to establish and maintain order and dominance over children, Ariès insists that religion "taught parents that they were spiritual guardians, that they were responsible before God for the souls, and indeed the bodies too, of their children" and continues by further asserting that "family and school together removed child from adult society."[11] In addition, Ariès contends that "the school shut up a childhood which had hitherto been free within an increasingly severe disciplinary system, which culminated in the eighteenth and nineteenth centuries ... The solicitude of family, Church, moralists and administrators deprived the child of freedom he had hitherto enjoyed among adults."[12] It is no mistake then that Shyamalan's central adult figures occupy these positions. They are more than simply parents: Malcolm Crowe (*The Sixth Sense*) is a child psychologist; David Dunn (*Unbreakable*) is a security guard; Graham Hess (*Signs*) is a pastor; Edward Walker (*The Village*) is a teacher and, essentially, lawgiver, as chief elder; Cleveland Heap (*Lady in the Water*) was a doctor; and Elliot Moore (*The Happening*) is a teacher. For Foucault, these positions are exactly the ones that were established in modern societies to sanction knowledge and control and discipline their populations.

The question then arises: what are the qualities children possess that may be read as so dangerous and evil a force that adults are required to quarantine and restrain them? Explaining why such institutions were established, Foucault's work coincides with Ariès'. Reversing Judeo-Christian principles, Foucault opens *Discipline & Punish* by proclaiming "the soul is the prison of the body."[13] Instead of being born in sin and, therefore, subject to punishment, the soul is born "out of methods of punishment, supervision, and constraint."[14] Fundamentally, he continues it is "produced permanently around, on, within the body by the functioning of a power that is exercised on those punished—and, in a general way, on those one supervises, trains and corrects; over madmen, children at home and at school, the colonized."[15] Here, the child is born into the world as a prisoner of culture; not yet culturally conditioned, the child represents a vital threat to society's order. The child is not born a subject: it becomes subject through social intervention. Still unaware of its community's rules, these culturally deficient beings are branded as not yet human. This might help explain why the child character in literature and film is often portrayed as "neither fully developed or fully undeveloped."[16] Socially, as well as physically weak, the child finds strength in this incompleteness and vulnerability; essentially, they do not yet belong to culture. Not yet assimilated into the social order, they hold a unique perception of the world in which they live and the problems and mysteries that exist within and around it. In their incompleteness, in their potential, and in their vision or understanding of the world, the child is a dangerous and potentially destabilizing threat to the social structure of their world and must be meticulously managed.

In this reading, M. Night Shyamalan's otherworldly creatures—whether they are ghosts, aliens, or folkloric monsters inhabiting the woods—are merely vehicles for luring out the visionary child from its controlled state and enabling the child's potential to be realized by both those with disciplinary power and the audience. In Shyamalan's context, the child's potential—its imagination, vision, and overall life force—is both humanity's saving grace and the child's own undoing. Parallel to the monstrous Other, the mysterious nature of the child's potential is equally terrifying; therefore, the child represents, or is at least temporarily transformed, into the Other. In fact, the child is actually the missing link between the Self and the Other: for example, in *The Sixth Sense*, Cole Sear sees and speaks to ghosts; in *Unbreakable*, Joseph Dunn sees his dad as possessor of superhuman strength; and in *Signs*, the Hess children believe and begin to decode alien activity. Making the strange familiar is the only force capable of realizing that the good and evil projected elsewhere—into the constructed grotesque—is actually in ourselves. These child figures are so dangerous, not because they are necessarily rebelling from any political or social system, but because they reframe and reconceptualize the very questions that their respective communities' systems attempt to answer. They expose cultural contradictions.

Several critics have already pointed out the importance of ambiguity to Shyamalan's narratives and imagery.[17] In his essay "Spellbound in Darkness: Shyamalan's Epistemological Twist," David Sterritt contends,

As an open-minded outlook based on resistance to the simplistic lure of either/ or logic, ambiguity can be a powerful tool; as an irresolute reaction to the ever-present fears, uncertainties, and futilities of the human condition, it can be a refuge from decision and a pretext for sloppy, constricted, and childishly magical thinking.[18]

What makes Shyamalan's films interesting—what provides mystery to the secrets of the communities portrayed as well as the cinematic narrative—is that they require magical thinking. Sterritt reads the "elusive ghosts," "the ungovernable body," "the murderous, coldblooded aliens," "the apparitions of the forest," etc. as the "*liminal* phenomena" in the body of work.[19] But these entities are merely the Other half of the binary. Again, through this reading, it is the child who allows these structures to become visible. Even in 2008's *The Happening*, it is young Jess that exposes the duality of good wife-mother and bad girl-slut potentially extent in Alma Moore's psyche. Here the deadly toxins only extend a metaphor for love/marriage or guilt/anxiety.

Cole Sear, the child that "sees dead people" in *The Sixth Sense* is perhaps the most complicated and dynamic model that Shyamalan creates. Although afraid of the ghosts he encounters, his access to their knowledge also makes him a threatening force himself. In one of the more popular scenes of the film, we see Cole tucked tightly into his bed, head peaking just above the covers, confessing his secret to his psychiatrist, Malcolm Crowe. However, it is easy to forget that Cole is not portrayed as merely a victim. For example, he shows signs of anger and aggression, rebelling from authority in the classroom when his teacher publicly debases one of his responses to a question concerning what their school was once used as. Cole breaks from the politically correct response of "a courthouse" and offers a much more descriptive answer: "They used to hang people here … They'd pull the people in, crying and kissing their families 'bye. People watching would spit at them."[20] At this, all of the students stop and stare, and the teacher, Mr Cunningham, gives a condescending grin. Cole is quick to respond, breaking his childlike persona by reprimanding him for giving the look. Reminding his teacher of how badly such behavior makes people feel, Cole repeatedly shouts "Stuttering Stanley," the name the man was teased with during his school days. While the rest of the class is shocked, silent, Mr Cunningham breaks out of a stutter to return Cole to his rightful place in the social order: "Shut up, you Freak!"[21]

The contagious Cole coaxes out this response. And aggression is met with aggression. Cole's actions, brought on by his own feelings of alienation and insecurity, and presumably aided by the information of a nearby—and invisible—ghost, reveal breaks in social etiquette: first, in the teacher's subtle look substantiating his authority over the boy, the classroom, and historical knowledge and, second, in the teacher's outburst, which reveals both his own sense of weakness and inadequacy and his potential anger, violence, and loss of authority. As Cole later realizes, with the help of Malcolm, the ghosts he sees generally do not intend to bring harm; instead, they merely hope to communicate and to find resolution in their former lives.

In approaching instead of running from these ghosts, Cole, and the audience, understands that the real fissures in order is not in the spirits whose presence defy science and logic but in adult characters' thinking and actions. Cole's conversations with these paranormal entities reveal a stepmother's conspiracy to poison and murder her stepdaughter and his own mother's failure to come to terms with his grandmother's death. Cole's intervention brings resolution and order to these scenes and leads to his psychologist's reconciliation with his work, his marriage, and his death. Aviva Briefel, in her article "What Some Ghosts Don't Know: Spectral Incognizance And The Horror Film" notes that, at the end of the film, Cole takes over "Malcolm's identity as psychiatrist when he realizes that he can attenuate his own trauma if he encourages the ghosts around him to talk about their problems."[22] Here, Cole does play mediator between living and dead, Self and Other—this is especially visible in the final car scene between Cole and his mother, as well as the "surprise" ending with Malcolm and his wife. However, at no point does the audience get the sense that Cole, through his gift/ curse, will rise to a position of social authority—like that held by a psychiatrist.

The protagonist, here, and arguably in all of Shyamalan's films is the aforementioned adult male authority figure, struggling with the pains of a tragic past and with the desire to maintain his sense of understanding and control. It is on his journey of redemption that the narratives are based, and it is from his perspective that the audience sees the world and the child. In *Imagining the Child in Modern Jewish Fiction*, Naomi Sokoloff points out that the "sensations and perception of childhood are to some extent always irretrievable to [adult] memory and articulation."[23] Hence, the child is a necessary component to make this journey. So what Shyamalan offers us in the child figure, in his "Once upon a time" tales, is a look into the disintegration of the Self and the surrounding disorder and, perhaps, a surviving glimmer of hope pointing towards a new order. *The Village* is a bit of a departure then in the Shyamalan model for a few reasons. First, it is the only film where the children compete with the

Symbolic Father's point of view. Second, it explicitly reveals the adult authority as the monstrous Other that lurks in the woods. Lastly, there are three central child figures, which allow Shyamalan to play with established archetypes, thus emphasizing social hierarchy in the village even more. Moreover, because it is, seemingly, set in a small and isolated and deeply hierarchized American town sometime in the early nineteenth century just prior to the Industrial Revolution, *The Village* most resembles the Foucaultian view of social order described above.

Before Ivy Walker departs for the Towns to obtain medicines for her dying fiancé Lucius, her father Edward shares the secret of "Those we do not speak of," the evil creatures that reside in the woods surrounding the village, by leading her into a barn "that is not to be used." Inside, Ivy is frightened by touching one of the mysterious creatures, which are, in fact, only costumes or "farce," as her father quickly explains their origins. He confesses that all rituals, sounds, and stories related to the creatures were created to keep the villagers from venturing into the woods towards the Towns, a place taught by the elders to be full of evil and corruption. While this is shocking for Ivy, for the audience, the more striking revelation registers soon after when Ivy climbs a wall which is supposed to lead to her destination. As she scales her way to the top, the camera cuts back to the village where her parents are unlocking a box containing the secret to the community's founding. As the couple scans through various newspaper clippings, a voice over of each elder, similar to a Noir confessional, narrates the evil and injustice each experienced which caused them to leave behind their homes and establish the village. After gazing down upon an old photograph of the elders in a 1970s American setting, the camera returns to Ivy, who has now reached the other side and is greeted by a modern day world: a security guard complete with an SUV and a sounding siren. The true portrait of the village is complete once the SUV, with "Walker Wildlife Preserve" painted on its door, rolls into view.

Not only did the elders create this dark mythology surrounding the woodland monsters, they founded a whole new community (and culture), encoding narratives such as those about the Towns and their pasts (many of which are in fact rarely spoken about and masked in vagueness) to maintain order and civility. This invented culture offers the elders a possibility to escape the loss and "darkness" felt in their previous lives; that is to say, it provides them with direct access to a power dictating social action and oppressing entities they consider evil. By suppressing creativity and limiting freedoms, the elders attempt to construct a simple and innocent society without evil and violence. In the essay "Contemporary Theories of Power and Subjectivity," Elizabeth Grosz defines such a social order as "the domain constituting social law, language and exchange."[24] She explains that this order is governed by "the Other," which she describes as "not a person but a place, a locus from which language emanates and is given meaning."[25] Drawing upon a Lacanian model of psychoanalysis, the post-feminist work incorporates another interesting point to the analysis of the social order of the village.

Grosz elaborates that "the Other is incarnated in human experience in the figure of the Symbolic Father's authority that real father's invoke to institute the law."[26] Fundamental to patriarchy, this sentiment is quite relevant to the governing order in *The Village*. Although the group of elders that preside over the community is comprised of both men and women, it is one man who leads most internal discussions as well as public functions. Edward Walker leads blessings at mealtime, teaches children at school (thereby promoting and developing the ideologies instituted by the elders), and, despite insisting that elders take turns presiding over meetings, acts as a guide and counselor among his peers. When Lucius Hunt asks about the Towns, indirectly questioning the council's ruling forbidding him to travel there for medicines, and suspects secrets and deception among the elders, his mother immediately insists that they speak with Edward Walker. As the audience discovers in the end, Walker not only suggested the founding of the village, but also supplied the capital making the establishment both possible and secret. And Walker acts alone in the decision to send his daughter to the Towns.

Here, Ivy Walker, Lucius Hunt, and Noah Percy each serve as typical Shyamalan children. *The Village* is unique from the other films discussed in this essay because the children analyzed here have already reached puberty and are rapidly approaching adulthood. However, they may still be considered a part of childhood for several factors. First, they are socially subordinate to the elders and sheltered as children; since they are not part of the elders' subculture, they do not have access to any knowledge concerning the village, the Towns, and Those we do not speak of. These characters are all innocent, in one sense of the word or another, and neither married nor sexually active which essentially supports a sense of purity or blamelessness (that is, they are not seen as adults). Most importantly, they are in one sense or another culturally incomplete; they are outsiders. Again, it is this condition that allows them to achieve ambiguous status and shift between the administration and creatures of the woods. They are socially subordinate, innocent, blameless, and—when compared to the elders—culturally incomplete. Yet their curiosity, bravery, or willingness to enter forbidden lands and to potentially expose truths and disrupt social hierarchies makes them both threatening and beneficial.

From his first introduction at the dinner table, Noah Percy is immediately perceived as odd. While the echoing shrieks and howls from the nearby woods silence and halt the rest of the community, Noah wildly chuckles and applauds. This lewd behavior instantly distinguishes him apart from his townsfolk. The next scene in which he appears shows that he is, in fact, of a simpler mind than his peers. He is caught harassing two peers by jabbing and swinging a stick at them. Although a fight breaks out between the children to constrain him, Ivy quickly brings it to an end and reminds Noah that the elders would have locked him in "the quiet room," a small one room building used for confinement and isolation as a disciplinary response. "If you will not go into the quiet room we must strike a deal," Ivy secretly suggests, and in doing so also deviates from the community's rules. With a handshake and a friendly kiss, Noah promises "never to hit anyone ever again." [27] The scene progression then follows the two on a race down the knoll where Noah almost immediately reveals that he has broken other community laws by treading within the forbidden ground and picking (and not burying) berries of the bad color, which attracts Those we do not speak of.

His shrieks, out-of-place hysterics, and propensity to violence clearly position Noah as an outsider when juxtaposed to the rest of his community. For the audience, he might be positioned as "slow," "dim-witted," or even mad. In his anthropological studies, Clifford Geertz separates "small children, boors, simpletons, the insane, [and] the flagrantly immoral" from culture, identifying them as Other, or "not yet" human. [28] Foucault asserts that the asylum was arranged so that the insane were transformed into children. Applying a new system of education, "the asylum would keep the insane in the imperative fiction of the family; the madman remains a minor, and for a long time reason will retain for him the aspect of the Father." [29] It is only after he stabs Lucius with a knife that Noah is confined to his prison-like cell. The action demonstrates the elders' loss of power at controlling violent acts and serves as impetus for Ivy's journey to the Towns. Noah's escape from his prison with one of the monster suits completes his transformation from innocent jester to violent ogre. For challenging the elders' laws and donning one of their authoritative monster suits, Noah must perish. When word of Noah's death reaches the elders, Edward

Walker's immediate response, while mournful and sensitive, celebrates the incident that "has made our stories real. Noah has given us a chance to continue this place."[30]

While Noah's madness keeps him distinct, it is Lucius' bravery, selflessness, and calmness that distinguish him. At his first appearance, Lucius interrupts the elders' meeting (unaware to his mother) to ask permission to depart for the Towns to retrieve new medicine so that future fatalities may be prevented. While he maintains a respectful tone, his plea logically outlines his safe departure and return which undermines the village's beliefs and regulations and questions the authority of the elders. The camera cuts from Lucius reading his formally written request to a quiet and nervous circle of elders staring back. Lucius' departure from standard modes of thought becomes more apparent in his following scenes. The next scene demonstrates his bravery and free-thinking attitude. While joining his frightened friend Finton Coin on the look-out tower, Lucius asks, "Do you ever think of the Towns?" An anxious Coin shivers, blankly gazing out into the darkness, replying, "What for? They are wicked places where wicked people live. That's all."[31]

For his inquisitive spirit and fearlessness towards the mysteries of the woods, Lucius is cast as an outsider. While his peers are laughing and noisily playing games together around the village, Lucius is cast alone, quiet, and usually working at his blacksmith shop. Edward Walker's eldest daughter Kitty admits her attraction for him in an early scene, describing him as "different than the other boys. He doesn't joke or bounce about."[32] His position outside his peer group allows Lucius a certain level of access into the elders' status. Although he doesn't understand the secrets of the Village, he is certainly aware of them; part of this knowledge is derived directly from the elders—notably August Nicholson and his mother Alice—who share the violent stories of murdered loved ones with him and draw attention to the suspicious locked boxes placed in the corner of their houses' common rooms. In one heated conversation with his mother, Lucius snaps, "There are secrets in every corner of this village. Do you not feel it? Do you not see it?"[33] and lunges towards the box and demands they open it and reveal the painful past to him. Obedient as he is, upon his mother's request, Lucius leaves the box undisturbed.

Ivy, like Lucius, is kind and good-hearted. And, like Lucius, she is separate from the rest of the children, not because of her blindness but because of her maturity. She plays guardian for the children of the house when the elders are secretly posing as the woodland creatures and, in many aspects mother, breaking up rough-housing in the courtyard and comforting her sister Kitty when her marriage proposal to Lucius is rejected. Despite her blindness, she maneuvers well around town and has a special sense to detect light and color emitted from the virtuous character of her father and Lucius.

Ivy's perception, while under-developed in the film, is a trait linking all of Shyamalan's indigo children and serves as a bridge between these children and the dangerous forces that threaten order. And, while this perception is used to protect or nurture their loved ones, it is also this characteristic that constructs the *difference* of the child. On this convention, Lebeau contends,

> At once a moment in the emergence of psychic life and a state of mind and being that never goes away, it may be that the *infans* has a special, and probably finally elusive, tie to the various technologies of vision that have come to pervade the experience of everday life throughout the twentieth century, and beyond ... each [child] comes to carry the delights, as well as the terrors, of an elsewhere, of a way of being otherwise. Bordering on an otherness within, a space and time that we have all known without knowing it, this is a child that must be left behind—or, more dramatically put to death, to murder—if we are to find our way into the worlds of language, culture, and community, but that we must, too, continually, renegotiate.[34]

And this is where Shyamalan's child is unique from convention. While the figure has much in common with—or possesses too much knowledge of—the monstrous, it is not monstrous itself. But death is not the only option for escape. In Shyamalan's model, the family unit is meant to be read as a safe and coveted structure. When the monstrous Other is realized or defeated, all may return to the "natural" order of things, to the patriarchal structure originally in place.

The Other in *The Village*, Those we do not speak of, is meant to symbolize the wickedness, the greed and violence, in the world. The audience is again meant to direct their empathy towards the elders, people who know tragedy and, by constructing the village, offer the opportunity to shield knowledge of such horrors from their children. Fear was the impetus for creating this community, and it is fear that keeps their children from wandering into the woods and discovering the secret of the town's founding. Edward Walker is an intelligent and stoic man and a good teacher. While he has created this folklore surrounding the creatures, he is also sympathetic to his students, encouraging critical thinking skills in respect to recent events and assuring them that they will not be harmed. But he is deeply affected by the children's fear and the death of one villager's son. In addition, he is time and again impressed by Lucius. In a note to the council, before the entire town, Lucius, seated in the back of the room hunched forward and in tears, confesses to stepping into the forbidden woods. Deeply moved, Walker kneels before him: "Fear not. You are fearless in a way I shall never know."[35] Such acts make Walker reconsider his actions, his past. Walker sees Lucius and Ivy as the future leaders of the village. The maturity, the compassion, and the love that they share and the hurt Ivy feels after Lucius is stabbed infects the Elder so greatly that it leads to his confession to Ivy and his consent—without consultation or approval from the council—to have her leave for the Towns to obtain medicine. In defense of his actions, he proffers,

> "Who do you think will continue this place, this life? Do you plan to live forever? It is in them that our future lies, it is in Ivy and Lucius that this way of life will continue. Yes, I have risked; I hope I am always able to risk everything for the just and right cause. If we did not make this decision, we could never again call ourselves innocent, and that in the end is what we have protected here, innocence! That I'm not ready to give up."[36]

It is in Ivy's journey to the Towns, in the hidden community's near exposure and deconstruction, and in the death of Noah that the village may survive. It has reunited the Elders and served as a confirmation as to what they are doing, what this way of life means to them, and what this way of life will mean to generations to come.

Despite the gifts or powers each child possesses, Shyamalan's stories are not about them, and this power is eventually put down. Foucault notes that the modern family is no longer just a "system of relations" or a "mechanism for the transmission of property," but has become "a dense, saturated, permanent, continuous physical environment which envelops, maintains, and develops the child's body."[37] Momentarily, the child figure emerges from its compliant role and is able to subvert traditional hierarchical roles. For example, Ivy and Lucius are able to confront tragedy while their parents attempt to ignore and flee it. In responding to Ivy's question as to how he is able to be so brave, Lucius responds, "I don't think of what might happen, only what must be done."[38] Similarly, the overwhelmed and grief-stricken mother of Cole, is often consoled, and ultimately healed, by her nine-year-old son. The Hess children similarly fend for themselves while their father copes with the loss of his wife and his faith. Cleveland Heap finds peace in his family's death after meeting Story. Elliot and Alma Moore are able to rekindle their love.

This reconstruction of identity in the protagonist and in the family structure is best seen in *Unbreakable*. For the opening sequence on the train, the camera takes the position of a child, peeping upward between the seats, witness to the deconstructing family: David Dunn takes off his wedding band and begins to flirt with the woman sitting next to him. The following sequence shifts from David's flirting to David's son Joseph who is home flipping through channels until he finds the wreck on the news. The color and brightness that fill the domestic scene flips back to David in a grayish tinted light at the hospital. Emerging as the only survivor, and without a scratch, he exists as alien. An artificial light shadows the faces of the family as the three leave together. The questions that David faces concerning his own identity as survivor mirrors the uncertain fate of his family.

It is only in meeting Elijah Price, a high brow comic book art dealer, that David's identity begins to come into view. Binaries of light and shadow, of good and evil, are quickly apparent as Elijah explains David's true self: a man with uncanny strength and supernatural instinct to sense crimes, both past and future. Through his son's persistent faith in the magic of comic book mythology and in him as a man and father, David is able to access his forgotten past and realize the truth in Elijah's assertions of his identity. After rescuing a family victimized by a violent break-in, David feels secure with himself and his uniqueness, and he returns home to the bed where his wife was sleeping. The stoic, uninterested façade he has recently maintained in their marriage is wiped clear as he cuddles beside her and childishly whimpers, "I had a nightmare …"[39] The following morning, the patriarchal order is restored and Joseph, happily, returns to his passive role as child. Meanwhile, the audience gleans a sense of achievement in Elijah as well. Although he is headed to jail for his series of terrorist schemes, through Joseph and his devout belief in the grand narratives of the comics he has grown up with, he is pleased to finally know his place, his sense of purpose: "Now that we know who you are … I know who I am – I'm not a mistake! It all makes sense, in the comics you know who the arch villain is going to be? He's the exact opposite of the hero! And most time's they're friends like you, and me. I should've known way back when. You know why, David? Because of the kids! They called me Mr Glass!"[40]

M. Night Shyamalan's films have been criticized as being overly-sentimental with "uncomfortable pattern[s] … that fell apart when exposed to outside logic."[41] But it is this pattern that defines and exposes the structures of which we are all part. Like the characters he creates, we are all subject to the dread of loss and the fears of violence. Yet the writer-director senses something unique in children. While often deemed the most fragile, the most victimized, of society, he sees them as occupying a space that also has the most courage, the most resilience, and the most knowledge. Perhaps it is because their modes of thought, of faith in humanity are less tainted by tragedy and "outside logic." Love, faith, and trust cannot exist in a single model of narrative. And for Shyamalan, the child infects, bringing tension offering freedom. *The Sixth Sense*'s Cole offers solace to the dead and their families, to his mother, his teacher, and his psychiatrist Malcolm; *Signs*' Hess children reunites their family and aids their father's return to faith in God and the church; David and Elijah must each embrace his childhood memories to discover their true selves in *Unbreakable*; and the young nymph Story in *Lady in the Water* offers resolution to an apartment manager grieving over his family's murder. And each film contains the paradoxical nature of the contagion. Durkheim remarks that "Passion individualizes, yet is also enslaves. Our sensations are essentially individual; yet we are more personal the more we are freed from our senses and able to think and act with concepts."[42] For Shyamalan, law is unavoidable, and this is not a bad thing. The relationships within that order are necessary for our progression as people. What the child offers is a break from the cultural logic we are all tied to, a chance to see these structures and renegotiate our relationships with them. Because Shyamalan's figure is positioned simultaneously as one of us and not, they are able to guide to us to see the world otherwise.

Notes

1   *Lady in the Water*, dir. M. Night Shyamalan (2006; Burbank, CA: Warner Home Video, 2006), DVD.

2   Philip Davis, *The Victorians: The Oxford English Literary History. Vol. 8, 1830–1880* (New York: Oxford University Press, 2002), 337.

3   Elizabeth Tucker, "Changing Concepts of Childhood: Children's Folklore Scholarship Since The Late Nineteenth Century," *The Journal of American Folklore*, 498 (2012): 389–410.

4   Patrick C. Collier, "'Our Silly Lies': Ideological Fictions in M. Night Shyamalan's *The Village*," *Journal of Narrative Theory*, 38, no. 2 (2008): 273.

5   Michel Foucault, *Discipline and Punish: The Birth of the Prison*, trans. Alan Sheridan (New York: Vintage, 1995), 199.

6 Mary Douglas, *Purity and Danger: An Analysis of Concept of Pollution and Taboo* (London: Routledge & Kegan Paul, 2005), 123–31.

7 Julia Kristeva, *Powers of Horror*, trans. Leon Roudiez (New York: Columbia University Press, 1984), 77.

8 Marie Winn, *Children without Childhood* (New York: Pantheon, 1983), 16–17.

9 Vicky Lebeau, *Childhood and Cinema* (London: Reaktion Books, 2008), 170.

10 Lloyd DeMause (ed.), *The History of Childhood* (New York: Psychohistory Press, 1974), 1.

11 Philippe Ariès, *Centuries of Childhood: A Social History of Family Life*, trans. Robert Baldick (New York: Knopf, 1962), 412.

12 Ibid., 412–13.

13 Foucault, *Discipline & Punish*, 30.

14 Ibid., 29.

15 Ibid.

16 Ian Wojcik-Andrews, *Children's Films: History, Ideology, Pedagogy, Theory* (New York: Garland, 2000), 46.

17 Patrick C. Collier, "'Our Silly Lies'"; Kirsten Moana Thompson, "*Signs* of the End of the World: Apocalyptic Dread," in *Apocalyptic Dread: American Film at the Turn of the Millennium* (Albany, NY: State University of New York Press, 2007), 127–44; Jeffrey A.Weinstock (ed.), *Critical Approaches to the Films of M. Night Shyamalan: Spoiler Warnings* (New York: Palgrave Macmillan, 2010).

18 David Sterritt, "Spellbound in Darkness: Shyamalan's Epistemological Twist," in Jeffrey A. Weinstock (ed.), *Critical Approaches to the Films of M. Night Shyamalan: Spoiler Warnings* (New York: Palgrave Macmillan, 2010), 55.

19 Ibid., 60, 55.

20 *The Sixth Sense*, dir. M. Night Shyamalan (2006; Burbank, CA: Warner Home Video, 2006), DVD.

21 Ibid.

22 Aviva Briefel, "What Some Ghosts Don't Know: Spectral Incognizance And The Horror Film," *Narrative* 17, no. 1 (2009): 97.

23 Naomi B. Sokoloff, *Imagining the Child in Modern Jewish Fiction* (Baltimore: Johns Hopkins University Press, 1992), 112.

24 Elizabeth Grosz, "Contemporary Theories of Power and Subjectivity," in Sneja Gunew (ed.), *Feminist Knowledge: Critique and Construct* (London: Routledge, 1990), 72.

25 Ibid., (73).

26 Ibid.

27 *The Village*, dir. M. Night Shyamalan (2004; Burbank, CA: Touchstone, 2005), DVD.

28   Clifford Geertz, *The Interpretation of Cultures* (New York: Basic, 1973), 52.

29   Michel Foucault, *Madness and Civilization: A History of Insanity in the Age of Reason* (New York: Vintage, 1988), 254.

30   *The Village.*

31   Ibid.

32   Ibid.

33   Ibid.

34   Lebeau, *Childhood and Cinema*, 84.

35   *The Village.*

36   *The Village.*

37   Michel Foucault, *Power/Knowledge: Selected Interviews and Other Writings, 1972-1977*, (ed.) C. Gordon (Brighton: Harvester Press, 1980), 172–3.

38   *The Village.*

39   *Unbreakable*, dir. M. Night Shyamalan (2000; Burbank, CA: Touchstone, 2001), DVD.

40   Ibid.

41   Michael Agger, "Village Idiot: The Case Against M. Night Shyamalan," *Slate* 30, July 2004. http://img.slate.com

42   Emile Durkheim, *The Elementary Forms of the Religious Life*, trans. Joseph Ward Swain (New York: Free Press, 1965), 307.

Bibliography

Agger, Michael. "Village Idiot: The Case Against M. Night Shyamalan." *Slate* 30 July 2004. http://img.slate.com

Ariès, Philippe. *Centuries of Childhood: A Social History of Family Life.* Trans. Robert Baldick. New York: Knopf, 1962.

Bann, Stephen. "The Sense of the Past: Image, Text, and Object in the Formation of Historical Consciousness in Nineteenth-Century Britain." In H. Aram Vesser (ed.), *The New Historicism.* 102–15. New York: Routledge, 1989.

Briefel, Aviva. "What Some Ghosts Don't Know: Spectral Incognizance And The Horror Film." *Narrative* 17, no. 1 (2009): 95–110.

Collier, Patrick C. "'Our Silly Lies': Ideological Fictions in M. Night Shyamalan's *The Village.*" *Journal of Narrative Theory* 38, no. 2 (2008): 269–92.

Davis, Philip. *The Victorians.* The Oxford English Literary History. Vol. 8, 1830–80. New York: Oxford University Press, 2002.

DeMause, Lloyd (ed.), *The History of Childhood.* New York: Psychohistory Press, 1974.

Derry, Charles. *Dark Dreams 2.0: A Psychological History of the Modern Horror Film from the 1950s to the 21st Century*. Jefferson, NC: McFarland, 2009.

Douglas, Mary. *Implicit Meanings*. London: Routledge & Kegan Paul, 1993.

—*Purity and Danger: An Analysis of Concept of Pollution and Taboo*. London: Routledge & Kegan Paul, 2005.

Durkheim, Emile. *The Elementary Forms of the Religious Life*. Trans. Joseph Ward Swain. New York: Free Press, 1965.

Foucault, Michel. *Discipline & Punish: The Birth of the Prison*. Trans. Alan Sheridan. New York: Vintage, 1995.

—*Madness and Civilization: A History of Insanity in the Age of Reason*. New York: Vintage, 1988.

—*The Order of Things: An Archaeology of the Human Sciences*. New York: Vintage, 1994.

—*Power/Knowledge: Selected Interviews and Other Writings, 1972–1977*. C. Gordon (ed.). Brighton: Harvester Press, 1980.

Geertz, Clifford. *The Interpretation of Cultures*. New York: Basic, 1973.

Grosz, Elizabeth. "Contemporary Theories of Power and Subjectivity." In Sneja Gunew (ed.), *Feminist Knowledge: Critique and Construct*. 59–128. London: Routledge, 1990.

Jackson, Kathy Merlock. *Images of Children in American Film: A Sociocultural Analysis*. London: Scarecrow Press, 1986.

Kristeva, Julia. *Powers of Horror*. Trans. Leon Roudiez. New York: Columbia University Press, 1984.

Lacan, Jacques. *Écrits: A Selection*. Trans. Bruce Fink. New York: W. W. Norton, 2004.

Lebeau, Vicky. *Childhood and Cinema*. London: Reaktion Books, 2008.

Nipp, Jessica. "From Despair to Hope, From Fear to Redemption: Religious Transformation in *The Sixth Sense*." *Currents in Theology and Mission* 32, no. 4 (August 2005): 276 (15). *Expanded Academic Index*. Infotrac. Van Pelt Library, University of Pennsylvania. http://infotrac.galegroup.com

Rosen, Elizabeth. "Reaching Out to the Other Side: Problematic Families in the Films of M. Night Shyamalan." In Jeffrey A. Weinstock (ed.), *Critical Approaches to the Films of M. Night Shyamalan: Spoiler Warnings*. 19–33. New York: Palgrave Macmillan, 2010.

Shary, Timothy. *Generation Multiplex: The Image of Youth in Contemporary American Cinema*. Austin: University of Texas Press, 2004.

The Sixth Sense. Dir. M. Night Shyamalan. 1999. Burbank, CA: Hollywood Pictures Home Entertainment, 2002. DVD.

Sokoloff, Naomi B. *Imagining the Child in Modern Jewish Fiction*. Baltimore: Johns Hopkins University Press, 1992.

Sterritt, David. "Spellbound in Darkness: Shyamalan's Epistemological Twist." In Jeffrey

A. Weinstock (ed.), *Critical Approaches to the Films of M. Night Shyamalan: Spoiler Warnings*. 53–69. New York: Palgrave Macmillan, 2010.

Suransky, Valerie Polakow. *The Erosion of Childhood*. Chicago: University of Chicago Press, 1982.

Thompson, Kirsten Moana. "*Signs* of the End of the World: Apocalyptic Dread." *Apocalyptic Dread: American Film at the Turn of the Millennium*, 127–44. Albany, NY: State University of New York Press, 2007.

Tucker, Elizabeth. "Changing Concepts of Childhood: Children's Folklore Scholarship Since The Late Nineteenth Century." *The Journal of American Folklore* 498 (2012): 389–410.

Unbreakable. Dir. M. Night Shyamalan. 2000. Burbank, CA: Touchstone, 2001. DVD.

The Village. Dir. M. Night Shyamalan. 2004. Burbank, CA: Touchstone Home Video, 2005. DVD.

Weinstock, Jeffrey A. (ed.), *Critical Approaches to the Films of M. Night Shyamalan: Spoiler Warnings*. New York: Palgrave Macmillan, 2010.

Winn, Marie. *Children without Childhood*. New York: Pantheon, 1983.

Wojcik-Andrews, Ian. *Children's Films: History, Ideology, Pedagogy, Theory*. New York: Garland, 2000.

2

The Monstrous Masculine: Abjection and Todd Solondz's *Happiness*

Adam P. Wadenius
Napa Valley College

Horror and the abject

There is a scene in Todd Solondz's *Happiness* that echoes the dread and fascination that consumes the spectator when watching Norman Bates, the protagonist of Alfred Hitchcock's horror classic *Psycho*, as he shifts worriedly from right to left after pushing Marion Crane's car into the murky waters of a swamp. Bill, the deviant, yet empathetic pedophile of *Happiness*, has prepared a tuna sandwich for his son's friend, Johnny, who is sleeping over for the night. After lacing the tuna with a sleeping pill, having earlier drugged his wife and sons with similarly laced ice cream sundaes, his gaze moves back and forth between the boy and the sandwich, as he waits for Johnny to divert his occupied attention to the fishy snack. An uncanny anticipation develops, akin to the feeling that resonates when Norman looks at Marion's car, her body entombed in the trunk, as it momentarily sticks in the muddy swamp. The simultaneous sense of repulsion and relief that fills the spectator when the car resumes its descent is similarly evoked when Johnny, falling victim to Bill's deception, looks cautiously into the tuna sandwich and takes a bite. Both Marion and Johnny are unsuspecting victims of a brutal crime carried out at the hands of a monster with whom the spectator momentarily identifies. And while *Psycho* is in keeping with the dominant motif of the popular horror film that requires the feminine body to serve as the site of monstrosity (e.g. Norman is "possessed" by Mother, and performs her outbursts of jealous rage), in *Happiness* it is the deviant masculine body, in its multiple guises, that is ultimately produced as monstrous.

In *Powers of Horror: An Essay on Abjection*, Julia Kristeva analyzes the conditions that make personal and social identity possible, positing a phase in the construction of subjectivity that requires a separation from the mother. This *abjection* takes place in the semiotic space of the mother/child symbiosis, a pre-symbolic level, prior to the subject's entry into language. In this space, the oral and anal drives of the child are regulated by its relationship with the maternal body.[1] The abject is "not a quality in itself," but a relationship to a boundary, representing "the object jettisoned out of that boundary, its other side, a margin."[2] The abject is tied to the fluids of childhood (excrement, vomit, blood), and to a lack of control and shamelessness. Experiencing the abject induces a simultaneous fear and fascination, a return to the space of the maternal semiotic, to "the place where meaning collapses."[3] In her book *The Monstrous Feminine: Film, Feminism, Psychoanalysis*, Barbara Creed draws upon Kristeva's theory of abjection to argue that the horror film represents woman's reproductive functions as abject in order to produce her as monstrous. The genre's ideological project, she writes, is an attempt to "bring about a confrontation with the abject," ultimately to expel it and "redraw the boundaries between the human and non-human."[4] She posits that the horror film is linked to Kristeva's theory through its abundance of abject imagery, its treatment of boundary crossing, and its construction of the maternal figure as the monstrous feminine.[5] The male body on the other hand, is represented as monstrous only when it assumes characteristics that are associated with the female body; his monstrosity is defined by the characteristics that make him not male.[6]

The thematic thread that permeates Todd Solondz's *Happiness* is deviant masculinity, and each male in the film is burdened with a particular sexual dysfunction that gradually comes to light through displays of perverse or obscene behavior. Situated among them is Billy Maplewood, the adolescent boy whose burgeoning sexuality emerges as the primary focus of the narrative. In mapping Billy's horrific trajectory towards maturity, the film's project is an abject representation of the specific rites of passage that he must undergo in order to accede to manhood. As both an application of, and a reimagining of, Creed's concepts, *Happiness* addresses its theme of abject masculinity through the generic conventions of the horror film, adopting a fluid strategy that adheres to, and then traverses the boundaries of her thesis. Masculinity is constructed as monstrous in terms of the very characteristics that shape Billy's experience of becoming a man. The spectator is invited to identify with him on this journey into manhood, as he explores the limits of his body and its sexual and reproductive functions, at the same time as he explores the limits of the law of the father.

At face value, *Happiness* would seem to elude classification as a horror film. Its outer appearance is that of black comedy, though resonating beneath its facade of suburban anxiety is a narrative that employs the shock tactics of horror, evoking an effect on the body of the spectator that is in keeping with the traditional appeal of the genre. Abject signifiers (e.g. death, vomit, excrement, semen) penetrate the mise-en-scène, and the inappropriate relationship that develops between Bill and Billy situates the father and son on the side of the abject. Billy must navigate and eventually come to accept a path to maturity that is fraught with the deviance represented by his father, who comes to signify the collapse of the boundary between normal and abnormal sexual desire.[7] In her chapter on *The Exorcist*, Creed argues that representations of the monstrous feminine are constructed through the female subject's rejection of the paternal order, and her refusal to "take up her place in the proper symbolic" is represented as a return to the semiotic.[8] She arrives at this point by first explaining that this denial of the father is also construed as a failure on his part to ensure the separation between the mother and child. A similar breakdown in the paternal function produces a representation of the abject in *Happiness*. Bill's failure to respect the border that separates normal and abnormal sexuality positions him as abject and his inability to enforce the symbolic law ultimately signals its collapse. His example of monstrous masculinity is proffered to Billy as a rite of passage into manhood. Accepting this cue from his father, Billy likewise violates the border of normative sexual behavior. He passes into maturity with his first ejaculation, his semen marking a collapse of the symbolic law, as Bill fails to prohibit the incestuous bond that Billy enters into with his mother at the film's climax. The typical horror film attempts to resolve this conflict in patriarchal authority, working to "separate out the symbolic order from all that threatens its stability," via the restoration of the law of the father, and by the repression of the abject maternal element.[9] In *Happiness*, there is no such resolution for patriarchy, as embodied by Bill, and thus the film concludes with the symbolic order in chaos and the failure of the paternal constructed as abject masculinity.

Conventional horror

Central to the horror film is the theme of the nuclear family in crisis, and *Happiness* employs this basic narrative strategy, exploring the horrific nature of a family invaded by male monstrosity. We are introduced to the Maplewoods.

Bill is a psychiatrist and father, struggling to control his nascent pedophilic urges. He is married to Trish, a vapidly domestic housewife, and together they have two children, Billy and Timmy. In his *Introduction to the American Horror Film*, Robin Wood contends that a society built on monogamy and family demands the repression of an enormous amount of sexual energy, and its return to culture takes shape as our nightmarish visions that find expression in the horror film.[10] He argues for the centrality of the family unit, identifying the primary narrative conflict in horror films as an issue linked to or triggered by familial or sexual tension.[11] On the exterior, the Maplewood's fit the ideal patriarchal mold. They are, as Trish puts it, a family who "has it all." Their seemingly ideal suburban lifestyle is soon ruptured, however, as Bill's repressed deviant masculinity gradually comes to light. This disruption at the heart of the Maplewood family serves as the central crisis of the film, out of which the surrounding narrative action develops.

Wood contends that the release of sexuality in horror films is typically presented as perverse and excessive, and such is the case in *Happiness*.[12] At the center of every horror film is a monster. In *Happiness* a monstrous masculinity haunts its characters, finding its core representation in Bill. In his taxonomy of the modern horror film, David J. Russell suggests that serial killers, maniacs, and other human figures who appear monstrous to the audience are classifiable as "deviant."[13] These deviant monsters threaten normality through acts of abnormality and transgression, challenging socially constructed rules of acceptable behavior. The males in *Happiness* are unable either to assert or to control their respective sexual drives, conditions that ultimately lead to displays of their deviant, repudiated compulsions. Fraught with sexual desire for young boys, Bill's unchecked libidinal urges manifest during several conversations with his son, Billy, in which he offers answers to questions about sex and male anatomy. Just as their talks should be drawing to a close however, he fractures the boundary of responsible parenting with inappropriate questions of his own that hint at a need to act out his frustrated sexual desires with the boy. His lack of control and disregard for the boundaries of proper sexual behavior mark him as deviant. The film depicts two specific instances in which Bill acquiesces to his pedophilic impulses. The first, is the aforementioned "tuna sandwich" scene, where he drugs and rapes Billy's friend Johnny Grasso during a sleepover. His second encounter is with Ronald Farber, another one of his Billy's schoolmates. When Billy mentions that Ronald's parents have gone on vacation and left him alone for the week, Bill drives to Ronald's house and takes advantage of the young boy. Neither scenario is played out onscreen, however, as their horrific nature is only alluded to by an ominous fade to black. Instead, Bill's malicious intentions are given visual representation in a dream sequence that he describes to his therapist.

Bill's fantasy begins in a lush green park where the sun is shining and the birds are chirping. A couple is jogging together along a gravel trail, and another walks hand in hand through the grass while a calming melody dominates the soundscape. The camera pans left, revealing more couples lounging together on a bench and picnicking in the sunlight. The peaceful setting is abruptly cut short as Bill comes into frame holding a machine-gun. He cocks his weapon and stalks through the park pumping bullets into the frightened couples, stopping as the camera zooms out to capture him in long shot, standing amidst a scattering of bloody, dead bodies. Wood writes that dreams are the embodiment of one's repressed desires, those that the conscious mind rejects.[14] Bill's dream is a violent representation of the conflict between his drive to fulfill his obligation as a husband and father, and his subconscious desire to have improper sexual relations with young boys. The former gives in to the latter, and his pedophilic impulses take over, finding expression as a murderous outburst against normative couples that offers only a momentary feeling of release. Just after describing the fantasy, Bill is asked by his psychiatrist how it makes him feel. "Much better," he says. "I wake up happy... feeling good."[15] After his session, he goes to a local convenience mart and buys a copy of a teen magazine. In the parking lot, he masturbates to a picture of a young boy in the rear seat of his car. Coupled with the sense of relief he feels after recounting the nightmare, his display of perverse self-gratification is only a temporarily mechanism for assuaging his repressed urges. Bill is eventually consumed by his perverse desire, the brutality of his fantasized shootout inflicted on to Johnny Grasso and Ronald Farber, through two equally vicious acts of rape.

Perverse sexuality is on display from the very onset of the film, and true to the conventions of the popular horror genre, this signals a return of the repressed deviance that exists at the core of masculinity in the film. The spectator is introduced to Allen through a verbal recounting of his sadistic sexual fantasy, in which he longs to tie up his neighbor Helen and "pump, pump, pump her" so hard that his "dick shoots right through her."[16] His overabundance of testosterone is exuded as raw, sexual aggression; however, his conception of masculinity is so heavily associated with the orgasmic capacity of his genitalia that he is rendered impotent in the company of women. Confused as to what to do in their presence, he has instead regressed from female contact to making obscene phone calls and masturbating excessively, depicted in abject detail in the film. Lenny's affliction is his extreme apathy, requesting a separation from his wife and continually affirming throughout the film that he is "in love with no one." When Mona, his now estranged wife, tells him not to feel guilty after the two have a brief sexual encounter in her apartment, his listless reply is that he "doesn't feel anything."[17] His presence throughout the film is an eerie foreshadowing of the late stages of the male experience, a figure whose deviance has left him totally devoid of emotion, a symbol of patriarchy in decline. Perverse sexual behavior perforates the boundaries of the film's primary male characters, spilling out on to the secondary and peripheral players as well. Pedro, the seemingly well-intentioned doorman is revealed as a hostile rapist, forcing himself sexually upon Christina; Joe is a homophobic father who, suspecting his son is gay, wants to buy him a prostitute; Andy is without control of his masculinity, pitifully reduced to infantility; and Vlad is a testosterone-fuelled philanderer, taking advantage of Joy's naiveté to use her for sex. There is no reprieve from deviance for the males in *Happiness*, an aspect of the narrative that proves essential towards an affirmation of the film's primary thematic focus.

In his scathing critique of the film, Andrew Lewis Conn remarks that *Happiness* is nothing more than a series of "shock tactics" that sink to the level of "the stabbings and beheadings of the splatter film."[18] He overlooks the film's theme of deviant masculinity, dismissing its abject imagery as mere mechanical devices, superfluous to the progression of the film's narrative. Conn likens the film to action movies such as *Armageddon* and *Speed 2*, suggesting that its failure to engage the spectator rests in its inability to support affable and empathetic characters for one to identify with. It is, however, the precise implementation of taboo subject matter that functions to give *Happiness* its unique sense of horror. In his discussion of David Cronenberg's *Shivers*, Robin Wood writes of the film's "breaking of every sexual-social taboo – promiscuity, lesbianism, homosexuality, age-difference and finally, incest."[19] In much the same way that Cronenberg's film is driven by specific instances of abnormal sexual behavior, *Happiness* systematically builds its acts of sexual deviance one on top of another as a strategy towards what Wood calls, an "accumulation of horrors." The physical effects of the horror film on the body of the spectator mark its primary allure as a popular genre, and *Happiness*' project is to provoke sensations of disgust with its images of masturbation, death, sexual impropriety, and incest. This defilement is methodically revealed as the narrative progresses, gradually laying the groundwork for a horrifying portrait of abject masculinity.

Blurred boundaries

The concept of the border in horror films is essential to a production of the monstrous, and Creed writes that anything that "crosses or threatens to cross the border" is abject.[20] The construction of monstrosity in *Happiness* takes place at the border that separates normal and abnormal sexuality.[21] The opening sequence of the film is a cue to the spectator that the standards of a rational and controlled masculinity are out of balance and no longer respected.

The film opens with a couple sharing an awkward pause as they sit together in an upscale restaurant. Joy has just broken-up with Andy, who, teary-eyed and shaken, asks if it is because of someone else. "No" she replies, "it's just you," a statement that cuts right to the heart of his inadequacy as a man. Instead of accepting her decision with the decorum expected of a man, he instead lashes out with a string of hateful remarks, evoking the abject with his supposition that she thinks he is "shit." His childlike response to Joy's rejection is an indicator that he has failed to live up to the standards of patriarchal masculinity, which in popular films is "usually associated with being large, loud, and active, with non-emotional aggression."[22] The scene is played out as if the two have exchanged gender roles, with Joy adopting the aggressive, forthright attitude, and Andy assuming the role of the vulnerable, jilted lover. The scene also signals a crossing-over into a foreign space, where masculinity is unsettled, and out of control. The film establishes its primary theme of male deviance with the male subject signifying the abject in his inability to perform proper masculinity.

The symbolic order sustains itself by maintaining its borders, and of all the characters in the film, Bill is the monstrous center whose deviant transgressions most clearly point to the fragility of the symbolic order. Early in the film his son Billy approaches him to ask what the word "come" means. Admitting that he has tried masturbation, Billy has not yet been able to come, evidence that he has yet to surmount the most significant step in his sexual development, his first ejaculation. Bill responds as any father might, with an honest, clinical answer to his question. Billy continues to express frustration at not knowing what to do, and Bill then oversteps the boundaries of the situation when he asks, "Do you want me to show you?" Later in the film the two are sitting in the family room, and Billy hesitantly inquires about the size of his penis. Again Bill offers sincere, fatherly advice, and again he fails to control his urges when asking, "Do you want me to measure?" Kristeva writes that the abject "does not respect borders, positions, rules" and Bill continually violates the borders of responsible fathering.[23] These moments are marked as rites of passage for Billy, providing a deviant model for his conception of the "symbolic boundaries and meanings" of proper masculinity.[24] His curiosity about sex and manhood is repeatedly met with answers that steer him toward an abject path.

Bill's representation in the film is one that both repels and attracts, evoking parallel feelings of pity and disgust. The deranged monster of the horror film is often its emotional center, positioned as a sympathetic character with whom the audience is asked to identify.[25] There is a sense of compassion felt for Bill as he tries to teach Billy what it is to be a man, but this compassion is equaled by the outrage that is provoked when his genuine advances venture beyond the bounds of decent parenting. His identity as a loving father and hardworking husband is fractured by the abject urges that have persisted beyond his control, corrupting Billy's path to manhood. Bill is the "amoral oscillator," at once conforming to one set of moral principles that define him as father and husband, and secretly flaunting them with his deviant behaviors.[26] Bill signifies perverse sexuality, and his transgressions against proper symbolic masculinity mark him as abject, calling attention to the fragility of the law through his disregard for the border that separates normal and abnormal sexual desire.

In the closing moments of the film, after Bill's crimes of pedophilia have been made public, he sits with Billy for one last father/son discussion. The children at school have been talking, and Billy asks if the rumors and accusations that he is a "serial rapist" and "pervert" are true. Bill candidly describes the sexual acts he committed with Johnny and Ronald. "I touched them," he admits, "I fucked them." Billy asks whether or not he would ever want to share a similar encounter with him, asking, "Would you ever fuck me?" Bill declines, saying, "No, I'd jerk-off instead."[27] Overwhelmed with emotion, Billy's only response is to weep in the face of Bill's brutal honesty. Chris Chang, in his article "Cruel To Be Kind," criticizes Solondz for what he calls an "insistence on ambiguity" in such a critical moment in the film, accusing him of sidestepping the issue of whether Billy's tears are over the horrific events that have transpired, or Bill's refusal to engage in sexual behavior with him.[28] Kristeva writes that above all, abjection is ambiguity.[29] It is the absence of borders, the in-between that lacks a definable object thus disturbing "identity, system, order."[30] This void pushes the subject to seek out the symbolic structure, offering a sense of delineation against the loathsome, horrific body that exists at its foundation. Billy's outburst is neither a horrified judgment nor a jealous protest of his father's affections; rather, it is a recognition of the abject and deviant model of masculinity being offered to him. For Billy, this is the moment in which he is faced with the abject, with that which he must acknowledge and accept in himself as he navigates his treacherous path to maturity. The ambiguity surrounding this sequence is crucial to a representation of abjection in the film. As the two sit together in the darkened space of the living room, the dungeon-like atmosphere evokes an uncanny similarity to Frankenstein's laboratory. Bill is frequently masked in shadow, like the creature or monster that lurks in so many popular horror films. This visual motif is emphasized in key moments such as this throughout the film, and it is here that Bill has given life to a monstrous creation of his own. The boundary that once delineated father and son has dissolved, revealing them as dual representations of the monstrous masculine.

Abject semen

On a social level, Kristeva posits that a confrontation with the feminine is equivalent to a confrontation with the abject. The maternal authority is charged with separating out and organizing the fluids and wastes that the child experiences in its early stages. This formative relationship with the mother is defined by this "primal mapping" of the body, during which the child exists in a realm without guilt or shame, in opposition to the symbolic.[31] The mother lays out a foundation on to which the paternal law "concatenates an order … precisely by repressing the maternal authority and the corporeal mapping that abuts against them."[32] As a means of purifying the abject, the symbolic order supports interdictions against incest and defilement rituals, marking the body's "clean and proper" boundaries.[33] These symbolic mechanisms function to exclude the abject from personal and social identity, offering protection from the threat of dissolution.

The abject is that which has been "jettisoned from the symbolic system," what the body must "permanently thrust aside in order to live."[34] Creed's contention is that the popular horror film acts as a modern form of defilement rite, attempting to purify the abject through an encounter with the maternal body. Its project is to saturate the film text with images of defilement, pointing to the fragility of the symbolic order, evoking the loathsome allure of abjection.[35] The horror film provides an arena for spectators to consume these images, signaling a desire for the "perverse pleasure" experienced in confronting the abject, which is equaled by the desire to expel it upon satiation.[36] In keeping with the horror film's propensity for the shocking, *Happiness* supplies an appreciable amount of abject imagery.

Blood, death, sexual impropriety, and incest permeate the film space, finding expression through deviant masculine behavior. Unable to bear the pain of Joy's rejection, Andy's cold, pale corpse is uncovered after committing suicide by consuming a cocktail of pills and vodka. Christina grabs a hold of Pedro's neck after he attacks her, snapping it backwards and killing him instantly. "I had to cut up his body and plastic-bag all the parts," she says when speaking about his remains. "There's still some left in my freezer."[37] Bill's nightmarish shooting spree provides the most vicious images of murder in the film, leaving behind a trail of bloody wounds and corpses. These dead and decaying bodies in *Happiness* signify the ultimate collapse of boundaries, the "utmost of abjection … death infecting life."[38]

The blood that leaks from Bill's victim Johnny marks the abject in just this way. The morning after his sleepover at Billy's, Johnny remarks that he's not feeling very well, and he vomits viscous white goo on to the kitchen table. Later that day he finds blood in his stool, and at the hospital his parents discover that he has been raped. Johnny is doubly bound by abjection. His expulsion of abject waste points to the collapse of his body's proper borders, while at the same time signaling his violation of the "interdiction against love of the same" via the improper sexual relationship forced upon him by Bill.[39] His vomit and bloody stool and the breach of his body evoke the abject, and at the same time they signify Bill's horrific crime of rape. Kristeva writes that those who perpetrate crimes against the law are abject: "the traitor, the liar, the criminal with a good conscience, the shameless rapist, the killer who claims he is a savior."[40] Johnny's sickness points to Bill's abject criminality, and to the corrupt masculinity that has been awakened in him; horrifically, the interior of the male body is made visible via an encounter with abject masculinity.

In her book *Cinema's Missing Children*, Emma Wilson posits a repulsive similarity between Johnny's sickness at the breakfast table and Allen's sadistic sexual fantasies.[41] Allen's desire to "pump" Helen so hard that his "dick shoots right through her … and (his) cum squirts out of her mouth,"[42] evokes a strange association between vomiting and ejaculation in the film. After an episode in which he makes an obscene phone call to Helen from his desk at work, Allen vomits when his neighbor Christina comes to visit him with information about Pedro's death. This mirrors an earlier lewd phone call that he places to Joy where he masturbates while talking to her, his semen captured in abject close-up as he ejaculates against the wall. Throughout the film, vomit and ejaculate are represented as vile by-products of an encounter with abject masculinity. This same sickness befalls Bill after his rape of Ronald Farber. He returns home to find Trish on the couch watching television. "I think I have to lie down," he says. "I hope you're not coming down with whatever Johnny Grasso had," she replies.[43] What makes Bill sick, however, is that which he cannot cure. His affliction is an uncontrollable, deviant sexual makeup that is inherent to him as a man, and shared by the rest of the male characters in the film.

Allen is also linked to Billy in the film, and he in many ways foreshadows— as an uncanny doppelganger of sorts—the man Billy will become. The two are bound together not only by their physical similarities (both have chubby, awkward bodies and bespectacled faces) and their individual masturbatory episodes, but each also shares an intimate relationship with Bill. When Allen is describing the vile, abject fantasies he has about performing with his neighbor Helen, Bill sits across from him, looking on with what seems to be genuine concern. His gaze, however, is insincere, and a subjective voiceover reveals that he is only pretending to listen while instead thinking about a list of errands he needs to finish. To the contrary, when talking with Billy, he is open and attentive, his forthrightness pushing beyond the acceptable limits of proper fathering. Throughout the course of both relationships, the abject flow of sexual impropriety is ignored between men. Bill abuses his responsibility as Billy's father, continually crossing the boundaries of proper parenting when talking to him about sex and manhood. He is similarly positioned as a father figure to Allen, and he neglects his obligation as a psychiatrist to counsel him through his perverse sexual fantasies. In both cases, abject masculinity is treated as unremarkable. It passes between men as something inherent in their masculine makeup, unnoticed but ever present.

Allen and Billy are further tied to each other through the graphic expulsion of abject fluids, their semen. Kristeva writes that polluting objects fall into two types: excremental and menstrual.[44] Both types emanate from the subject's relationship with the maternal body, excremental objects endangering from without and menstrual blood threatening from within. Excremental fluids signify a split between the maternal authority and the paternal symbolic. They point back to a time when the child's relationship with the mother was unbound by feelings of embarrassment and shame, set apart as a realm characterized by his "untrammelled pleasure in 'playing' with the body and its wastes."[45] These feelings are surmounted upon the subject's entry into the symbolic, during which the exclusion of filth is "promoted to the ritual level of defilement," marking the sacred order of the body's "self and clean."[46]

Defilement is expelled from the "pores and openings" of the body, pointing to the fragility of its borders, as that which "gives rise to abjection."[47] Impurities such as urine, blood, sperm, and excrement are those that obscure the borders of the body and are "subject to ritual acts whose purpose is to ward off defilement."[48] Kristeva writes that, "any secretion or discharge, anything that leaks out of the feminine or masculine body, defiles."[49] She notes, however, that not everything within one's body contaminates, and although sperm "belongs to the borders of the body," it cannot represent the abject because it "contains no polluting value."[50] The presence of semen in *Happiness*, however, does come to signify the abject, because it is contextualized as filthy, unclean. It is ascribed a polluted value because it represents a non-normative masculinity. This is evidenced not only by the specific focus put on Billy's quest to come, but also by the way in which it manifests itself in the film physically in Billy and Allen's abject cumshots, and symbolically in Johnny's ejaculatory vomiting and Bill's unrestrained gunfire. *Happiness* is explicitly about semen and about the way in which it contaminates proper masculinity. Semen signifies the sickness that haunts the male body in the film, polluting him from within, and represented as abjected masculinity upon its expulsion.

The monstrous masculine

The closing sequence of the film begins with Billy standing alone on a balcony outside of his grandmother's new condominium. Looking down on to the pool area below, he spies a woman laying out a towel in preparation for sunbathing. His eyes devour her voluptuous figure, the scant bikini accentuating her curves, as she sits and opens a tube of sunscreen. He watches as she massages the lotion along her arms and over her breasts, his mouth agape as she turns over on to her stomach, softly untying her top to start tanning. In a state of arousal, and with no regard for the boundaries of the situation, Billy begins to masturbate on the open balcony while watching her sunbathe. Taking a cue from Bill's deviant model of behavior, Billy's instinctual response when faced with the stimulation of a nearly naked woman is to immediately gratify his urges in plain view on the balcony, regardless of the potential consequences.

Creed posits that woman's monstrosity in the horror film is derived from her physical, sexual and biological attributes. She adds that man cannot "give birth, lactate or menstruate," thus rendering his fathering and reproductive functions incapable of signifying monstrosity.[51] The perverse characteristics that define masculinity in *Happiness* however, are explicitly related to Bill's perverse conception of fatherhood, and to Billy's comprehension of his newly acquired reproductive capabilities. Bill ignores the boundaries of proper father/son relations throughout the film, proffering his perverse conception of masculinity unto Billy. Upon realizing his father's fallibility, Billy is able to accept the notion of his own masculinity as abject, engaging in behavior similar to that of his deviant counterparts in the film. He achieves his first orgasm while masturbating in a setting where his respect for the boundaries of normal sexuality is disregarded, signaling his passage into an abject maturity. In *Happiness*, the deviant nature of the male body and its features are put on display and represented as abject, producing masculinity as monstrous.

Immediately after his transgression on the balcony, a vivid close-up captures Billy's semen as it drips on to the guardrail, and the family dog Cookie scuttles over to lap up the milky substance. Running back into the dining room, Cookie rushes over to Trish and gives her an unexpected sign of affection, licking her on the face and mouth. Trish's interaction with the dog is a vivid evocation of the abject, their abnormal contact functioning to symbolically unite Billy with his mother in an incestuous relationship, signified by the transfer of his semen to her via the dog's kiss. This illicit encounter is alluded to earlier in the scene by the half-finished glass of milk that sits in front of his chair at the dinner table. Kristeva writes that milk binds the mother to the child, thus connoting incest.[52] As a symbol of the semiotic, Billy's consumption of milk just prior to his revelation on the balcony implies his desire to reconnect with the maternal.[53] He regresses to the early relationship with his mother, to the realm where guilt and embarrassment cease to exist. The spectator is immersed in the "vortex of summons and repulsion" that characterizes the abject, situated in a state of disgusted pleasure, stirred by the experience of a violation of the incest taboo.[54]

The prohibition against incest protects the subject from a return to the pre-Oedipal, a paternal function that acts as a rejection of the abject. Incest represents a breakdown of symbolic law, and Billy's improper union with his

mother is a consequence of Bill's failure as a father. His absence at the film's
conclusion, in conjunction with the pitiful image of Lenny at the dinner table
signifies a rupture in the paternal order. Creed argues that the popular horror
film is an attempt to stage an encounter with the abject, only to annihilate its
threat to the symbolic and restore the boundaries of normality.[55] Such is not the
case in *Happiness*. The film stages a collapse of the symbolic order, signaling
horror as an encounter with the perverse characteristics of the monstrous male
figure. Where the traditional horror film functions to redraw its boundaries
and repudiate the monstrous element, the paternal crisis in *Happiness* remains
unresolved. Incest marks Billy as unclean, and his abject passage into manhood
ultimately symbolizes the inherent deviance that exists at the core of masculinity in the film.

A portrait of horror

The horror film's milieu is its violation of boundaries, its pleasure in perversity,
and its revelry in the breaking of cultural taboos. *Happiness* traverses these
grounds in its exploration of the monstrous masculine, staging a collapse of
the paternal order via Billy's horrific adolescent trajectory. In his essay "The W/
Hole and the Abject," Phil Powrie points to the perverse masculinity of Gaspar
Noe's *Seul contre tous* as a crucial component in the film's radical exploration
of abjection. He argues that the sordid "variations" of the film's protagonist
negotiates a delicate equilibrium between a confirmation and a refutation of
the abject.[56] *Happiness'* construction of monstrous masculinity has the same
subversive potential, working within and around the borders of the popular
horror film to expose the inherent deviance of the male subject, pointing to an
encounter with the male body as an encounter with the abject.

In the final moments of the film, after his transgression on the balcony,
Billy follows Cookie into the dining room and looks toward his family, proudly
exclaiming, "I came." Their heads whirl around and look back in stunned
silence as they realize for the first time that like his father, Billy too, has become
a monster. The closing image of Norman in *Psycho* imparts a similar representation of monstrosity, with its chilling juxtaposition of his mother's corpse,
Marion's car being pulled from the water, and his devious, smiling face staring
back at the spectator. Like Bill, Billy and the rest of the men in *Happiness*,
Norman is positioned as abject because of his criminality, his refusal to let go

of the maternal, and his disregard for sexual borders. Hitchcock's film marks a significant turning point in the evolution of the horror film. Its subversive approach to the genre reinvented traditional conceptions of the monster, transforming him from an external, physical being to an internalized, psychological threat. As a horrifying portrait of a deranged serial killer, *Psycho* arouses concerns about one's ethical boundaries, implicating the spectator as capable of crime and murder. *Happiness'* grim vision of the decline of patriarchal authority is equally menacing, and Bill's paternal failings and Billy's regression to the semiotic similarly position the spectator to identify with the monstrous masculinity embodied by this father and son at the margin of their sexual identities.

Notes

1   Kelly Oliver, *Reading Kristeva* (Bloomington: Indiana University Press, 1993), 34.

2   Julia Kristeva, *Powers of Horror: An Essay on Abjection* (New York: Columbia University Press, 1982), 69.

3   Ibid., 2.

4   Barbara Creed, *The Monstrous Feminine: Film, Feminism, Psychoanalysis* (New York: Routledge, 1993), 46.

5   Ibid., 11.

6   Ibid., 118.

7   Ibid., 39.

8   Ibid., 38.

9   Ibid., 46.

10   Robin Wood, *American Nightmare: Essays on the Horror Film.* (Toronto: Festival of Festivals, 1979), 10, 15.

11   Ibid., 17.

12   Ibid., 21.

13   David J. Russell, "Monster Roundup: Reintegrating the Horror Genre," in Nick Browne (ed.), *Refiguring American Film Genres* (Berkeley: University of California Press, 1998), 241.

14   Wood, *American Nightmare*, 13.

15   *Happiness*, dir. Todd Solondz (Burbank, CA: Good Machine Productions, 1998), Film.

16   Ibid.

17   Ibid.

18   Andrew Lewis Conn, "The Bad Review *Happiness* Deserves or: The Tyranny of Critic-Proof Movies," *Film Comment*, 35, no. 1 (1999): 71.

19   Wood, *American Nightmare*, 24.

20   Creed, *Monstrous Feminine*, 10–11.

21   Ibid.

22   Harry M. Benshoff and Sean Griffin, *America on Film: Representing Race, Class, Gender, and Sexuality at the Movies* (Hoboken: Wiley Blackwell, 2009), 205.

23   Kristeva, *Powers of Horror*, 4.

24   Chet Meeks, "Gay and Straight Rites of Passage," in Steven Seidman, Nancy Fischer, and Chet Meeks (eds), *Introducing the New Sexuality Studies* (New York: Routledge, 2011), 58.

25   Wood, *American Nightmare*, 15.

26   John Lechte, *Julia Kristeva* (New York: Routledge, 1990), 160.

27   *Happiness.*

28   Chris Chang, "Cruel to Be Kind: A Brief History of Todd Solondz," *Film Comment*, 34, no. 5 (September-October, 1998): 75.

29   Kristeva, *Powers of Horror*, 9.

30   Ibid., 4.

31   Creed, *Monstrous Feminine*, 38, 40.

32   Kristeva, *Powers of Horror*, 72.

33   Ibid., 102.

34   Ibid., 3, 65.

35   Creed, *Monstrous Feminine*, 43–4.

36   Ibid., 10.

37   *Happiness.*

38   Kristeva, *Powers of Horror*, 4.

39   Ibid., 102.

40   Ibid., 4.

41   Emma Wilson, *Cinema's Missing Children* (New York: Wallflower Press, 2003), 49.

42   *Happiness.*

43   Ibid.

44   Kristeva, *Powers of Horror*, 71.

45   Creed, *Monstrous Feminine*, 13.

46   Kristeva, *Powers of Horror*, 65.

47   Ibid., 108.

48   Lechte, *Julia Kristeva*, 160.

49   Kristeva, *Powers of Horror*, 102.

50   Ibid., 71.

51   Barbara Creed, *Phallic Panic: Film, Horror and the Primal Uncanny* (Melbourne: Melbourne University Publishing, 2005), 16.

52   Kristeva, *Powers of Horror*, 105.

53   Allison Weir, "Identification with the Divided Mother: Kristeva's Ambivalence," in Kelly Oliver (ed.), *Ethics, Politics & Difference in Julia Kristeva's Writings* (New York: Routledge, 1993), 82.

54   Kristeva, *Powers of Horror*, 1.

55   Creed, *Monstrous Feminine*,14.

56   Phil Powrie,"The W/Hole and the Abject," in Phil Powrie, (ed.) *The Trouble with Men: Masculinities in European and Hollywood Cinema* (New York: Wallflower Press, 2004), 215.

Bibiliography

Benshoff, Harry M. and Sean Griffin. *America on Film: Representing Race, Class, Gender, and Sexuality at the Movies.* Hoboken: Wiley Blackwell, 2009.

Chang, Chris. "Cruel to Be Kind: A Brief History of Todd Solondz." *Film Comment*, 34, no. 5 (September-October, 1998).

Creed, Barbara. *The Monstrous Feminine: Film, Feminism, Psychoanalysis.* New York: Routledge, 1993.

—*Phallic Panic: Film, Horror and the Primal Uncanny.* Melbourne: Melbourne University Publishing, 2005.

—"Dark Desires: Male Masochism in the Horror Film," in *Screening the Male: Exploring, Masculinities in Hollywood Cinema*, Steven Cohan and Ina Rae Hark (eds), New York: Routledge, 1993.

—"Horror and the Monstrous-Feminine: An Imaginary Abjection," in Barry Keith Grant (ed.), *The Dread of Difference.* Texas: University of Texas Press, 1996.

Happiness. Dir. Todd Solondz. Burbank, CA: Good Machine Productions, 1998.

Kristeva, Julia. *Powers of Horror: An Essay on Abjection.* New York: Columbia University Press, 1982.

Lechte, John. *Julia Kristeva.* New York: Routledge, 1990.

Lewis Conn, Andrew. "The Bad Review *Happiness* Deserves or: The Tyranny of Critic-Proof Movies," *Film Comment*, vol. 35, no. 1, January, 1999.

Meeks, Chet. "Gay and Straight Rites of Passage," in Steven Seidman, Nancy Fischer, and Chet Meeks (eds), *Introducing the New Sexuality Studies.* New York: Routledge, 2011.

Oliver, Kelly. *Reading Kristeva*, Bloomington: Indiana University Press, 1993.

Powrie, Phil. "The W/Hole and the Abject," in Phil Powrie (ed.), *The Trouble with Men: Masculinities in European and Hollywood Cinema.* New York: Wallflower Press, 2004.

Russell, David J. "Monster Roundup: Reintegrating the Horror Genre," in Nick Browne (ed.) *Refiguring American Film Genres.* Berkeley: University of California Press, 1998.

Weir, Allison. "Identification with the Divided Mother: Kristeva's Ambivalence," in Kelly Oliver (ed.), *Ethics, Politics & Difference in Julia Kristeva's Writings*. New York: Routledge, 1993.

Wilson, Emma. *Cinema's Missing Children*. New York: Wallflower Press, 2003.

Wood, Robin. *American Nightmare: Essays on the Horror Film*. Toronto: Festival of Festivals, 1979.

3

Only a Child: Spectacles of
Innocence in the *Lolita* Films

Brian Walter
St. Louis College of Pharmacy

In a 1958 letter to Putnam editor Walter Minton, Vladimir Nabokov expressed great concern over the burgeoning notoriety of his controversial novel *Lolita*. In particular, the author insisted that the producers of any future film version not try to cast the title role realistically: "I would veto the use of a real child. Let them find a dwarfess."[1] Among other things, such surprisingly conventional, automatic constraint in an author who seriously considered naming his next novel *The Happy Atheist*[2] highlights the special (and disturbingly) erotic capacity of the film image.[3] Nabokov lends his narrator, Humbert Humbert, a remarkably supple and playfully romantic prose style to deploy in exonerating and celebrating his illicit relationship with a decidedly under-aged child, a gorgeous writerly affect that can famously disarm the reader's moral judgment.[4] Nevertheless, the author who makes Humbert's nympholepsy so compelling on the page insisted that the screen counterpart of his novel should forswear strategies or effects that might similarly eroticize a minor. Nabokov's rather unlikely interdiction thus begs several telling questions about the complex relationship between the spectator and the film image in general and between the spectator and the film image of the child in particular: what would make the prospect of an adult playing Humbert's nymphet more acceptable or reassuring than a child? And whom would it reassure: the viewer (who might respond sexually to the image?) or the filmmakers, whose consciences would find it troubling to make such images available to anyone who purchased a ticket? What impulses and appetites does the film image feed that a character comprised of a series of printed words does not or cannot? Does the illusion of the film image so helplessly pander to the viewer that a child who played Lolita on screen would inevitably become a victim in her real life off it? How and why might the spectator develop a sense of ownership and prerogative over the image?

Such questions about the troubling and (at least potentially) erotic transactions between the film image and its spectator have engaged various critics and theorists, from Münsterberg to Mulvey and beyond, throughout the century-plus history of the medium. But where an early theorist like Münsterberg decried the image's ability to corrupt the innocent or insufficiently guarded viewer,[5] more recent theory has tended to focus on the voyeuristic qualities of the spectator's gaze and (usually) his self-serving consumption of the image, the power of looking augmented by the power of not being available to a reciprocal gaze from the viewed object. If, for a Münsterberg, the film image cast a dangerously powerful spell over the viewer, for a Mulvey, especially in her well-known 1975 essay "Visual Pleasure and Narrative Cinema" and the hungry liberty of the male gaze that it characterizes, the viewer all too powerfully appropriates and consumes the objects on the screen, particularly women. Mulvey's influential essay effectively indicts the film image for catering to the debauched appetites of an untouchable, invulnerable viewer.[6]

The presence of a child on screen would only seem to complicate the dynamic. In her book *Childhood and Cinema*, Vicky Lebeau embeds the complex effects of filming children within the traditions of Victorian child imagery, which early film was steeped in and which has ever since (as Lebeau persuasively argues) informed the feature film's treatment of children. In particular, while discussing Victorian illustrator Kate Greenaway, Lebeau suggests that photographic images of children galvanized nostalgia as a crucial form of consumption in narrative film:

> Greenaway, one of the most famous illustrators of and for children, represents the child *for* the adult: capturing the childishness of children – 'Greenaway's images looked childlike', as Anne Higgonet put it – her pictures solicit adult interest in looking at the child and her world. These 'seductively pretty pictures', as one critic has very recently described them, captivate their adult audience with a spectacle of childhood, childhood as a spectacle, that can be difficult to distinguish from a scene of seduction: of the adult by the *image* of a child.[7]

This "seduction" of the adult viewer by the filmed child would seem to ally Lebeau more closely with Münsterberg than with Mulvey. But Lebeau's fuller discussion of the popularity of children-focused scenarios in early film (especially ones that emphasized their states of undress)—not to mention the connection she draws between the seductiveness of Greenaway's images and the repeated directions of her friend John Ruskin to undrape the child subjects for the camera and his resulting pleasure—brings her much closer to Mulvey's position As such, the spectator submits only to an illusory "seduction," a false powerlessness before an image that the viewer seeks out, pays for, and consumes. A seduction, of course, only qualifies as such when the seducee resists the seducer (at least at first), whereas the film viewer is the one seeking out the helplessly pre-determined film image.

Lolita would seem to lend itself perfectly (if rather dauntingly) to such dubious "seduction," with a narrator in Humbert Humbert who simultaneously repulses, tantalizes, and engrosses the reader. Nabokov himself once described Humbert neatly as a "vain and cruel wretch who manages to appear 'touching'" (Nabokov 1973, 94), an eager voyeur who itemizes the object of his lust with remarkable visual acuity and thoroughness. But Nabokov also manages to ironize Humbert's perspective, to allow glimpses of the "real" child, Dolores Haze, to emerge subtly from Humbert's fanciful embroiderings. Anyone who would adapt Humbert's memoir for the screen must therefore, in some way, tackle the ironies within which Nabokov so trickily immerses Humbert's perspective. Ewa Mazierska has usefully connected the challenge of adapting *Lolita* for the screen to two important strains in the critical responses to the novel: romance vs realism. As she writes:

> The filmmaker can try to make a realistic or unrealistic film of it (for example, in a form of parody or an 'intertextual collage.') He or she can give in to Humbert's 'dominant vision' and depict him as a romantic lover, even a passive victim of the nymphet's sexual power, and a poet whose subtlety distinguishes him from the social mainstream. Conversely, Humbert can be depicted as a "neurotic scoundrel" who not only rapes, manipulates, and enslaves a child, but almost until the end of his life hides his actions behind a barrage of ornamental language.[8]

Mazierska soon suggests a third (theoretical) approach, one that would allow Humbert the winning romantic to coexist with Humbert the sordid criminal,[9] but regardless of the specific approach taken, the relationship between the image and the viewer will depend heavily on Humbert's success as a seductive or otherwise appealing figure.

Hand-in-hand with Humbert's appeal is that of the title character, although here, the filmmaker can draw on what Lisa Olson and Andrew Scahill have described as "one of the most common and endearing tropes in film … the lost and Othered child."[10] Like Lebeau, Olson and Scahill connect the uses of children on screen to the adult viewer's efforts to construct his own identity within the viewing experience, the child's unstable position lending itself all the more to this effort: "The Othered child has occupied the interstice within an identity that is constructed for them via adults, and when such children strain against adult constructions, they become marginalized, outside the idealized notions of what children should be."[11] Humbert's memoir abounds with such exploitive desire to hold the child fast within imaginative constructions that allow him to play a variety of flattering roles, the other to his exalted and often exasperated romantic champion:

> She had entered my world, umber and black Humberland, with rash curiosity; she surveyed it with a shrug of amused distaste; and it seemed to me now that she was ready to turn away from it with something akin to plain repulsion. Never did she vibrate under my touch, and a strident 'what d'you think you are doing?' was all I got for my pains. To the wonderland I had to offer, my fool preferred the corniest movies, the most cloying fudge. To think that between a Hamburger and a Humburger, she would – invariably, with icy precision – plump for the former. There is nothing more atrociously cruel than an adored child.[12]

In the case of the character Lolita, the endearing marginalization that Olson and Scahill ascribe to the lost child other must fight literally against Humbert's efforts to trap her into the fantasy role of the nymphet, the cruelly adored child.

Turning to the two film adaptations of *Lolita*, made by very different filmmakers at very different points in the history of American pop culture, the viewer finds that they present Lolita specifically and children and childhood in general with notably different levels of irony. Both films adapt the first-person perspective of the book partly by granting Humbert numerous voice-over comments, and both employ point-of-view images of Lolita from Humbert's perspective to encourage the viewer, at times, to see the "nymphet" through her ardent pursuer's eyes. But the similarities soon give way to the differences. In his 1962 film, Stanley Kubrick worked to set Lolita in complex visual and dramatic contexts that fully acknowledge Humbert's obsessively appetitive and controlling presence but which also, crucially, limit the authority he would assert over her. In sharp contrast, Adrian Lyne caters in his 1997 film especially to Humbert's gaze and, by extension, to a viewer who seeks in images of Lolita a similarly charged image of a child's sexual availability, delimited knowledge, and quasi-innocent initiative. In both films, the child's innocence serves simultaneously as subject and object, the stuff of often comic spectacles, but the nature of the comic effect varies greatly. Kubrick's film consistently makes the child's pursuer at least equally the object of the viewer's laughter, undermining the knowing adult whose voiceover might otherwise establish a special confidence with the spectator. In telling contrast, Lyne spotlights Lolita's childish qualities for the adult's impassioned response, effectively alienating the viewer from the child even as he insinuates Humbert's perspective.

Together, the two films offer different visions of (to return to Lebeau's terms) the adult's seduction by the image of a child. Lolita does cater to Humbert's possessive imagination in each film, but not nearly so equally to any such impulse in the viewer. The changes she undergoes from Kubrick's film, which appeared near the end of the Hollywood studio era, to Lyne's film, which appeared relatively early in the age of the Internet, suggest that the films targeted different taboos: for the earlier film, it is the adult Humbert's appetite for the child Lolita, which Kubrick holds up for comic undermining, that scandalizes. But for the later film, it is the sexual provocativeness of the girl that is to shock and titillate, the innocence and license she so brazenly combines inciting her poor adult victim to his helpless crimes of love. For the later film, Lolita becomes, more or less, the femme fatale that Humbert frequently jokes about her being in the book, a wanton, willful, even deadly temptress whose most childlike qualities only provoke the helplessly besotted Humbert all the more (at least as he would have it). As a result of these differences, the child actually emerges in much better shape from the older than from the recent film, despite the latter's designs on enlightened "realism."[13]

How did they ever make a film of *Lolita*?

The marketing campaign for Stanley Kubrick's 1962 film of Nabokov's novel made heavy use of a coy come-on line of a question: how did they ever make a film of *Lolita*? The question not only panders to a knowing (and presumably male) viewer, but also, once again, underscores the special potency of the film image; it may be all well and good to tell such a story in mere words, but to put it on screen is to push the bounds of (sexual) propriety.

In any event, Kubrick and producer James Harris used Nabokov's screenplay to make a remarkably straightforward version of the story, one that is much less coy than its tag line. The visual treatment of the title character acknowledges and even, at times, emphasizes sexual possibility and allure, but, rather remarkably, in ways that manage never simply to place her at Humbert's or the viewer's easy disposal. The film effectively embeds her sexuality within a capacious innocence that complicates Humbert's otherwise natural authority as both the voice of the narrative and the successfully predatory adult.

In Lolita's carefully-constructed debut, the film immediately and effectively combines innocence with deliberate sexuality. Lolita first appears quite exposed in her backyard, reclining within a static frame in just a two-piece bathing suit, but projecting perfect comfort in her skin, even under Humbert's hungry eye. Kubrick's treatment of this signal passage from the book makes Lolita a worthy foil for Humbert, neutering the authority of his palpable appetite. Kubrick begins to build toward this effect immediately, cutting to a full shot of Lolita sunning herself *before* Humbert enters, so that she is looking at him before he can see her. The whole scene that ensues, therefore, proceeds more from her perspective than his. Also, Kubrick supplies his Lolita with a radio that she has set to the kind of popular music that leaves Humbert in the novel helplessly uncomprehending, a repulsive aural equivalent (as he characterizes it) to the cloying fudge that Lolita constantly eats.[14] Kubrick therefore arranges Lolita not simply for Humbert's or the viewer's visual pleasure, but also, precisely, for her own simple enjoyment, relaxed and self-assured in a way that Humbert markedly is not. Also, importantly, her mother, Charlotte, remains in the frame with Humbert, pressurizing his attempts to steal glances at the unembarrassed girl in the bikini, making *him* the comic spectacle as he struggles not to expose his lurid attentions while the girl confidently lowers her sunglasses to look him over. Crucially, then, Kubrick in no way elides Humbert's immediate and unseemly lust nor the frankness of the child's erotic interest and self-presentation. Nevertheless, both the editing and the mise-en-scène treat the child as an independent subject in her own right (not merely an object) in an arrangement that at once acknowledges both her relative innocence in the encounter and her entirely plausible recognition of the adult's lascivious gaze.

The subsequent scene uses an equally simple set-up to achieve an equally complex (and welcome) impression of the child's innocence. The scene opens with a jarring cut from a close-up of the girl's knowing smile in her backyard to a shot from a vintage horror film,[15] the camera dollying in rapidly on a monster ripping a bandage off his grotesquely disfigured face, an unmistakable reference to the previous scene's exposure of the monster in Humbert. Kubrick

Lolita. Directed by Stanley Kubrick. 1962.

then cuts to a tight-medium oblique shot of Humbert sandwiched between mother and daughter in the front seat of the family sedan at the drive-in. This set-up clearly invites the viewer to compare the respective responses of all three characters to the shocking images of the horror film. And all three register comparable transfixture, but with subtle, telling differences that emphasize the child's innocence without circumscribing it within Humbert's appetite. Lolita's expression remains remarkably unprotected, even unconscious, as Humbert smiles slightly at her side, appreciating the irony of the monster's unmasking more than mother or daughter. Charlotte, in the meantime, watches horrified but helplessly captive, noticeably wrinkling her nose and mouth with a repulsion that neither Humbert nor her daughter experiences. The child remains open, even innocent, before the horrifying image, suggesting that her mother's disgust arises from age, experience, and acculturation, a response that the child only learns in time. Some new onscreen horror causes mother and daughter to grab simultaneously for Humbert's hands, one on each knee, before all three withdraw their hands at the same time. Once again, then, the child emerges from the scene unmistakably more appealing than either of the adults, less calculating and notably more vulnerable. The child's innocence here in fact exposes the sexual possessiveness and manipulation of both the adults who share the screen with her, winning chuckles at their expense rather than suffering them at her own.

Another early scene which complicates the impression of childhood innocence has Lolita counting the revolutions she is making with her hula hoop while Humbert watches over the top of a book. Lolita stands directly in Humbert's line of sight, turned just far enough away from him to make it nearly impossible for her to see him, leaving it unclear whether she knows of his ill-disguised and palpably hungry gaze. But more important for the effect of this scene is the tight framing the camera initially takes on Humbert, the lower half of his face covered by the book but his eyes exposed as he watches a child who is initially offscreen, whose actions therefore initially constitute a mystery to the viewer. The spectator, in fact, would not even know that she is present but for her rhythmic counting, which is audible when the camera first shows Humbert's face. The counting makes it clear that she is repeating some sort of physical action over and over, but the nature of her endeavors remains a tantalizing mystery until the camera obligingly pulls back (more or less along Humbert's line of sight) sufficiently far to bring her gyrations into view. Humbert slowly lowers the book more or less in concert with the camera's removal to the more distant vantage point, his eyes locked on Lolita, leaving him oblivious as Charlotte enters from the house and startles both him and Lolita by taking his photo.

The brief hula hoop scene constitutes the second consecutive shot sequence— the entire scene unfolding in a single shot—typifying Humbert's time in the Haze household before Lolita departs for camp. Like the one that preceded it (a scene in which a white-nightgowned Lolita comes downstairs to bid good night to Humbert and Charlotte as they play chess), this shot sequence cleverly outlines the triangle of mutually exploitive relations that binds the three cohab-itants. It begins by pairing two members of the threesome in the foreground (Humbert with one of the women) while the third (the other female) intrudes gradually or eventually from the deep background of the frame, crossing a significant distance before she reaches the other two. This repeated set-up lets the viewer see what Humbert cannot, limiting his awareness and authority and bestowing an agency and independence on both mother and daughter that they would otherwise lack. Moreover, Humbert emerges as a kind of comic innocent himself, so completely (and salaciously) absorbed in the hula-hoop spectacle that he does not even notice Charlotte until the camera shutter clicks. The predator turns prey precisely in his predations, as helpless and vulnerable to Charlotte's visual consumption as his child quarry is to his (and even more so in that Charlotte captures an image of him in his unconscious state, memorializing his comical innocence).

But perhaps still more important in the hula hoop scene is the child's simple but resonant imaginative freedom. Lolita's play may spark the nympholept's erotic response, but it remains nevertheless completely and plausibly innocent. The child plays by testing her physical abilities, counting to apparently see how long she can keep the hoop aloft, perhaps to break a personal record—recreation with the subtly serious purpose of measuring one's growing control over one's body. But the rhythmic swaying of her hips—traditionally, of course, a site of sexualized attention—work just as well for the male predator who watches, transfixed by this spectacle of innocent sexuality. Still more cunningly, Kubrick sets up the scene to expose much more of Humbert's flesh than Lolita's, the self-styled enchanted hunter sitting in an open robe with his chest partly and his crossed legs completely exposed, so that the spectacle of sexualized innocence operates as much on its consumer as on its putative vehicle.

Perhaps most importantly, this ingeniously simple 30-second shot sequence finally liberates the spectacle of innocence, opening it up to new possibilities. Lolita is every bit as much an object here of sexualized attention as she is a child subject innocently enjoying simple bodily play, but instead of catering to the adult's erotic exploitation, the scene manages perhaps still more to honor the child's absorption. And this expansive effect depends, to a great degree, on the illusion of movement provided by a series of rapidly moving still images, for the majority of the frames that comprise the shot—especially those preceding Charlotte's intrusion that so surprises both Lolita and Humbert—would, if viewed individually, arrest the child's play for Humbert's voyeuristically ideal

Lolita. Directed by Stanley Kubrick. 1962.

vantage point, mere feet away while she turns in a direction that renders him invisible to her. But the combined effect of her counting, heard before she appears in the frame, and the casual, even bored demeanor with which she pursues the exercise, holds her free from the viewer's simple targeting as a naïf next to the more knowing (and therefore potentially more appealing) Humbert.

With these and many similar images, Kubrick cleverly creates safe space within both the frame and the dramatic context outside of Humbert's powerfully controlling gaze. In this safe space, Lolita is free to remain a child, to engage in unthinking and appealing play, an innocent rather than the ignorant vulgarian that Humbert often describes in the novel. Other subtle visual strategies only enhance this important dynamic. Kubrick rarely uses close-ups or shallow focus shots, for example, further thwarting or at least complicating Humbert's obsession, the wider framings consistently incorporating the settings in sufficient detail to ensure that the child seldom appears isolated within her pursuer's power. The generally high-key lighting, typical of comedies, also helps to deprive Humbert's presence and obsessive perspective of much of the forcefulness they can so easily exert. Kubrick enmeshes Humbert's sordid relationship with Lolita in a visually and dramatically complex mise-en-scène that protects the innocent child in Lolita, no matter how earnestly and even effectively Humbert manages (at least at times) to realize his exploitive fantasies with her. There are simply too many eyes watching Humbert watch Lolita within Kubrick's film for the nympholept to enjoy anything like free rein with her. As a result, when she rejects his final invitation to run away with him, Lolita shows simply and profoundly that she has grown into her own person, one who no longer relies on her stepfather—in sharp contrast to the tragically nostalgic coda that Humbert makes of this final encounter in the book (and which the later film allows him to have on screen).

Humbert's movie

Three-and-a-half decades after Kubrick's film appeared, Adrian Lyne brought out a vastly different vision of Nabokov's book, one that adheres much more closely to the storyline as Humbert so fancifully records it. The movie combines an impressively faithful plot with Lyne's signature glossy camera style to present a much more sexually aggressive and manipulative Lolita than her predecessor in Kubrick's film. In consequence, when she acts innocently, she ends up isolating herself, even alienating the viewer, whom Lyne clearly imagines to be more taken with Humbert's agonized romanticism than with the object of his hungry gaze herself. Lyne's film, in other words (and among other things), serves up precisely the kind of seduction that Lebeau detects in Kate Greenaway's illustrations: of the adult seduced by the *image* of childhood, the carefully packaged spectacle of a child's innocence. Humbert much more effectively mediates and therefore controls the viewer's experience of his "nymphet," exerting (as both a cause and a result) much greater authority in Lyne's version. Lyne himself, in talking of his film, declared it "Humbert's movie,"[16] an attempt to find a visual language that could serve as a true counterpart to the improbably romantic eloquence that Nabokov bestowed upon his vain, cruel wretch of a narrator. In the process, Lyne's film engages one of the other farthest-reaching legacies of Freud's sexual theories, as Lebeau characterizes it: children's innocence is defined not just by sexuality in general, but specifically by their sexual interest and curiosity,[17] so that (in the case of this film, at least) the child's innocence matters primarily in the way it offers itself up to Humbert's erotic response. The film therefore presents spectacles of innocence that humble and objectify the child while flattering the predatory adult.

Lyne establishes this pattern with Lolita's debut in the backyard, paging through a movie magazine as the spray from a rhythmically spinning sprinkler plasters her dress to her body (a convenient effect for Humbert's impassioned response). Lyne's Lolita is thoughtlessly, even helplessly sexual in her innocence. Whereas Kubrick has the child exert considerable control over her status and effect to make the adult gazer at least as vulnerable as she is, Lyne serves up the child's innocence as an extraordinary visual spectacle for Humbert's and the viewer's consumption. She is lying on her stomach paging slowly through a movie magazine, oblivious to the drenching both she and the magazine are receiving. Completely soaked by the time the viewer sees her, she must have been lying in the sprinkler's spray for a long time oblivious of her dress – a register of the child's literalness and unconcern for social conventions. To allow the sprinkler also to spray the magazine (even a trashy pop culture publication) further drives home her breezy, heedless disposition.

Other elements of Lyne's treatment enhance the spectacle. Humbert stares wide-eyed and helpless at Lolita, arrested by her mere appearance, while her mother—in direct contrast to her counterpart in the earlier film—conveniently removes herself from the frame. Nevertheless, the child continues to page idly through the magazine, allowing this strange adult to feast his predatory gaze as

Lolita. Directed by Adrian Lyne. 1997.

long as he likes. When she does finally look at him, it is only to smile broadly, displaying not only her retainer but an improbable welcome for his eager, hungry gaze. Seeking the most pronounced erotic effect for Humbert, Lyne presents Lolita as an extraordinarily subservient fantasy, the child as happily willing visual victim, her innocent backyard idyll geared entirely for the adult's wolfish appetites.

Lyne's Lolita does not always feed Humbert's salacious attention so directly, but other images still achieve similar effects. Lyne repeatedly, almost obsessively, captures Lolita eating, drinking, or chewing, using the child's simple appetites to emphasize Humbert's keen perceptions. Early in the film, for instance, Humbert follows her downstairs to find her sitting obliviously bare-legged in front of the open refrigerator, eating ice cream and playfully doling out raspberries one to a fingertip before plucking them off one-by-one. Lyne crosscuts shots of Humbert watching from the kitchen doorway with shots of the girl consuming her snack, dollying the camera in closer and closer on Humbert's smile as the child picks slowly picks the berries off her fingers, finally giving herself a stark white "mustache" of cream to crudely cap off the shot, followed only by a last image of Humbert's smile in tight medium, the camera finally at rest.

The refrigerator scene aggressively transforms the child's independence and creativity into a voyeuristic feast for Humbert (and the viewer). Considered entirely in their own rights, Lolita's actions from the beginning of the sequence to the end once again (and rather joyously) free her from social convention, showing how fully and comfortably she inhabits her body and how charmingly she will satisfy it. For example, she appears bare-legged before the refrigerator, even though she is wearing pajama bottoms at the beginning of the sequence; Lyne even incorporates a quasi-explanatory shot of Humbert discovering the bottoms on the upstairs landing before he heads down to the kitchen to find her at the refrigerator. But if this costuming change makes her a more vulnerable and tantalizing prospect for the stalker lodger with whom she now shares a bathroom, she would actually dispense with the bottoms simply because they are too long for her (as an earlier insert shot has shown, a couple inches of the fabric trailing on the floor). As a child plausibly would, therefore, she has simply freed herself of their encumbrance not in the privacy of her room, but right where it occurs to her to solve the problem—on the landing before she heads down to the kitchen. It is hardly a surprise then, that when this oblivious, even brazen child eats, she not only flouts all possible table manners, but also turns the imperative of hunger into play, adding tactile and visual pleasure with the raspberry-finger ritual.

But in Lyne's treatment, the child's charming midnight snack does little but feed Humbert's (and potentially the viewer's) appetites. Further, it urges the viewer not so much to enjoy her innocence and creativity for their own sake, but rather for the lascivious pleasure they afford to Humbert. The careful low-key lighting of the scene envelops the bodies of the actors in fetchingly soft shadows, while a romantic piano-and-strings air plays non-diegetically over the soundtrack, insinuating the lyrical ache of Humbert's palpable desire; with all these effects in play, only an unusually decisive and independent viewer could detach from Humbert's perspective at all. As the camera glides in closer and closer to Humbert, it also privileges his perspective all the more. The camera has merely cut in closer on *her* action, suggesting a given quality to what she is doing, consigning it, in fact, to the status of a flat spectacle. But for Humbert, the camera moves in slow and weightless, its movement subtly drawing out his dawning recognition of her obliviously sensual behavior. In the end, even the revelation of Lolita's milk mustache does not matter in itself, but only in Humbert's appreciative recognition of it as the emblem of a sex act he craves so frankly in the novel, referring nostalgically at one point to the "magic and might of her own soft mouth."[18] In Lyne's treatment, then, the child's creativity and innocence only ensure her picturesque defenselessness, heedless (unlike the adult who watches her so openly) of the erotic potential and implications of eating, her very existence mattering only in the way it stokes Humbert's predatory fantasies.

A more subtle but equally telling spectacle of innocence takes place when Humbert picks up Lolita from Camp Climax after Charlotte's death. The opening shots of Humbert's arrival at the camp stir up a vortex of girlish activity around the visual locus of the lone adult male, standing tall and relatively dignified in blue suit and hat within the frame. The girls all wear a uniform of white t-shirts and short shorts, and while they are lively and playful, they tend to move horizontally across the frame within fixed depths; Humbert, in contrast, tends to move vertically backward or forward within the depth of the frame. This visual clash between Humbert and the other girls works subtly to romanticize Lolita's carefully withheld appearance at the end of the sequence, lugging her oversized trunk up a hill in a trajectory that mirrors Humbert's, perpendicular to the horizontal flatness of the frame. Still more dreamily, Lolita appears entirely alone in these shots—the only shots in the camp sequence that allow a girl to appear by herself. The singles of Lolita here make for a (luridly) romantic reunion, feeding Humbert's (and the viewer's) most self-serving fantasies.

As for the child's innocence here—the aspect of the image that Lyne devises to make the viewer smile with Humbert—it stems subtly from Lolita's unthinking decision to lug the enormous chest up the steep, leaf-strewn road. The first time we have seen this trunk in an earlier scene, Lolita is carrying it to the car to head off to camp—but only with the help of Louise, the Haze household maid; it is simply too big and awkward for her to handle easily by herself. So why would she lug it up the hill by herself when she could have asked one of her fellow campers for help? Or still more easily, why wouldn't she have Humbert drive the car down the road to pick it up? Considered carefully, this scene makes little sense; if Lolita thought to get help when carrying the trunk downstairs, she would presumably think to get (easily available) help to transport it uphill—except that, by lugging it up the steep incline, she singles herself out happily from the rest of the campers for Humbert's joyful recognition and welcome. Once again, then, the child's innocence contrives an erotic spectacle for Humbert's and the viewer's consumption.

If Kubrick's vision is fundamentally comedic—a world in which no person is an island, where social relations surround and to some degree govern even the most cunningly secretive predator—Lyne's is much more conventionally tragic, isolating both Humbert and Lolita largely according to Humbert's wishes and designs. While the later film does occasionally threaten him with exposure, Humbert's true nemeses here are (1) Lolita's willfulness and (2) his rival, Clare Quilty, another lone nympholept with designs on Lolita. In service to this vision, Lyne's film consistently reduces Lolita's imaginative playfulness to the status of a sensual and comic spectacle, rendering innocence as an unfortunate or, at best, humorous deficit. Humbert's final vision of Lolita encapsulates both the insights and the costs of the film's literalist approach: as he looks at the married, pregnant, bespectacled Dolly Schiller standing at the door of the shack she shares with her husband, Humbert suddenly replaces the expecting mother with an image of Lolita as a smiling nymphet one last time, clad in the short blue shorts she has worn much earlier in the film to throw herself into his arms for their first kiss, her red hair once again in braids, swinging herself in beatific slow motion from the supports of the decrepit porch. The child, as Nabokov has Humbert put it in the novel, has been safely solipsized in Lyne's film, her happily eroticized image available at any point for the adult's imaginary invocation, for his own purposes, regardless of the reality she actually presents or embodies.

Lolita *Infans*

A surprisingly wide gulf separates Kubrick's vision of Lolita from Lyne's. In many ways, it seems as if Lyne's film takes several steps backward by treating the child's innocent but palpable sexuality as an inflammatory spectacle, as if the very idea that a child could initiate sex acts is the key revelation. Kubrick's film, by contrast, seems to accept, even embrace, the child's sexual awareness from Lolita's very first appearance, granting her authority at least equal to that of her adult pursuer even as the film constructs a child's innocently imaginative world within her actions. Quite apart from the often-remarked fact that Sue Lyon, the actress who played the title role for Kubrick, both looks and actually was a year or two older (at the respective times of filming) than Dominique Swain, her successor in Lyne's film, the earlier film's child appealingly combines sexuality with pre-adult imaginativeness, exerting control over her own sexuality in sharp contrast to her later much sadder counterpart, a child whose impulses and behavior are dismally enchained to Humbert's appetites.

What do these differences imply about the respective cultural moments and milieus of the two films? If Vicky Lebeau is right to suggest, in *Childhood and*

Cinema, that film has traditionally presented children in ways that encourage the spectator to find flatteringly powerful images of him or herself on screen, then what kinds of mirrors do these films offer us? For Lebeau, this transaction requires the filmed child to embody an inarticulate, unacculturated phase of existence that must come to an end, the stage of the *infans*, the "human infant – helpless, dependent, speechless … – [who] is born into the adult world of language, meaning, and desire."[19] The filmed child, in Lebeau's searching characterization, therefore emerges as a tantalizing, elusive figure for the spectator, unknowingly purveying crucial knowledge and feeding a troubling fatalism:

> First times, first things: the idiom of the *infans*, its fascination, can be found at work across the field of vision: in the very structure of looking in cinema, in the image of the child, as each comes to carry the delights, as well as the terrors, of an elsewhere, of a way of being otherwise. Bordering on an otherness within, a space and time that we have all known without knowing it, this is a child that must be left behind – or, more dramatically, put to death, to murder – if we are to find our way into the worlds of language, culture and community, but that we must, too, continually renegotiate.[20]

If the filmed child holds up a mirror to the viewer as offering a specialized site of nostalgia, affirmation, and foreboding, then it seems fair to say that Kubrick's mirror is (perhaps ironically, given his reputation for an austerely dark vision) considerably more hopeful and inviting than Lyne's, which largely reduces the child to a vehicle of agonizingly precocious sexuality. For Lyne (as for Humbert), Lolita's "otherness" as a child seems to consist of her inability to understand the fantastic sexual power she wields, whereas for Kubrick, Lolita's sexuality is merely a natural part of the person, existing along with and even within her childlike qualities. Childhood (for Kubrick, anyway) need not be a defect that adult maturity simply has to amend.

Nabokov's Humbert struggles with this idea as well. In the novel, when Lolita taunts him for not having kissed her yet, he cautions himself (and the reader) to remember that "she is only a child,"[21] coaching himself to act the adult who appreciates the limits of her understanding, to recognize and even protect the innocent she remains even as she flirts and initiates a kind of sex-play with him. Lyne's *Lolita* effectively confirms this perspective, consigning her to the status of a lesser being—*only* a child—whereas Kubrick's older and much less literally faithful film manages to achieve something greater: Kubrick's Lolita is not only a child, but remarkably and appealingly a child, a creature of much greater capacity and promise than her eventual counterpart ever gets a chance to be.

Notes

1 Dmitri Nabokov and Matthew J. Bruccoli (eds), *Vladimir Nabokov: Selected Letters 1940–1977* (San Diego: Harcourt Brace Jovanovich, 1989), 261. The author would like to thank Brian Boyd for referring him to the source of this quotation.

2 Ibid., 212.

3 Nabokov's next published novel was *Pale Fire* (1962).

4 For a useful overview of the moral dilemmas that the novel's reader faces, see Ellen Pifer's entry "*Lolita*" in Vladimir E. Alexandrov (ed.), *The Garland Companion to Vladimir Nabokov* (New York and London: Garland Publishing, Inc., 1995), 305–21. For a more specific consideration of Humbert's potent Romantic appeal, see my "It was Lilith He Longed For: Romanticism and the Legacies of *Lolita*" in Andrea Ruthven and Gabriela Madlo (eds), *Women as Angel, Women as Evil* (Oxford: Inter-Disciplinary Press, 2012), 141–53.

5 Film theorist Vicky Lebeau discusses Münsterberg's concerns about the damaging effects of cinema on children. See especially Vicky Lebeau, *Childhood and Cinema* (London: Reaktion Books, 2008), 44–8.

6 Laura Mulvey, "Visual Pleasure and Narrative Cinema," in Leo Braudy and Marshall Cohen (eds), *Film Theory and Criticism, 5th edn* (New York: Oxford University Press, 1999), 833–44. See especially pp. 837–43.

7 Lebeau, Childhood and Cinema, 87.

8 Ewa Mazierska, *Nabokov's Cinematic Afterlife* (Jefferson, NC and London: McFarland and Company, Inc., 2011), 18.

9 Ibid., 19.

10 Debbile Olson and Andrew Scahill (eds). *Lost and Othered Children in Contemporary Cinema* (Plymouth: Lexington Books, 2012), ix–x.

11 Ibid., x.

12 Vladimir Nabokov, *Novels 1955–1962* (New York: Library of America, 1996), 155.

13 In making this argument, I depart drastically from Mazierska's reading of Kubrick's film, as her insistence that Kubrick's innate misogyny elides Lolita's presence in the film misses out (in my viewing of the film) on important visual, editing, and narrative elements that allow the child to emerge as an appealing character in her own right. See Mazierska, *Nabokov's Cinematic Afterlife*, (2011), 27–31.

14 Nabokov, *Novels,* 138.

15 Vickers identifies the film as *The Curse of Frankenstein* (Hammer Productions,

1957). See: Graham Vickers, *Chasing Lolita* (Chicago: Chicago Review Press, 2008), 115.

16   Quoted in Ben Svetkey's "Girl Trouble," *Entertainment Weekly*, 9 August 1996, http://www.ew.com

17   Lebeau, Childhood and Cinema, 99–102.

18   Nabokov, *Novels*, 172.

19   Lebeau, Childhood and Cinema, 64.

20   Lebeau, Childhood and Cinema, 84.

21   Nabokov, *Novels*, 105.

Bibliography

Lebeau, Vicky. *Childhood and Cinema*. London: Reaktion Books, 2008.

Lolita. Dir. Stanley Kubrick. 1962. Burbank, CA: Warner Home Video, 2000. DVD.

—Dir. Adrian Lyne. 1997. Burbank, CA: Trimark Home Video, 2007. DVD.

Mazierska, Ewa. *Nabokov's Cinematic Afterlife*. Jefferson, North Carolina, and London: McFarland and Company, Inc., 2011.

Mulvey, Laura. "Visual Pleasure and Narrative Cinema." In Leo Braudy and Marshall Cohen (eds), *Film Theory and Criticism, 5th edn,* 833–44. New York: Oxford University Press, 1999.

Nabokov, Dmitri and Matthew J. Bruccoli (eds). *Vladimir Nabokov: Selected Letters 1940–1977*. San Diego: Harcourt Brace Jovanovich, 1989.

Nabokov, Vladimir. *Novels 1955–1962*. New York: Library of America, 1996.

—*Strong Opinions*. 1973. Reprint, New York: Vintage International, 1990.

Olson, Debbie and Scahill, Andrew (eds). *Lost and Othered Children in Contemporary Cinema*. Plymouth: Lexington Books, 2012.

Pifer, Ellen. "Lolita." Vladimir E. Alexandrov (ed.), In *The Garland Companion to Vladimir Nabokov*, 305–21. New York and London: Garland Publishing, Inc., 1995.

Svetkey, Ben. "Girl Trouble." *Entertainment Weekly*. August 9 1996. http://entertainmentweekly.com

Vickers, Graham. *Chasing Lolita*. Chicago: Chicago Review Press, 2008.

Walter, Brian D. "It was Lilith He Longed For: Romanticism and the Legacies of Lolita." In Andrea Ruthven and Gabriela Madlo (eds), *Women as Angel, Women as Evil*, 141–53. Oxford: Inter-Disciplinary Press, 2012.

Part Two

Childhood as Text

4

The "Rubbing Off" of "Art and Beauty": Child Citizenship, Literary Engagement, and the Anglo-American Playground and Play Center Movement

Michelle Beissel Heath
University of Nebraska, Kearney

In 2011, KaBOOM!, a nonprofit organization dedicated to building playgrounds, celebrated its fifteenth birthday by building its two thousandth playground. KaBOOM's aim of creating more play spaces for children is noble and has had political and commercial appeal: the current and former first ladies have lent visibility to its cause, and it has even generated its own Ben & Jerry's ice cream flavor.[1] But the organization's fun-promoting purpose reveals a darker side: it exists because of a perceived need to "save play." Similar concerns appear in fears over the allure of video and computer games, shrinking playground budgets, and poor playground upkeep. For Richard Louv and those involved with Elizabeth Goodenough's documentary film project "Where Do the Children Play?," the fear is a lost connection with nature.[2] For still others, such as Gill Valentine, the fear is lost independence, lost "street cultures," and ultimately lost experiences key to identity-formation.[3] At the same time as organizations like KaBOOM are building playgrounds to promote play, there are those who oppose playgrounds based on concerns that their uniformity actually inhibits children's free play, as well as the sense that playgrounds are spaces created by adults to contain and control children. Valentine, for example, argues that playground space is not "real" public space, but privatized "public" space, while John R. Gillis mourns that "increasingly super-vised" parks and playgrounds create "islanded" children "systematically excluded from the former mainlands of urban and suburban existence, especially the streets and other public spaces."[4] Indeed, Gillis proposes that the boundaries between adult and child worlds need to be more fluid. This would, he suggests, not only benefit children: it would improve the world for adults, as adults do not otherwise "know children as complex beings" and as what he calls "mainlands have become inhospitable for many adults as well as children."[5] Gillis emphasizes the importance of adult voices and acknowledgment of adult needs in creating shared spaces between adults and children, while those like Valentine, Louise Chawla, and David Driskell acknowledge that children's voices need to be heard more, particularly in the planning of such spaces. They call upon U.N. initiatives such as the Convention on the Rights of the Child to help achieve this.[6] Playgrounds, in other words, symbolize significant, contradictory problems for childhood and play today: kids playing outside do not really have their own spaces; kids playing outside are too isolated in their own spaces away from adults; kids are being kept out of the streets; kids are too much on the streets; kids do not play outside and are missing a connection with nature; and kids do play outside but are subject to adult interference even there.

What I wish to suggest from this brief overview of some of the recent criticism of children's play spaces is not that any of these positions are right or wrong—indeed, there is validity to many, if not all of them, contradictory as they are—but to point to continuity between them and the early discourse of the Anglo-American playground and play center movement. Concerns over playgrounds today overlook anxieties shared with the past with respect to child citizenship.[7] In this chapter I will examine the discourse of the early Anglo-American play movement alongside the discourse of play today to propose some of the reasons public play spaces became and remain central sites in notions and anxieties of citizenship. These reasons are related, as Karen Coats might suggest, to the fact that citizenship is a form of subjectivity and therefore "has resonances of both agency and subservience," that it is itself contradictory and complex and "beholden to the forces of its environment and in many ways limited by the possibilities of its time and culture, though it has some power to change and expand those possibilities."[8] I will argue, however, that these reasons reflect not only an inheritance left over from the Anglo-American play movement, but also children's symbolic potential for adults and a consistent aligning of play with literature.

The early play movement and the discourse of citizenship

It is generally admitted that a motivation behind the Anglo-American play movement at the turn of the nineteenth and twentieth centuries (from roughly the 1880s to about 1920) was to produce good citizens. Marta Gutman and Ning de Coninck-Smith observe that "at the beginning of the [twentieth] century, organized play on dedicated spaces was intended to socialize immigrant and working-class children, to inculcate gender norms, and to create a foundation for citizenship in democratic societies."[9] Dominick Cavallo's study of the early US playground movement also highlights the movement's socializing and civilizing efforts.[10] However, Cavallo critiques the movement's objectives by suggesting the intention was to take control of play from children and families in favor of the state. Some of Cavallo's claims—notably that of unilateral agreement within the movement that play should be supervised and organized—have been recently and rightly contested in an article by Ocean Howell, who claims that the influence of urban developers and other stakeholders in creating playgrounds should not be ignored. Howell goes too far, however, in claiming that "the socialization agenda" was "the most controversial aspect of the movement," although he is correct that the need for play to be supervised by trained volunteers or paid employees was not universally agreed upon.[11] The centrality of good citizenship to the movement can be gleaned through the very titles of articles offered in the proceedings and periodicals of the early Playground Association of America. Such articles include "Play as a School of the Citizen" (1907), "The Playground as a Phase of Social Reform" (1909), "Can the Child Survive Civilization?" (1909), "Play as an Antidote to Civilization" (1911), "Higher Standards of Citizenship Made Possible by Rural Recreation Centers" (1912), "The Schoolhouse Recreation Center as an Attempt to Aid Immigrants in Adjusting Themselves to American Conditions" (1912), "The Relation of Play to a Civilization of Power" (1913), and "Recreation as a Fundamental Element of Democracy" (1913). Belief in the movement as churning out good citizens is displayed repeatedly by play movement leaders and others. For example, in the February 1909 issue of *The Playground*, a monthly journal published by the association, The Philadelphia Grand Jury and Judge Staake endorsed the public playground through the claim that it "stands for body and character building and produces better children, homes, morals, and citizens."[12] Notably, these attempts at citizen- and character-building were just as contradictory as the discourse of the playground movement is today. Kenneth Kidd, in *Making American Boys* (2004), indicates that the very term "boy"—and I might add "child"—in the US has been and is often construed to mean white, middle class, straight, and Christian (generally protestant). If this point is taken into consideration, it becomes clear that The Philadelphia Grand

Jury's and Judge Staake's comments about "character building" are paradoxical and elusive, if not willfully naïve. According to Kidd,

> Native-born boys were a relatively secure form or embodiment of character, more so than, say, immigrant men who were arriving in droves. The success manuals and the boyology primers [of the time, from the late 1800s to about 1920] don't just ensure that this population of native-born, WASP boys can develop and claim character, they also ensure that character will belong solely to this particular group. Targeting this particular group of American subjects not only bestowed privilege but also checked the fungibility of such a generic and vague term.[13]

Such privileging and assumptions about boyhood, as Annette Wannamaker has observed, ensure that "women, gay men, and men of color can never, of course, fully gain access to subjectivity because they cannot transcend positions marked as Other."[14] When discussing children and play, play movement advocates often had "native-born," white, middle class, straight, Christian boys in mind—as the grand jury and Judge Staake likely do, given that "body" and "character building" tended to be applied more to "normative" boys rather than girls and Others. But those who were attracted to play sites in reality, as play advocates and organizers also had to admit, included Others, among them heterogeneous girls and immigrants.

Overall, the play movement's origins are rooted in worries over the roles of immigrants and the lower and working classes, and hope placed in recreation promoted through such ideas as the "People's Palace" (1896), which were encouraged by social problem novels such as English writer Walter Besant's *All Sorts and Conditions of Men* (1882). Origins can also be traced, however, to other notable "civilizing" reform efforts of the period. These include the child study movement, "child saving," and the increasing acceptance of Friedrich Froebel's kindergarten. All of these efforts gained force through the success of settlement homes in the US and Britain, which were especially important to the play movement. These settlements included Jane Addams' Hull House in Chicago, Toynbee Hall in London, and Mrs Humphry Ward's Passmore Edwards settlement in London, which was inspired in part by Mrs Ward's own religious social-problem novel, *Robert Elsmere* (1888). The Passmore Edwards Settlement was in fact the direct origin of the play center movement in Britain. After the failure of her religious settlement efforts, Mrs Ward redirected her vision to the part of her settlement that was thriving: a children's playroom. She then spent much of her life vigorously fundraising for play centers, opening play centers for able as well as disabled children, and encouraging the play movement on both sides of the Atlantic. She borrowed ideas from the US to open vacation schools and attempted, not quite successfully, to promote organized playgrounds and open school playgrounds in Britain. She even served as an honorary member of the Playground Association of America, helping to form within that association a circle of prominent citizens including literary figures. Other prominent members included honorary member US president Theodore Roosevelt and founding member Jane Addams. In its rhetoric and representatives, the play movement strove to enmesh itself in ideals of citizenship and citizen-building.

Past and present anxieties in the civilizing discourse of play

Playground discourse in the first part of the twentieth century and that of the first part of the twenty-first century tellingly display competing concerns that children need spaces of their own and that sharing play benefits adults and children alike. In *Concerning Children* (1901), US writer Charlotte Perkins Gilman, for instance, mourned lack of space and consideration bestowed on children: "a visitor from another planet, examining our houses, streets, furniture, and machinery," she observes, "would not gather much evidence of childhood as a large or important factor in human life."[15] Perkins Gilman expresses pleasure in the fact that "children's playgrounds are beginning to appear at last among people who have long maintained public parks and gardens for adults,"[16] but in her view the division between adult and child worlds evident today to Gillis was not in place at the end of the nineteenth century. Instead, there was only an adult world and, prophetically channeling Virginia Woolf's claims for women a few decades later, she suggests that children need room of their own. Lack of boundaries between adult and child worlds was not, however, viewed negatively by all. The very first article in the 1907 proceedings of the first play conference, held in Chicago after the founding of the American Playground Association, highlights how "everybody played."[17] Children and variously aged adults all played, and there was a sense that there should not be any spectators for, according to Dwight H. Perkins, then architect for the Chicago Board of Education, "every one of us ought to get into the game somewhere."[18] Such a belief was also expressed at the 1916 International Recreation Conference when Joseph Lee, president of the playground association at the time, remarked that

"Froebel's great word was: 'Come, let us play with our children' to which may be added in this day of the conscious re-birth of the community: 'Come, let us play with our neighbors.' The two together make a good play program."[19]

Early in the twentieth century as today, mixing child and adult play was viewed as beneficial not only for personal needs for play, but also for good citizenship and societal survival as waves of immigration, industrialization, and increased urbanization produced concerns. Thomas H. Russell, an early twentieth-century play advocate, voiced the movement's sense that churches and immigrant groups found playgrounds to be rich sites, an observation that calls attention to the movement's expectation that the effects of playgrounds are not confined to children and adolescents. Parents at playgrounds and organized activities, Russell commented in 1914, "find that they are drawn into social intercourse on common ground" and "are themselves educated and trained to take part in civic affairs."[20] This contradicts Kidd's reflection that adults, for many reformers, were unreformable[21]; certainly for many play and "child saving" advocates, adults could be saved—through their children. E. B. De Groot, a leader in the early play movement and part of Chicago's exemplary South Park System, made just as explicit the bubble-up effect of healthy citizenship he saw playgrounds as promoting: "dirt upon the hands and faces of the children of the streets rub off when it comes in contact with the bathing facilities of the park. Likewise," he insists, "do art and beauty 'rub off' in contact with young folks in the park and are no doubt carried to homes in expressions of home improvement."[22] Lawrence Veiller phrased it even more forcefully in 1907: "I take it, we are all agreed that the main purpose of having children is to educate and develop their parents, and from this point of view we should not lose sight of the developing power that the playground has upon the older generation."[23] Through their children and their children's play, adults and especially adults from the immigrant, working, and lower classes were envisioned as benefitting from the civilizing efforts of playgrounds. In place today are similar views. According to Suzanne H. Crohurst Lennard, in her chapter in Goodenough's *A Place for Play* (2008), "because of their natural playfulness, the presence of children within varied social groups often helps adults to be more sociable."[24] In her view, children and their play help people with different cultural and ethnic backgrounds and values to get along. Joan Almon, also writing in Goodenough's volume, more broadly believes that "in our stressful times, play is needed at all ages" and that watching their children play helps parents to relax.[25]

Almon's and Crohurst Lennard's views underscore the degree to which children, play, and public play spaces are still related to notions of "civilization" today. Indeed, the present-day arguments and anxieties over playgrounds I outlined at the beginning of this chapter could almost be taken verbatim from late nineteenth- and early twentieth-century playground and play center discussions. Immigrant and working-class areas in the US and Britain still tend today to have few public places for children and a need for such spaces is still generally acknowledged. In her 2008 case study of the immigrant-heavy area of Sunnyside in New York, for example, Susan Turner Meiklejohn points out that "Sunnyside has less recreational space per person than just about anywhere in New York City" and that those in Sunnyside "are very aware of the lack of public play spaces for children."[26] Sophie Watson makes similar observations in 2006 in her case study of two groups of London schoolchildren.[27] Jenny Holt, remembering her own British childhood, remarks that "my school in the 1980s had nothing but a square of tarmac and a field."[28]

Anxieties over children's safety and juvenile delinquency are also as prominent today as they were in early twentieth-century discussions. Exaggerated media attention has contributed to adult fears of kidnapping and abuse, leading to a presumed rise in children staying indoors. Gang violence is also a continued concern today. Both of these concerns are strikingly reminiscent of early twentieth-century anxieties. Russell observed in 1914 that an impetus for the play movement was the realization that "thousands of children were found to be growing up in the streets, coming into conflict with the police, and their hope of useful manhood and womanhood being destroyed."[29] Through playgrounds and organized play, he insisted, "tough gang leaders" with criminal records could be "transformed into forces for good."[30] Mrs Ward's play center fund-raising appeals in London's *The Times* early in the twentieth century repeatedly stress easing parental anxiety about their children's after-school safety: "I could easily fill a column with unsought testimonials," she states in a 1914 plea, "given by parents, often the poorest of the poor, to the good which play centers have done for their children, and to the relief brought to their own minds by the thought that Tommy and Louie are safe and happy in those dangerous hours."[31] Despite the promises of children having street cultures of their own, in the early twentieth century streets were, as today, often viewed as dangerous for children. Not only were children's moral and physical safety at risk from juvenile delinquency, but children's lives were endangered by encounters with the newly introduced automobiles. According to Viviana A. Zelizer, "by 1910 accidents had become the leading cause of death for children ages five to fourteen."[32] World War I Zeppelin bombings and enforced blackouts only enhanced those dangers in London.

Concerns over children's play needs, child safety, and the usefulness of public play spaces in "civilizing" children are all manifest in considerations of supervised play today. While supervised play is viewed suspiciously by some as, for example, limiting children, others find in it an ideal means to provide "safe" play and to encourage "civilized" behavior. In 2007, *The New York Times* announced the creation of an "Imagination Playground" in New York employing trained "play workers" based on a "concept" "popular in Europe."[33] The *Times* does not connect these play workers to early twentieth-century play organizers or even to the adventure play movement that began in the middle of the twentieth century, but the article does emphasize parental approval of such play workers. One parent, for instance, indicated that "well-trained and carefully screened workers could help children develop manners, engage their imagination, and most important, provide an extra layer of security."[34] As the parent's comments indicate, public play spaces like "Imagination Playground" are still considered civilizing sites, places to encourage "good manners" while keeping children busy and "secure."

Cultivating citizenship through child crowds and public play spaces

In addition to providing "safe" and "civilizing" fun, play centers and playgrounds served day care needs. In 1914, for example, Mrs Ward indicated part of the success of her centers was due to "the wide prevalence in all the poorer districts of married women's work."[35] She also commented upon the need to provide cots for the baby sisters and brothers young girls often brought with them when they came to play. Similar observations were made in the US. That same year playground association members observed that "in Seward Park mothers were in the habit of putting their children to sleep and then going away, so that the teacher in charge really had a nursery on her hands."[36] Organizers tried to discourage the dropping-off of children by transforming playgrounds into shared spaces where mothers would bring "sewing, knitting, crocheting," or other occupations with them and by "provid[ing] books for them to read while their infants are sleeping."[37] But the need was overwhelming. One playground association member reflected, "one principal said to me last summer," presumably the summer of 1913, "'What shall I do? I have thirty-eight babies who want to sleep, and only eighteen hammocks.'"[38]

Such displays of tremendous need make apparent some of the ways in which public play spaces became obvious sites for citizenship development. They did so through the idea of the "crowd." A striking feature of photographs and descriptions in play movement documents is obvious demand evidenced by masses of thronging children. In 1920, Mrs Janet Trevelyan, Mrs Ward's youngest daughter, describes in detail some of the crowds she dealt with at the Passmore Edwards settlement: "one evening," she observes, "I had to cram in 136 [children] 'sitting on seventy-six chairs, two hot-water stoves, and one small table,' as my diary of the time reminds me, so that it really was too tight a fit, and although they heard me out they broke into wild riots at the end, stormed the platform out of sheer relief from cramp, and reduced me to behave 'like Ajax on his ship.'"[39] The anxieties over "pandemonium" and maintaining order she acknowledges were far from unusual. The crammed-together 136 children she describes was actually a relatively small number. In a December 21, 1914 letter to the editor of *The Times*, Mrs Ward notes that one evening she encountered 1,400 children at a play center, 412 playing in one room alone.[40] The play centers were so popular that administrators had to resort to taking children in by shifts and to distributing "tickets" of admission to children on merit, need (including parental pleas), and first-come-first-served bases. US playground association materials detail similar demand. In 1908, for example, daily attendance figures at Brooklyn playgrounds ranged from 200 at Greenpoint Park to 2,000 at New Lots Playground and McLaughlin Park.[41] In attendance at the opening of Jones Park in East St. Louis, Illinois, on June 12, 1914, were 25,000 people. Over 5,000 of them made use of the swimming pool.[42]

Descriptions of such crowded scenes by play movement advocates are revealing. In both the US and Britain throughout the nineteenth century, crowds were increasingly common in public life and public imaginations, and took on a variety of meanings. There were revolutionary crowds, evocative in early nineteenth-century Anglo-American imaginations with the French Revolution and later with the Chartist movement, which were potentially dangerous politically and physically. There were democratic crowds, the mass of "the people" pivotal to democratic societies. There were also consumer crowds, gatherings of people at commercial sites such as shopping spaces and entertainment venues and indicative of increasingly urban life.[43] Conceptions of crowds became simultaneously common and democratic, the essence of democratic citizenship and potentially threatening—as of course were children. Our conceptions of children are often predicated on the idea of crowd or multiplicity: more than with the plural of adult, "adults," or even the ideas of "men" and "women," the word "children" conjures up an image of a crowd or a swarm, or at the very least a group. A single child, "the child," may be an ideal and a symbol, but real children tend to be clustered into collective entities in our minds: in families, with siblings, in classrooms. That they should necessitate public space and spur "civilizing" discourse in this light makes perfect sense: since, in the Anglo-American tradition, crowds are public entities and a crucial part of democratic civilization, child crowds obviously warrant public spaces and civilizing attention to fulfill their democratic destinies. Cries for supervision to maintain order amidst the sheer physicality of crowd numbers also makes sense: crowds are potentially dangerous and even child crowds, as Trevelyan notes, can break into riot. Flag salutes, patriotic drills, and child "governments" at play sites are just a few of the means by which early twentieth-century play organizers sought both to keep order and to shape child crowds and individuals into "civilized," democratic ideals.

Why public spaces designed to inculcate "good citizenship" took the specific form of play spaces relates to various views of play itself. For many, play is simply what children do; therefore, encouraging children in their "natural" acts makes sense. Play is itself "irreducible" and an "irreducible" part of children's nature, as play philosopher Johan Huizinga would phrase it.[44] Play is also, however, connected for many to notions of performance, to acts of creation. In this case, then, it makes sense to connect play to the "creation" of "civilized" children. Indeed, as Robin Bernstein reminds us, "the Child Study Movement" "successfully promulgated the idea that children's imaginative practices, especially girls' play with dolls, could and should serve cultural purposes."[45] Bernstein cites Alice Minnie Herts Heniger, whose Children's Educational Theatre strove "to mold the behaviors and imaginations of immigrant and first-generation children so as to Americanize them, and through them, their families," as being "among those who believed in the power of children's imaginative play, as performance, literally to shape civilization."[46]

The performative, "creative" connection made regarding play at the turn of the nineteenth and twentieth centuries was even more poignantly apparent through the physical origin of playgrounds. At the end of the nineteenth century, play spaces were generally just empty lots or rooms; at best, they were gardens (hence, the idea of infant and child gardens). The first equipment generally introduced at play sites in fact kept to the original garden theme: sand gardens. Such a theme, as Morag Styles notes in her discussion of children's poetry, remains consistent with the alignment of childhood and nature.[47] It was only through the popularity of gymnastics that the equipment we tend to associate with playgrounds today found its way to play spaces. In their initial forms, children's play spaces were designed to create gardens of cultivated flowers, human and botanical, out of emptiness, if not out of desolation and waste. Indeed, the first public play sites startlingly demonstrate this, as they were often carved out of literal leftover spaces, including abandoned graveyards and prisons. For example, a note in London's *The Times* on 20 June 1900 announced the opening of a former burial ground as the Collier's Rents Recreational Ground and cited a Metropolitan Public Gardens Association representative as suggesting "that altogether they had laid out 102 open spaces in London, comprising 140 acres, at a cost of £46,000, but there were still 160 disused burial grounds, &c., which might well be turned into places for recreation."[48] Fifteen years earlier, *All the Year Round* celebrated the transformation of "Horsemonger Lane Gaol, once the dreariest of all London prisons" into "now, perhaps, the happiest spot of ground in all the metropolis" as a children's playground.[49] It still exists today as Newington Gardens, a public park. In 1908 Henry S. Curtis, one of the founders of the playground association, mapped Washington D.C.'s abandoned cemeteries with the hope of turning them into playgrounds, observing as he did so "that London had taken sixty-seven cemeteries within the last few years for playgrounds."[50] On both sides of the Atlantic, playgrounds were established on deserted sites and called upon to create and perform: to transform, through play, neglected places into gardens and to mold children into model democratic crowds, exemplary public figures, and ideal citizens.

Creative potential: Play and the power of stories

Insistent literary connections reinforced the civic, performative, and creative purposes embedded in playgrounds. Indeed, as early as 1874, *The Graphic* linked playgrounds both with graveyards and prominent literary figures: "It was, we believe, Charles Dickens who originated the idea of furnishing cockney children with playgrounds … But the scheme, though agitated for a while, was gradually dropped and heard of no more until the other day, when somebody [observed] that there is an old disused grave-ground in Drury Lane."[51] Throughout the

early twentieth century play sites continued such connections by housing books
and libraries and by offering storytelling sessions and theatrical productions
and reenactments. The Playground Association even assigned a committee to
investigate storytelling on the playground. In 1909, the committee defended
the value of "a good story" as protecting children "from the harmful literature
known as 'the penny dreadful,' the comic Sunday supplement, and sentimental
books," while insisting that "dramatic expression" is such "a valuable aid" that
"children should be encouraged to act out their favorite stories."[52] It also made
the presumed essential connection between playground and story explicit.
Listing what it saw as the "underlying principles" and "ideals" of the fledgling
playground movement, the committee reported that "in the end the playground
as a finished product should give beauty and perfection – not only to the body
of the child, but also to the soul ... The story reaches the spiritual child."[53] The
"purpose of the story" on the playground was to give children something "by
means of the imagination" to "strive to imitate," "to give high ideals which are
reproduced in character," such as "generosity, kindness, hospitality, courage,
heroism, chivalry, etc."[54]

Symbolizing this attempt to encourage "high ideals" through "imaginative
capabilities" and "good" literary connections is the tendency of early twentieth-
century playgrounds to be associated with literary texts and figures: examples
include "Little Dorrit's Playground" in Southwark; J. M. Barrie's playground
in Kensington Gardens; and Hans Christian Andersen, Lewis Carroll, and
Robert Louis Stevenson playgrounds in Oak Park, Illinois. These playgrounds
not only offered children public play spaces, but serve as a reminder of what
good literature was and what good citizens could do: be charitable, make sacri-
fices, overcome obstacles, explore and colonize the world, domesticate and
civilize, and become great authors or other prominent citizens. Little Dorrit's
Playground, for example, was established in 1902 on a disreputable space near
the prison where Dickens' father was confined for debts, reminding visitors both
of Dickens' achievements and of the difficulties he experienced on the way to
becoming a renowned author. J. M. Barrie's playground in Kensington Gardens
has today been remodeled and named the Diana, Princess of Wales' Memorial
Playground, but its literary connection flourishes: Peter Pan, complete with
pirate ship and teepees, is the inspiration for the playground's theme. Barrie's
Peter Pan stories, along with the empire-building and adventure-prone novels
and stories of his contemporaries Stevenson and Rudyard Kipling (also popular
at play site story hours and with play movement leaders), may seem resistant

to adult intervention, but they are in fact filled with proper ideals of British citizenship. Peter Pan may be derisive of adults, but when, in *Peter and Wendy* (1911), the lost boys and the Darling children are threatened by the unpatriotic pirates in Neverland, they all know what they must do: Curly must cry "Rule Britannia!," John and Michael must affirm their allegiance to the king, and Wendy must prepare the boys to "die like English gentlemen."[55] Fairy tales, including Carroll's *Alice* books, meanwhile, were useful for play site performances and for encouraging domesticity for girls. The January 1914 issue of *The Playground* includes photographed reenactments from Dayton, Ohio, of Wonderland's Mad Tea Party and Snow White with a few dwarves.[56] A "Play Day" in Johnstown, Pennsylvania, in 1916 involved "between 12,000 and 13,000 people" "who were entertained at sunset by *Mother Goose in Fairyland*, participated in by about five hundred children."[57] Snow White, like many other fairy tale figures, is tellingly domestic, at least in the Grimm Brothers' portrayals of her.[58] Alice's adventures of the garden-party (tea, croquet, dancing, and cards) are also notably those of a typical Victorian upper-middle-class girl. With a thimble in her pocket, Alice is in fact an ideal girl citizen for play organizers who promoted sewing among their activities for girls.[59]

Mrs Ward, the early play movement's most prominent literary figure, also epitomized gendered aspects of good citizenship, as well as the creative potential of play and stories. Her literary and social work demonstrate the power of storytelling, linked with play, as a creative act influencing real-world people and events, a feature which made it so attractive to play organizers. In her only children's novel, the obscure but domestic *Milly and Olly* (1881), Mrs Ward not only offers strong foreshadowing of her play center movement (the book's pages are filled with praises of kindergartens and play), but vicariously transforms herself into an idealized female adult citizen. Mrs Ward, unlike Jane Addams, chose not to live at her settlement house. Preferring genteel surroundings, she deftly transferred direct play center responsibilities to her daughters and others. She delighted, however, in sweeping in at odd moments to perform good deeds and solve problems so as to, as her biographer John Sutherland puts it, "enhance the 'Fairy Godmother' role" she imagined for herself.[60] This was a role straight out of her children's book: her character Aunt Emma is beloved by children, but distant from their daily lives; she is a figure who is visited or visits at holidays, tells stories, solves domestic problems, and then leaves. She is even asked by one of the children, as Mrs Ward seems to have wanted to have been asked, "were you ever a fairy godmother?"[61] Aunt Emma's role as fairy godmother, storyteller, and player is further demonstrated when she appears unexpectedly on a rainy day with gifts of toys and "a story-telling game."[62] Both Mrs Ward and Aunt Emma see obvious links between stories and play, strive to make stories into play and play into stories, and to make play and fiction into reality and reality into play and fiction. For Mrs Ward this meant trying to transform *Robert Elsmere* into a social movement and trying to transform herself into an Aunt Emma.

Tellingly, creative possibilities and power seemingly inherent in the linking of stories and play is not lost on play advocates today. All of the early twentieth-century playgrounds cited above exist still today and play today is still adamantly connected with "good" literature. In New Orleans' City Park, children can wander down Jack and Jill's hill-shaped slide, embark on adventures in Peter Pan's ship, and surround themselves with representations of other classic figures and themes from fairy tales, nursery rhymes, and children's literature in a play space called "Storyland." At the Strong National Museum of Play in Rochester, New York, children can play in "Reading Adventureland" and meander along "the yellow brick road" to places including "Upside-Down Nonsense House" and "Fairy Tale Forest." Universal Studios' Harry Potter-themed park, Disney's amusement parks, and the Dickens World theme park also foreground literary couplings. Even the explanatory discourse has not altered significantly: echoing the early twentieth-century playground association's storytelling committee, Almon justifies links between stories and play by crediting imagination. To play, she says, children "need healthy nourishment for their imaginations in the form of storytelling, including fairy tales and nature tales."[63]

What *is* lost

Ironically, though the power and potential of linking stories and play is not lost to play advocates today, the sense of their own storytelling and "gifting" is. Playworkers pride themselves on giving children "unadulterated" play but do not always realize the fictions they are creating. In one of her playwork descriptions, for example, Penny Wilson excitedly explains the process of a playworker allowing a child to toss colored chalk into water and then "describ[ing] in words which the child cannot voice, the things they are watching together: the bubbles rising, the chalks changing colour and drifting lazily to the bottom of the pool."[64] Supplying the adult's voice to fill the child's supposed lack is not only "adulterating," but also a form of storytelling, providing a narrative of what is supposedly "seen" by both child and adult, a story the voiceless child cannot verify. Such adulteration and storytelling are also on display in the insistence of some play advocates today that children have forgotten how to play but that, as Almon phrases it, they "can be brought back to it" by seeing "that adults value play" and with "help in re-entering the space of play."[65] Similar sentiments were also commonly expressed in early twentieth-century play movement discourse: play organizers then suggested, for instance, that children needed to be "taught to play as carefully as they are taught to read, cipher, and spell."[66] In such scenarios, both today and in the past, adults become not only fairy godparents like Mrs Ward and her fictional Aunt Emma ("gifting" play to children), but arbiters of play—authorities in what play is and what it is not. A danger, of course, is that what adults want play to be is based on their own sense of what children need and want to be good citizens and human beings, what adults' sense of good citizens and human beings are, what adults' own desires are to "help" children or to give meaning to their own lives, and what adults' nostalgia is with respect to their own childhood play. In other words, play critics and advocates today and early in the twentieth century both rely on their own imaginative and fictional creations to form stories of ideal children and play.

Such creations, based almost exclusively on adult perceptions and memories, tend remarkably to fight against change and to mistake older notions as "new" ideas. Richard Louv's "Leave No Child Inside" campaign and the children's garden trend promoted by Anna Halverson and her colleagues today, for example, both notably tend to ignore the fact that they are just repeating the past: in the Anglo-American play movement, play started with children's gardens and with the belief that children needed nature.[67] Indeed, Kidd reminds us not only of the ways in which current fears of a "boy crisis" have evolved out of earlier movements, but also of the late nineteenth- and early twentieth-century practice of relocating large numbers of children from urban to rural environments in a system known as "placing out."[68] The Children's Aid Society alone relocated about 90,000 children from New York City between 1853–90, he suggests.[69] He also notes that "reformers sometimes shipped kids to the country for a day or so, in the hopes that brief exposure to the 'great outdoors' might work wonders. 'Country Weeks' and 'Fresh Air' funds were financed by major newspapers."[70] Placing out efforts were far from controversial and evidence regarding their benefit to children is mixed. Some relocated children, for example, did find loving homes, but many found themselves merely laboring hands in alien lands, and many were traumatically separated from siblings, sometimes forever. If nature movements and children's gardens were not the answer a century ago (and the subsequent shut down of placing out programs and the development of the still-problematic foster system today indicate this), how can we be so confident they will work now? In their discussions of play today, critics often hint at a presumed golden age of children's play, an age that seems to have existed mere decades ago, but as Colin Ward reminded us in 1978, "every generation assumes that the street games of its youth have been destroyed by the modern city."[71]

Ignoring the discourse of the earlier play movement enables us to forget these details and to overlook insights we might otherwise glean as to what might be harmful, and what beneficial, to children and adults today. We may forget, for example, that the stories we may create about childhood and play may actually essentialize children, not take into account potential complexity and variety. In our attempts to do right, we may neglect to remember our own nostalgia and neediness: today, as was the case early in the twentieth century, we are still in danger of generalizing children and childhood, of assuming, for instance, that because some children form beneficial street cultures, all children should, or because many children reap benefits through connections with nature, all children will. Forcing children outside can be just as islanding, to borrow Gillis' term, as locking them indoors. We also tend to forget, in narratives and discourse of play and good citizenship today, to credit children's own agency and imaginative potentials, their own powers of resistance and story-making. We may be concerned about the quality and presence of play spaces today, and alarmed at the thought that play today involves video games and computers; however, children do still play. Time and again in history, children play regardless of the conditions in which they find themselves. As Peter and Iona Opie disturbingly remind us, even at Auschwitz during World War II, children played "a game called 'Going to the Gas Chamber.'"[72] We need not fear, then, that play is being "destroyed" or that children have "forgotten" how to play: children are playing— they just are not always playing what adults want them to. Indeed, even when we may most desperately wish they would refrain, children play.

We need to be cognizant, then, of our own desires and stories surrounding children's play: in what ways are our wishes for certain types of and spaces for play reflective of what is truly best for children, and in what ways are they merely reflective of our own nostalgic sense of what play should be, based on what we believe it has been? In his *A History of Children's Play and Play Environments*

(2010), Joe L. Frost claims that "a twenty-first century child saving movement" modeled after the early twentieth century "is sorely needed."[73] His evidence for such a need frequently turns to his own memories of a 1930s childhood and comparisons with nineteenth-century descriptions. He celebrates, for example, the presumed similarity between his childhood and that of the mid-nineteenth century depicted by C. D. Warner: "the differences in our experiences were that John drove oxen and I drove a team of mules, and while alone driving a wagon, one of my dearest friends at that time fell out and was killed when run over by a wheel. We all reveled in having a horse to ride, cows to chase, and games to play."[74] The unsettling shift in Frost's sentences from the death of a child to "we all reveled in" underscores the text's at-times blind nostalgia, its willingness to overlook potential harm—the tragedy of traumatic child death in this case—for the belief in the value of some types of "play" (Frost defines driving mules or oxen as play) over others. The death, it would seem, is nothing to, as Frost offers Warner's words, "a glorious feeling" "when a boy is for the first time given the long whip and permitted to drive the oxen."[75] Play, as Warner's and Frost's examples of ox and mule driving vividly demonstrate, reflects societal definitions and attitudes, including conceptions of maturity and "good" child citizenship, and must therefore necessarily change over time. Play must fit into the actual worlds children experience—for many children in the US and Britain today, for example, that world does not include mules and oxen. Nor should it necessarily include them. Attempts to alter or control play based on a sense of a past (generally nonexistent) ideal betrays both noble attempts to create better worlds ("art and beauty," for example, "rub[bing] off" and "bubbl[ing] up") for children and adult anxieties about change and about the future. Such attempts overlook fictions created about play, fictions at times bolstered by consistent linking of play, literary engagement, and good citizenship. Such attempts also ignore, at times, the reality that the story of play itself has a history and that children are more than just idealized individual symbols and potentially threatening crowds. Such attempts often ignore, too, the reality that children, as much as adults, shape the story of play.

Notes

1   "Highlights in KaBOOM! History," KaBOOM.org, http://kaboom.org [2013].

2   See Richard Louv, *Last Child in the Woods* (Chapel Hill, NC: Algonquin Books,

2005) and Elizabeth Goodenough (ed.), *Where Do the Children Play?: A Study Guide to the Film* (Michigan Public Media, 2007).

3   Gill Valentine, *Public Space and the Culture of Childhood* (Aldershot: Ashgate, 2004), 101.

4   Ibid., 102; John R. Gillis, "Epilogue: The Islanding of Children – Reshaping the Mythical Landscapes of Childhood" in Marta Gutman and Ning De-Coninck-Smith (eds), *Designing Modern Childhoods* (New Brunswick: Rutgers University Press, 2008), 316–30.

5   Gillis, "Epilogue," 327–8.

6   See, for example, Louise Chawla and David Driskell, "Having a Say about Where to Play: A Serious Way to Learn Democracy" in Elizabeth Goodenough (ed.), *A Place for Play* (Carmel Valley, CA: The National Institute for Play, 2008), 65–81.

7   For a more detailed consideration of child citizenship (and its historical evolution) itself, including aspects of its "imaginary" functions, see Courtney Weikle-Mills, *Imaginary Citizens: Child Readers and the Limits of American Independence, 1640–1868* (Baltimore: Johns Hopkins University Press, 2013).

8   Karen Coats, *Looking Glasses and Neverlands: Lacan, Desire, and Subjectivity in Children's Literature* (Iowa City: University of Iowa Press, 2004), 3.

9   Marta Gutman and Ning De Coninck-Smith, "Introduction: Good to Think With – History, Space, and Modern Childhood" in Marta Gutman and Ning De-Coninck-Smith (eds), *Designing Modern Childhoods* (New Brunswick: Rutgers University Press, 2008), 10.

10 Dominick Cavallo, *Muscles and Morals: Organized Playgrounds and Urban Reform, 1880–1920* (Philadelphia: University of Pennsylvania Press, 1981).

11 Ocean Howell, "Play Pays: Urban Land Politics and Playgrounds in the United States, 1900-1930," *Journal of Urban History* 34.6 (September 2008): 988, 961–94.

12 "The Philadelphia Grand Jury and Judge Staake Endorse the Playground Movement," *The Playground* 23 (February 1909): 4, 3–5.

13 Kenneth B. Kidd, *Making American Boys: Boyology and the Feral Tale* (Minneapolis: University of Minnesota Press, 2004), 71.

14 Annette Wannamaker, *Boys in Children's Literature and Popular Culture: Masculinity, Abjection, and the Fictional Child* (New York: Routledge, 2008), 31.

15 Charlotte Perkins Gilman, *Concerning Children* (Boston: Small, Maynard, and Co., 1901), 120.

16 Ibid., 120.

17 Graham Romeyn Taylor, "How They Played at Chicago" in *Proceedings of the Annual Playground Congress* (New York: Playground Association of America, 1907), 1, 1–10.

18 Cited ibid., 1–2.

19 Joseph Lee, back cover, *The Playground* 10.1 (April 1916).

20 Thomas H. Russell, *Stories of Boy Life* (Chicago: The Homewood Press, 1914), 177.

21 Kidd, *Making American Boys*, 94.

22 Cited in Russell, *Stories of Boy Life*, 189.

23 Lawrence Veiller, "The Social Value of Playgrounds in Crowded Districts" in *Proceedings of the Annual Playground Congress* (New York: Playground Association of America, 1907), 39, 37–40.

24 Suzanne H. Crowhurst Lennard, "The City as Playground" in Elizabeth Goodenough (ed.), *A Place for Play* (Carmel Valley, CA: The National Institute for Play, 2008), 209.

25 Joan Almon, "Entering the World of Play" in Elizabeth Goodenough (ed.), *A Place for Play* (Carmel Valley, CA: The National Institute for Play, 2008). 23.

26 Susan Turner Meiklejohn, "Sunnyside Gardens Today" in Elizabeth Goodenough, (ed.), *A Place for Play* (Carmel Valley, CA: The National Institute for Play, 2008), 221.

27 Sophie Watson, *City Publics: The (Dis)enchantments of Urban Encounters* (London: Routledge, 2006), 129–30.

28 Jenny Holt, "'Normal' versus 'Deviant' Play in Children's Literature: An Historical Overview," *The Lion and the Unicorn* 34.1 (January 2010): 54, notes 2, 34–56.

29 Russell, *Stories of Boy Life*, 174.

30 Ibid., 176.

31 Mary A. Ward (Mrs Humphry), "Evening Play Centres: A Better Playground than the Streets," *The Times*, February 6, 1914, 10.

32 Viviana A. Zelizer, *Pricing the Priceless Child* (New York: Basic Books Inc., 1985), 32.

33 Diane Cardwell, "New York Tries to Think Outside the Sandbox," *The New York Times,* January 10, 2007, A1.

34 Andy Newman, "New York City's Future Playground Gets a Nod From Present-Day Players," *The New York Times*, January 11, 2007, B5.

35 Ward, "Evening Play Centres: A Better Playground than the Streets," 10.

36 Edward W. Stitt, "Discussion of Article on Equipment by Henry S. Curtis, PhD, in *The Playground* for November," *The Playground* 7.12 (March 1914): 483, 482–6.

37 Ibid., 483–4.

38 Ibid., 484.

39 Janet Penrose Trevelyan, *Evening Play Centres for Children* (New York: E. P. Dutton and Co., 1920), 4.

40 Mary A. Ward (Mrs Humphry), "Evening Play Centres: Children and Darkened Streets," *The Times*, December 21, 1914, 10.

41 "Brooklyn," *The Playground* 17 (August 1908): 10.

42 Tampton Aubuchon, "Jones Park, East St. Louis, Illinois," *The Playground* 10.1 (April 1916): 35, 33–5.

43 For analyses of nineteenth-century crowds, see John Plotz, *The Crowd: British Literature and Public Politics* (Berkeley: University of California Press, 2000); Nicolaus Mills, *The Crowd in American Literature* (Baton Rouge: Louisiana State University Press, 1986); Mary Esteve, *The Aesthetics and Politics of the Crowd in American Literature* (Cambridge: Cambridge University Press, 2003).

44 Johan Huizinga, *Homo Ludens: A Study of the Play-Element in Culture* (London: Routledge & Kegan Paul, 1949), 7.

45 Robin Bernstein, *Racial Innocence: Performing American Childhood from Slavery to Civil Rights* (New York: New York University Press, 2011), 184.

46 Ibid., 184.

47 Morag Styles, *From the Garden to the Street: An Introduction to 300 Years of Poetry for Children* (London: Cassell, 1998).

48 Collier's "Rents Recreation Ground," *The Times*, June 20, 1900, 4.

49 "Our Playgrounds," *All the Year Round* 35.842 New Series (January 17, 1885): 342, 341–6.

50 Henry S. Curtis, "Washington Sites Available For Playgrounds," *The Playground* 12 (March 1908): 15, 14–20.

51 "Playgrounds in Town," *The Graphic*, February 7, 1874.

52 "Report of the Committee on Storytelling in the Playground" in *Proceedings of the Second Annual Playground Congress and Year Book* (New York: Playground Association of America, 1908), 336.

53 Ibid., 335.

54 Ibid., 335.

55 Barrie, J. M., *Peter and Wendy* in *Peter Pan: Peter and Wendy and Peter Pan in Kensington Gardens*, (ed.) Jack Zipes (1911; reprint, New York: Penguin Books, 2004), 120–1.

56 *The Playground* 7.10 (January 1914): 410–11.

57 Play Days," *The Playground* 10.1 (April 1916): 9, 8–9.

58 See, for example, Jack Zipes' comparisons of their 1810 and 1812 versions of the story in *When Dreams Come True* (New York: Routledge, 2007), 76–8.

59 Lewis Carroll (Charles Dodgson), *Alice's Adventures in Wonderland & Through the Looking-Glass* (1865 and 1871; reprint, New York: Signet Classic, 2000), 36.

60 John Sutherland, *Mrs Humphry Ward* (Oxford: Oxford University Press, 1990), 227.

61 Mary A. Ward (Mrs Humphry), *Milly and Olly* (London: Macmillan and Company, 1881), 82.

62 Ward, *Milly and Olly*, 143.

63 Almon, "Entering the World," 22.

64 Penny Wilson, "Playworkers and the Adventure Play Movement" in Elizabeth Goodenough (ed.), *Where Do the Children Play?: A Study Guide to the Film* (Michigan Public Media, 2007), 63–7.

65 Almon, "Entering the World," 22.

66 A. I. Decker, "Teaching Children to Play," *The Playground* 10.1 (April 1916): 28, 28–30.

67 See, for example, Anna Halverson, Nancy M. Wells, Donald A. Rakow, and Sonja Skelly, "The Growth of Children's Gardens" in Elizabeth Goodenough (ed.), *A Place for Play* (Carmel Valley, CA: The National Institute for Play, 2008), 161–72.

68 Kidd, *Making American Boys*, 95.

69 Ibid., 208, note 14.

70 Ibid., 208.

71 Colin Ward, *The Child in the City* (1978; reprint, London: Bedford Square Press, 1990), 73.

72 Iona Archibald and Peter Opie, *Children's Games in Street and Playground* (Oxford: Clarendon Press, 1969), 331.

73 Joe L. Frost, *A History of Children's Play and Play Environments: Toward a Contemporary Child-Saving Movement* (New York: Routledge, 2010), 83.

74 Ibid., 45.

75 Ibid., 45; C. D. Warner, *Being a Boy* (New York: Houghton Mifflin, 1877), 2–3.

Bibliography

Almon, Joan. "Entering the World of Play," in Elizabeth Goodenough (ed.), *A Place for Play*, 19–25. Carmel Valley, California: The National Institute for Play, 2008.

Aubuchon, Tampton. "Jones Park, East St. Louis, Illinois." *The Playground* 10, no. 1 (April 1916): 33–5.

Barrie, J. M. *Peter and Wendy* (1911), in Jack Zipes (ed.), *Peter Pan: Peter and Wendy and Peter Pan in Kensington Gardens*, 5–153. New York: Penguin Books, 2004.

Bernstein, Robin. *Racial Innocence: Performing American Childhood from Slavery to Civil Rights*. New York: New York University Press, 2011.

"Brooklyn." *The Playground* 17 (August 1908): 10.

Cardwell, Diane. "New York Tries to Think Outside the Sandbox." *The New York Times*, January 10, 2007: A1; B4.

Carroll, Lewis (Charles Dodgson) (1865, 1871). *Alice's Adventures in Wonderland & Through the Looking-Glass*. New York: Signet Classic, 2000.

Cavallo, Dominick. *Muscles and Morals: Organized Playgrounds and Urban Reform, 1880–1920*. Philadelphia: University of Pennsylvania Press, 1981.

Chawla, Louise and David Driskell. "Having a Say about Where to Play: A Serious Way to Learn Democracy," in Elizabeth Goodenough (ed.), *A Place for Play*, 65–81. Carmel Valley, CA: The National Institute for Play, 2008.

Coats, Karen. *Looking Glasses and Neverlands: Lacan, Desire, and Subjectivity in Children's Literature*. Iowa City: University of Iowa Press, 2004.

"Collier's Rents Recreation Ground." *The Times*, June 20, 1900: 4.

Crowhurst Lennard, Suzanne H. "The City as Playground," in Elizabeth Goodenough (ed.), *A Place for Play*, 207–11. Carmel Valley, CA: The National Institute for Play, 2008.

Curtis, Henry S. "Washington Sites Available For Playgrounds." *The Playground* 12 (March 1908): 14–20.

Decker, A. I. "Teaching Children to Play." *The Playground* 10, no. 1 (April 1916): 28–30.

Esteve, Mary. *The Aesthetics and Politics of the Crowd in American Literature*. Cambridge: Cambridge University Press, 2003.

Frost, Joe L. *A History of Children's Play and Play Environments: Toward a Contemporary Child-Saving Movement*. New York: Routledge, 2010.

Gillis, John R. "Epilogue: The Islanding of Children – Reshaping the Mythical Landscapes of Childhood," in Marta Gutman and Ning De-Coninck-Smith (eds), *Designing Modern Childhoods*, 316–30. New Brunswick: Rutgers University Press, 2008.

Goodenough, Elizabeth (ed), *Where Do the Children Play?: A Study Guide to the Film*. New York: Alliance for Childhood, 2007.

Gutman, Marta and Ning De Coninck-Smith. "Introduction: Good to Think With – History, Space, and Modern Childhood," in Marta Gutman and Ning De-Coninck-Smith (eds), *Designing Modern Childhoods*, 1–19. New Brunswick: Rutgers University Press, 2008.

Halverson, Anna, Nancy M. Wells, Donald A. Rakow, and Sonja Skelly. "The Growth of Children's Gardens," in Elizabeth Goodenough (ed.), *A Place for Play*, 161–72. Carmel Valley, CA: The National Institute for Play, 2008.

"Highlights in KaBOOM! History." kaboom.org. 2013. Available at http://kaboom.org/about_kaboom/our_story

Holt, Jenny. "'Normal' versus 'Deviant' Play in Children's Literature: An Historical Overview." *The Lion and the Unicorn* 34, no. 1 (January 2010): 34–56.

Howell, Ocean. "Play Pays: Urban Land Politics and Playgrounds in the United States, 1900–1930." *Journal of Urban History* 34, no. 6 (September 2008): 961–94.

Huizinga, Johan. *Homo Ludens: A Study of the Play-Element in Culture*. London: Routledge & Kegan Paul, 1949.

Kidd, Kenneth B. *Making American Boys: Boyology and the Feral Tale*. Minneapolis: University of Minnesota Press, 2004.

Lee, Joseph. Back cover to *The Playground* 10, no. 1 (April 1916).

Louv, Richard. *Last Child in the Woods*. Chapel Hill, NC: Algonquin Books, 2005.

Mills, Nicolaus. *The Crowd in American Literature*. Baton Rouge: Louisiana State University Press, 1986.

Newman, Andy. "New York City's Future Playground Gets a Nod From Present-Day Players." *The New York Times*, January 11, 2007: B1; B5.

Opie, Iona Archibald and Peter. *Children's Games in Street and Playground*. Oxford: Clarendon Press, 1969.

"Our Playgrounds." *All the Year Round* 842 (17 January 1885): 341–6.

Perkins Gilman, Charlotte. *Concerning Children*. Boston: Small, Maynard, & Co., 1901.

"The Philadelphia Grand Jury And Judge Staake Endorse the Playground Movement." *The Playground* 23 (February 1909): 3–5.

"Play Days." *The Playground* 10, no. 1 (April 1916): 8–9.

The Playground 7, no. 10 (January 1914): 410–11.

"Playgrounds in Town." *The Graphic*. February 7, 1874.

Plotz, John. *The Crowd: British Literature and Public Politics*. Berkeley: University of California Press, 2000.

"Report of the Committee on Storytelling in the Playground." *Proceedings of the Second Annual Playground Congress and Year Book*. New York: Playground Association of America, 1908.

Romeyn Taylor, Graham. "How They Played at Chicago." *Proceedings of the Annual Playground Congress*, 1–10. New York: Playground Association of America, 1907.

Russell, Thomas H. *Stories of Boy Life*. Chicago: The Homewood Press, 1914.

Stitt, Edward W. "Discussion of Article on Equipment by Henry S. Curtis, Ph.D., in *The Playground* for November." *The Playground* 7, no. 12 (March 1914): 482–6.

Styles, Morag. *From the Garden to the Street: An Introduction to 300 Years of Poetry for Children*. London: Cassell, 1998.

Sutherland, John. *Mrs Humphry Ward*. Oxford: Oxford University Press, 1990.

Trevelyan, Janet Penrose. *Evening Play Centres for Children*. New York: E. P. Dutton and Co., 1920.

Turner Meiklejohn, Susan. "Sunnyside Gardens Today," in Elizabeth Goodenough (ed.), *A Place for Play*, 215–28. Carmel Valley, CA: The National Institute for Play, 2008.

Valentine, Gill. *Public Space and the Culture of Childhood*. Aldershot: Ashgate, 2004.

Veiller, Lawrence. "The Social Value of Playgrounds in Crowded Districts." *Proceedings of the Annual Playground Congress*, 37–40. New York: Playground Association of America, 1907.

Wannamaker, Annette. *Boys in Children's Literature and Popular Culture: Masculinity, Abjection, and the Fictional Child*. New York: Routledge, 2008.

Ward, Colin. *The Child in the City*. 1978. New Edition. London: Bedford Square Press, 1990.

Ward, Mary A. (Mrs Humphry). "Evening Play Centres: A Better Playground than the Streets." *The Times*. February 6, 1914: 10.

—"Evening Play Centres: Children and Darkened Streets." *The Times*. December 21, 1914: 10.

—*Milly and Olly*. London: Macmillan and Co., 1881.

Warner, C. D. *Being a Boy*. New York: Houghton Mifflin, 1877.

Watson, Sophie. "Children's Publics," in *City Publics: The (Dis)enchantments of Urban Encounters*, 123–58. London: Routledge, 2006.

Weikle-Mills, Courtney. *Imaginary Citizens: Child Readers and the Limits of American Independence, 1640–1868*. Baltimore: Johns Hopkins University Press, 2013.

Wilson, Penny. "Playworkers and the Adventure Play Movement" in Elizabeth Goodenough (ed.), *Where Do the Children Play?: A Study Guide to the Film*, 63–7. Michigan: Public Media, 2007.

Zelizer, Viviana A. *Pricing the Priceless Child*. New York: Basic Books Inc., 1985.

Zipes, Jack. *When Dreams Come True*. New York: Routledge, 2007.

5

"The Studio World Surprised and Disturbed Ruth": The Diffident Stage Mother and the Difficult Child in a Post-War Novel by Noel Streatfeild

Sally Sims Stokes
The Catholic University of America

A seasoned actress who became a playwright, novelist, and social critic, Noel Streatfeild, OBE (1895–1986) will forever be associated with *Ballet Shoes: A Story of Three Children on the Stage*. This 1936 favorite continues in print, and is one of dozens of popular children's novels Streatfeild produced between the 1930s and the 1970s. Her believable characters and lively dialogue engaged countless mid-century children in Britain and around the globe who were eager to see inside the worlds of the performing arts and professional sports.

Streatfeild never intended to become a children's author, and was still fighting off that label in 1949.[1] She had begun publishing novels and short stories for adults in the early 1930s, with immediate success. Abusive parents, predatory producers, suicide, teenage pregnancy—Streatfeild considered them all, and won consistent critical praise.[2] She started writing children's books only grudgingly, surprised at her own knack for reaching younger readers.[3] *Ballet Shoes* set her on her way in 1936. That same year, Andrew Carnegie established the Carnegie Medal in Literature, to be awarded to an outstanding book for young readers. Streatfeild's *The Circus is Coming* received the Carnegie in 1939. By the early 1950s Noel Streatfeild was, according to the illustrator Shirley Hughes, "the doyenne of children's authors" in the UK.[4] Her stories have been translated into many languages, including Dutch, Finnish, Croatian, Polish, and Hebrew.

While trying her hand at screenwriting in the 1930s, Streatfeild lived in Los Angeles, and returned there from London after World War II. During both California stays, she studied child actors at Metro-Goldwyn-Mayer and 20th Century Fox in preparation for a children's book to be set in a motion picture studio. The result was *The Painted Garden: The Story of a Holiday in Hollywood*, first published in 1948 as a serial in *Collins Magazine for Boys and Girls*. Collins released the story as a children's novel in 1949. In *The Painted Garden*, Streatfeild presents the antics of an energetic London family living in Santa Monica, but she also probes poor attitudes, jealousy, and the child actor as commodity. Although Streatfeild attempted glibly to deny it, MGM served as the model for the book's Bee Bee Studios.[5] Parents of child film stars in *The Painted Garden* range from the overbearing British stage mother, Mrs Tuesday, to the humane and wise Midwesterners Mr and Mrs Doe. Consistent with the pattern in Streatfeild's children's novels about tennis, skating, dance, theater, and the circus, *The Painted Garden* plays down glamour in favor of a practical look at studio life, but does not diminish the excitement and gratification that athletes and show-people experience in their daily work.

In the 1970s, scholars began to address Streatfeild's larger contribution to British literature for children and adults. Angela Bull observes in her 1984 biography that one of Streatfeild's greatest strengths was as a chronicler of cultural trends and period details.[6] At the same time, Bull dismisses some of the books that best exemplify Streatfeild's skill at capturing the essence of an era. Bull is no fan of *The Painted Garden*, and she holds in especially low regard the 12 pulp romances for adult readers that Streatfeild produced under the pen name "Susan Scarlett" between 1938 and 1951. Bull calls these romances "secret progeny," and suggests that Streatfeild was ashamed of the lot.[7]

Some of the Scarletts, even those boasting skillful dialogue and nimble pacing, do adhere to a predictable template, and Streatfeild's irritation with the light romance genre shows in her strained portrayals of the ingénue, the scheming rival, and the obligatory happily-ever-afters. But having fulfilled the requirements of the Cinderella formula for adult female readers, Streatfeild pushes its boundaries to capture, with shrewd irony, the mood of Britain in wartime and during the early postwar period, and the movements and fads that shaped popular thinking of the day.[8]

Nancy Huse, in her 1994 Twayne survey of Streatfeild's work, discounts the Scarletts' historical value, and scarcely recognizes their content. Huse does apply Janice Radway's 1984 paradigm for reading popular romances, a rational exercise hindered by the fact that Susan Scarlett was Noel Streatfeild; and although she came to accept her status as a respected children's writer,

Streatfeild was in no way committed to drugstore fiction as an art form.[9] Her contract with Hodder and Stoughton for the Scarletts shows that she wanted her identity concealed; her secretary chided her for wasting her talents cranking out bargain books.[10] But potboiler romances kept food on the table, and provided a diversion for women confined to bomb shelters. In effect, these books supported the war effort by keeping up civilian morale.[11]

The first step of Radway's thirteen-tier "narrative structure of the ideal romance" consists of "the heroine's removal from a familiar, comfortable realm usually associated with her childhood and family."[12] In *Love in a Mist*, the last of the Scarletts, Streatfeild mounts Radway's first step to hook the reader: she ensures that Ruth Tring, the apparent heroine, is an outsider, an American who has left her home and job in Illinois and moved to the English town in which her husband Peter's family runs a grocery business. Besides Ruth, the other Tring daughters-in-law are the shallow, self-centered Anna and Doris, a free-thinker and ex-Communist who enjoys analyzing and classifying people according to her own system. Streatfeild keeps Radway's remaining dozen steps in view, but leaps away (with glee, one imagines) before scaling them. By including *Love in a Mist* among the Susan Scarlett dozen, she implicitly represents it as a romance novel,[13] all the while building out the story as a problem play—a drama that addresses societal issues of the times and that refuses to arrive at any absolute conclusion. In a lattice of topical themes and power struggles bolted to mind control and misread cues, she explores contemporary matters that she might have been less likely to test under her own name. In what might at first seem "fluff lit" for bored postwar housewives of 1951, she adeptly explores the mental health of a four-year-old actor and that of his mother, and she strolls boldly into a hot combat zone of the 1940s and 1950s: Childrearing techniques.

Shakespeare's works had a distinct influence on Streatfeild. Children in *Ballet Shoes* perform *A Midsummer Night's Dream*; in *Curtain Up* (1944), they present *The Tempest*. "Through her accounts," writes Bull, "shines such authentic awe and excitement that even the youngest readers can glimpse something of the thrilling quality of the plays."[14] Streatfeild had enrolled in 1919 at the Academy of Dramatic Art (later the Royal Academy) in Gower Street, London. On completing her course, she toured with Charles Doran's Shakespeare company until her challenge to his alleged exploitation of an underage performer led to her break with Doran in 1922.[15]

Along the way she must have become acquainted with F. S. Boas's treatises on the problem plays of Shakespeare and Ibsen: she had first discovered Ibsen's works after leaving the Academy, and devoured them with zeal.[16] She might also have known W. W. Lawrence's *Shakespeare's Problem Comedies* (1931); and she perhaps even glimpsed E. M. W. Tillyard's *Shakespeare's Problem Plays* (1949) before embarking on *Love in a Mist*.

Streatfeild was also a protégée of John Galsworthy, who had nominated her for membership in the P.E.N. Club on the basis of her first novel, *The Whicharts* (1931), an assault on the sordid and seamy side of the stage.[17] Galsworthy's words of wisdom to all playwrights, "Some Platitudes Concerning Drama" (1913), stress the value to humanity of Shakespeare's ability to hand the audience or reader the task of deciding the moral.[18]

Standard lists of Shakespeare's problem plays usually include *Measure for Measure, All's Well That Ends Well*, and *Troilus and Cressida*. Streatfeild titles *Love in a Mist*'s final chapter "A Fine Night, and All's Well," but she does not attempt a trite retelling of, or character substitutions from, *All's Well*. Yet her chapter title is a sly alert that *Love in a Mist* is a problem play, because whether all's well—and, if so, why, and by whose measure—will remain open to debate even after the Tring saga closes.

Streatfeild drafted six pages of character charts for *Love in a Mist*, but none presents a plan for the narrative.[19] Even so, *Love in a Mist* adheres to Tillyard's criteria for a problem play: an emphasis on "religious dogma or abstract speculation or both," and an "acute interest in observing and recording details of human nature.[20]

Streatfeild fulfills Tillyard's first criterion by supplying Ruth Tring with a "bible" in the form of a childrearing manual, and a priestly or godlike counselor (the manual's unnamed author); by having the family patriarch, Dad-Tring, press the next generation to accept Church of England practices; and by allowing celebrity worship to echo everywhere.[21] If we can take Tillyard to mean by "abstract speculation" a metaphysical inquiry into appearance versus reality, then in *Love in a Mist* a film studio will serve as the requisite icon of sham and fakery. The studio thus also meets Boas's 1896 bylaw that the problem plays should "introduce us into highly artificial societies."[22] Streatfeild's adroit, elusive premise—that cunning and misapprehension underlie all the action in *Love in a Mist*—rounds out the rest of Tillyard's requirement.

Tillyard's second standard goes without saying across the body of Streatfeild's work. It is especially piercing in *Love in a Mist*, which rides heavily on human beings' responses to the influence of popular culture and to power shifts within both a family and a workplace (the film studio).

Boas noted in 1896 that the artificial societies of the problem plays generate "abnormal conditions of brain and emotion."[23] Such conditions are a potent implement in Streatfeild's hands as she sows her narrative over a child's perceived mental state. In the language of flowers, love-in-a-mist (also called devil-in-the-bush) stands for "perplexity." Boas remarks that in the problem plays "we move along dim untrodden paths … ; we are excited, fascinated, perplexed, for the issues raised preclude a completely satisfactory outcome."[24] Wordplay and gardening were among Streatfeild's pet pursuits,[25] and for this novel, which offers plenty of perplexity, Streatfeild/Scarlett chose her title well.

W. W. Lawrence concludes that the themes in problem plays are presented "to probe the complicated interrelations of character and action, in a situation admitting of different ethical interpretations."[26] Vital to *Love in a Mist* is Streatfeild's studied refusal to give an explicit interpretation of a character's ethics. As Susan Scarlett, Streatfeild ultimately permits one character, Doris, to comprehend the agitation that drives the narrative and its side stories, but she sends mixed signals about Doris's purposes. Working beneath the mantle of a romance novel, Streatfeild writes above her projected audience, coaxing readers to warm to characters who *appear* to act for others' good, but who may have less splendid aims. She reveals prevailing circumstances that could influence a character's decisions, and then steps away, leaving the attentive reader to appraise that character's scruples without assistance from the author.

Love in a Mist reshapes Streatfeild's own brand of the family novel[27] to explore the ecology of misapprehension, collusion, and control within a multi-generational kinship unit. Early on, Ruth contemplates how set in their ways Mum-Tring and Dad-Tring are, and concludes that "'fun' was not a word people like the Trings knew anything about."[28] Ruth, Anna, and Doris are all unaware that Mum and Dad's version of fun is to settle into their armchairs in the evenings to toy with the family dynamic—to promote, and capitalize on, misunderstandings among the Tring boys and their wives.

Mum and Dad are such old darlings, it seems,[29] but it is their blithe little habit to plant tiny psychological bombs, not just for sheer entertainment value, but also to achieve specific results. Here is *The Tempest* overlaid upon pulp fiction, with Dad, whose craggy, "Cliffs-of-Dover" face marks him as Caliban. Mum might be Prospero, the maker of "as strange a maze as e'er men trod,"[30] and the furtive family doctor is perhaps their Ariel. Mum and Dad get first-rate jollies from spreading tales among the Tring sons and daughters-in-law, scattering just enough bad feeling to set one adult child against another; to force emotions to the surface; and to bring each young couple to accede unsuspectingly, and even gratefully, to the elder Trings' plans for them.

These mind tricks lend comedic effect, but Streatfeild's interest in family interactions, mental illness, and despair was genuine. The British psychiatrist Jeremy Holmes, in his afterword to the 2000 reprint of Streatfeild's 1945 adult novel *Saplings*, finds it noteworthy that Streatfeild, without any training in psychological studies, pegged rising trends in the evaluation of children who experience emotional trauma during World War II.[31] Holmes is an authority on another British psychiatrist, John Bowlby, author of *Maternal Care and Mental Health*. Bowlby produced this study in 1950 for the United Nations's program for the welfare of homeless children. There is every reason to assume that Streatfeild might have read, or at least taken an interest in, the Bowlby report. She had been a social worker in the southeast London borough of Deptford in the 1930s, and was later a member of the Woman's Voluntary Service. As a WVS worker and air raid warden, she put in grueling hours giving practical and emotional support to Londoners of all ages made homeless by German bombs. Her own flat was blown up in 1941.[32]

Jeremy Holmes had no cause to know of Streatfeild's "secret progeny," and he does not refer to any of the Scarletts in his essay. He is right that Streatfeild professed no expertise in psychology, psychiatry, psychoanalysis, or their foundations or terminology. It is likely, however, through her own family welfare efforts during World War II, that she knew the work of her contem-porary Anna Freud in London's Hampstead War Nurseries. Freud welcomed into institutional foster care children who had been separated from one or both parents during the war. These children became study subjects for Freud when she began to integrate the techniques of direct observation with her work in clinical child psychoanalysis.[33] Surely Streatfeild must also have been aware of Donald Winnicott, who worked with evacuated children in Oxfordshire. Winnicott's *Clinical Notes on the Disorders of Childhood* (1931) and a compi-lation of his BBC radio addresses, *Getting to Know Your Baby* (1945), were both imprints of Heinemann, which published Streatfeild's adult novels from 1931–9.

Love in a Mist is set in real historical time, and the fictional tantrum-prone four-year-old Paul Tring is a bellwether of the baby boom. Paul would have been among millions of children whose mothers were lapping up the advice of pedia-tricians, psychologists, early childhood educators, and the authors of a new surge of child-rearing texts in the late 1940s and early 1950s. Untold numbers of American women became disciples of the Yale Clinic of Child Development's

Arnold Gesell, whose hefty handbook, *Infant and Child in the Culture of Today*, was published in 1943, aimed at mothers and teachers, and offered, as is claimed on the dust jacket, "a realistic discussion of … techniques for … child guidance and psychological care in a democratic culture." Mothers also sought the expertise of Benjamin Spock, the now-legendary pediatrician and psychiatrist. Spock's *Common Sense Book of Baby and Child Care* was published in 1946—about the time Paul Tring would have been born.

In *Raising Baby by the Book: The Education of American Mothers*, Julia Grant observes,

> [W]hile Gesell and his fellow researchers were less likely than their psycho-analytic counterparts to attribute childhood problems to parental behaviors, both groups agreed that early childhood should be a time of relatively relaxed guidance and that parents should attempt to meet, rather than regulate, children's physical and emotional needs.[34]

A drawing in the first edition of Spock's *Baby and Child Care* bolsters Grant's point. The Spock illustration emphasizes that guiding a child away from a tippy lamp, rather than saying "No, no, don't touch," respects the toddler's natural curiosity about his or her world.[35]

Women who accepted the idea of giving Junior some blocks to divert his attention from Mother's new lamp were often at odds with in-laws and husbands who adhered to "spare the rod and spoil the child" philosophies.[36] Ruth Tring finds herself in this kind of predicament. She does her best to be cordial to Anna and Doris, but receives no support from either one when Paul's fits wear her down. Peter's response to Paul's tantrums is to toss cold water in the boy's face, and to threaten him with a belt. Ruth comprehends that the Trings and the school personnel think Paul is spoiled. All the adults, including Ruth, are unaware that older children are bullying Paul on the playground, and that Doris's Jimmie is a ringleader, with Anna's Wendy a satisfied spectator.

Ruth privately surmises that Americans are more enlightened about the latest trends in evaluating and treating children's mental health than are the British. Ruth's conclusions run counter to the research conducted by Bowlby, Winnicott, Anna Freud, and others in the 1940s, but point to the enormous middle-class appeal of the friendly, reassuring American manuals on the order of Gesell or Spock. We soon find Ruth in a bookshop, searching for a guide to "child neuroses." She purchases *The Mind and the Child*, an American parenting handbook strictly of Streatfeild's own invention. Ruth's initial browse through the book's chapters on infantile neurosis, maternal separation, and child psychoanalysis quickly becomes an obsession.

To "compensate" the child with an alternative activity in order to offset frustration is a central precept of *The Mind and the Child*. Ruth likes the author's suggestion that the parent help a child express him- or herself, and expand the young one's soul to overcome a narrow social environment. Ruth promptly recognizes that what she calls "the Tring mould," breeding generation after generation into the grocery trade, is a supreme example of a constrained environment. As her dependency on *The Mind and the Child* grows, Ruth imagines herself engaged in exclusive correspondence and conversations with the handbook's author.[37]

During one of Ruth's silent rambles on Paul's mental health, Streatfield steals in with the tidbit that the author of *The Mind and the Child* had "made it clear that he was a layman writing for laymen."[38] Here Streatfeild has raised the implicit question of how so-called expert advice can become codified and revered simply because it has been published. This question parallels another: why a child and his parents should become the subject of adulation or envy simply because the child is receiving money to act a part that will be captured on film for commercial consumption.[39] Both questions concern the childlike susceptibility of the adult mind to the promotion of popular media, whether self-help literature or film, and they are crucial to Streatfeild's narrative.

Under her author-friend's otherworldly direction, Ruth seeks the spiritual strength to help Paul conquer his outbursts. Help arrives when a studio rep spots Paul in a crowd as "just the child we want" for an upcoming motion picture, *Cast a Stone,* and urges Ruth to bring the little boy to Rose of England Studios for a screen test. This she does, without consulting Peter. Her own boldness astonishes Ruth. She is sure that her father-in-law thinks it effeminate for a boy to "play-act," and she expects that her husband will also disapprove. Anna has aspirations for Wendy to be in the movies, and Anna's nose goes severely out of joint when the film company selects Paul, not Wendy. Innocent of any such fantasies for her son, Ruth is focused solely on seeking therapeutic "compensation" for Paul, and hopes that letting him act in a movie will resolve this need. Ruth's "mist" will begin to lift when she learns that the film's director, Noel Water, has Paul in mind for the role of the young child Jonathan Bone, who, over the course of the film, will grow up to be a notorious thug.

Streatfeild deftly casts Ruth against type, ensuring an outright mismatch to the classic calculating, status-hungry stage mother whom she had already caricatured for children in the deliciously obnoxious Mrs Tuesday (*The Painted Garden*), and in one of her adult novels, Fanny Elk, who enters her little Flossie in a prettiest-child contest (*It Pays to Be Good*, 1936). Instead, Streatfeild lodges these pushy, desperate traits in Anna, a dim and silly woman who has projected film-star potential onto Wendy, while remaining blind to the simple joy her children take in madcap improvizational home theatricals under the direction of the maid, Iris. Anna, in her resentment of Paul's selection for *Cast a Stone*, completes the circle of what Doris terms the "yattering mob" of neighborhood mothers. Anna is convinced that this group is "sniggering behind her back because Ruth had got the chance she wanted."[40]

Streatfeild tentatively establishes Ruth as the quintessential American good mother while also implying that Ruth is being sucked in by the trends that thrive as parenting doctrine back home in the States, but that are still held at arm's length in her adopted country. Ruth beseeches her phantasmal advisor to condone Paul's movie role as a means to purging the boy's demons and helping him achieve emotional balance.[41] But a specter haunts her. She accepts that Paul has no idea that little Jonathan Bone, whose child self Paul portrays in the movie, will age into a baddie, but she believes that the attention showered on Paul in the studio is inflating his ego and that he has stopped differentiating between fact and fantasy. She is frightened that he will eventually absorb the traits of the deviant Jonathan. Indebted to the producers for giving Paul the opportunity to fulfill himself through acting, she frets that if she asks Noel Water to terminate Paul's contract, Water will retort, "What does the child's character matter, if it's a good movie?" Whether it matters, and what a stage parent should do about it, are two principal problems of this problem play.

The stage mother has been unlovingly portrayed in film, fiction, and theater—MGM's 1933 *Stage Mother*, based on the Bradford Ropes novel; Mama Rose in the more recent *Gypsy*—and has been captured in memoirs of such former child actors as Diana Serra Cary, known as Baby Peggy Montgomery, as well as in Nora Frankel's 2009 biography of Gypsy Rose Lee. In 1951, the same year *Love in a Mist* was published, the Italian producer Salvo d'Angelo and neorealist director Luchino Visconti collaborated on *Bellissima*, d'Angelo's send-up of the values that drive a mother, Maddalena Cecconi, to haul her daughter Maria to the casting-call meat market. After some consideration, Maddalena declines Cinecittà's offer of a part for little Maria.[42]

E. D. Nelson's 2001 article in the journal *Qualitative Sociology* establishes that a stage mother passes through definable intervals while they advance their goals for themselves and their children, even if the mother and child do not share such goals. Nelson labels the final interval "Letting Go." Nelson interviewed some mothers who had arrived at the "Letting Go" phase, during which they persuaded themselves that their children were not physically suited to continue in a specific pursuit—in Nelson's case study, preparing for a ballet career—and that it was time to withdraw them from the endless round of classes, auditions, and performances.[43] Ruth's "Letting Go" occurs in three parts: she realizes that although Paul seems to love acting, he has become more difficult and demanding; she develops a gnawing dread that her son could be emotionally compromised by acting the part of a child who matures into a criminal; and she begins to doubt her own self-worth.

During her Hollywood sojourn in 1947, Streatfeild had observed Margaret O'Brien in rehearsal at MGM. In production that year was *The Unfinished Dance*. Margaret played "Meg," whose mean-spirited backstage actions cause serious injury to another dancer. If Streatfeild saw Margaret rehearsing scenes for this film, here would have been her chance to muse, "What does the child's character matter, if it's a good movie?" and to consider whether Margaret O'Brien herself was negatively affected by performing Meg. It happens that Margaret recorded in her published diary how much fun she had making this movie. She enjoyed the dance sequences, and was pleased with the beautiful costumes.[44]

Margaret O'Brien's cheerful daybook exemplifies industry public relations devices that render actors "authentic" in order to further their star appeal,[45] but the entries do ring true, and give the impression that the ten-year-old diarist really did enjoy a happy childhood, filled with love, solid discipline, and lots of playing outside with her pals in the back yard of the relatively modest O'Brien home. One hopes Margaret suffered no emotional scars, but the searing recollections of some former child stars about the working conditions and pressures to which they were subjected cannot be ignored. In *The Cultural Significance of the Child Star*, Jane O'Connor calls attention to the powerlessness of the child celebrity to separate from his or her reputation as *wunderkind*, and later on, to shed the stigma of "former" as a modifier of "screen sensation."[46]

Of related interest is a report released in England just before the publication of *Love in a Mist*. In 1950, Parliament appointed an external committee to study an issue tangential not only to Ruth's doubts, but also to the ill deeds of Meg in *The Unfinished Dance*. The committee concerned itself with the consequences of exposing child actors to potentially traumatizing scenes—how, for example, an actress such as Margaret O'Brien might have been affected had she seen Meg's "victim" actually fall through a trap door. This seems to have been a fairly new question in 1950. The committee concluded that because of the fragmented nature of filming, it was unlikely that a youngster would be needed during violent or sadistic scenes; and that if a child did happen to be present, he or she would see the adult actors laughing and joking between takes, and would know that the scary scenes were make-believe. [47]

Streatfeild counters this stance in *Love in a Mist* by showing Paul's mistrust in the actors who play opposite him in the roles of the

> self-centered stepmother and his weak, charming father. Paul did not like the scenes with [these actors]; he half knew they were nice people really, but when [the script called for him] to [be] snubbed or disregarded, his hurt at such treatment showed on his face ....[48]

Of course this "hurt" is what Noel Water needs from Paul, and Water has been scrambling to sustain a "fairy tale atmosphere," alive with fanciful creations such as a mechanical stork that delivers kittens, to keep Paul on game. Indulging the child in this way is exactly what Ruth does not want. It is undermining her authority as a mother. She does not understand the "laws" of the studio "kingdom."[49] In her own mind, Ruth holds

> long, one-sided conversations with her friend, the author of *The Mind and the Child*. She [tells] him over and over again how Paul [is] reacting, and [queries] if that [is] what he would approve.... [Ruth says to herself,] "If there was a tendency to neurotic infantilism—which was what I feared—that surely is cured now. Maybe it was smart to put him into pictures. Maybe that was just what was needed to free his ego, and it surely has done that, for there's no stealing of mother love; right now it sometimes seems he doesn't need me at all."[50]

Ruth has now shifted focus from Paul's well-being to her own maternal needs. Even as her unease intensifies, she senses that Peter and his parents are not, after all, strenuously opposed to Paul's working in films, but she fails to discern why this is so. Ruth must remain in a mist a bit longer, because her stage mother stint is a contrivance for Susan Scarlett, and for that cagey pair, Dad-Tring and Mum-Tring. A "squib," Dad calls it, a small explosive that he and Mum have intentionally tossed in amongst their daughters-in-law to create some desirable fallout. Mum-Tring needs Ruth to outshine Anna. Anna's histrionics over Ruth's presumed opportunities for Paul at Rose of England are misplaced, but they allow Mum to maintain the pretense that she is just a vague, empathetic old woman, as she "stroked Anna's hair and spoke as she would have done to a child," all the while plotting Anna's future according to the Tring mold.[51]

Ruth's own guileless outpourings to Mum about *The Mind and the Child* while Mum rocks, knits, and schemes, add the term "compensate" to Mum's vocabulary. Dear old Mum sees that "compensating" Anna with a new hat for her disappointments will be a handy technique, but there will be even more in store for Anna in the end. Mum long ago learned that it is in her best interest to fit into the Tring mold. Having become a Tring wife herself, she will sculpt her daughters-in-law to be Tring wives, too.

Streatfeild sets the dominos of missed signals and dimmed motives to tumble on and on. Her characters' thoughts continue to reveal misplaced apprehensions, but she studiously prevents each player from understanding the thoughts of the others. She smoothly intimates that a character's action might be altruistic, or that it might be self-serving, but she does not dictate which it shall be. Mum now seems the lay expert of record as she works the mind of this or that adult child. But Mum is unaware that Ruth has built up the fortitude to "Let Go," and that she has bravely approached Noel Water. Ruth's slackening interest in keeping Paul in pictures could loosen Mum's hold on Anna, if Anna no longer has any reason to envy Ruth and to come crying to Mum-Tring about it.

Noel Water grasps that her anxieties about Paul have pulverized Ruth, but he does not see that Ruth's mission is to reclaim her authority as a parent. When Noel agrees to help her, Ruth, in turn, does not perceive that he may have multiple motives. There have been rumblings that Nicholas Dram, the actor who plays the adult Jonathan Bone, is resentful of talented child actors such as Paul. The screenplay does not absolutely demand flashbacks to Bone's childhood; the scenes featuring Paul could be cut without disrupting the story line. Dram is box-office gold, and Paul Tring is, as of the moment, conveniently a nobody. Streatfeild cannily casts Noel Water as both the hero/rescuer and the self-interested effete who will upend a child's contract to save his own job.

Let us now recall Doris to the scene, although she has been there all along, keeping up her hobby of analyzing and pegging all of her in-laws. Doris has been wondering whether she is getting everyone into the right box. She is starting to think Mum has more to her than meets the eye, and to wonder whether it is all sunshine and pink petals for Ruth at Rose of England. She drops by to see Ruth on the set, becoming the only adult character other than Ruth whom Streatfeild allows to traverse the boundary between the two universes— film and the family.[52]

At the studio, Doris's roles will coalesce. In a swift reallocation of power and insight, Streatfeild will take Doris from casual cataloguer to enlightened analyst.[53] Doris will invite Ruth to confide in her, and Doris will be rewarded: she will hear about Ruth's motherly reasons for placing Paul in films, and Ruth's sense of uselessness during the long, idle hours at Rose of England. Doris does not buy Ruth's judgment that Paul needs psychiatric treatment or "compensation," but she can grant that Paul might just have a good old-fashioned inferiority complex. Doris arrives at this conclusion via the equally good old-fashioned method of putting two and two together.

Even so, Doris has become, as she marvels, "interested in the bits of psycho-analysis [Mum] had picked up. Where had the old thing heard them?"[54] And Doris herself is not immune to their effects. Cozy chats with Mum begin to win her over, and she is now unsure whether she has been pigheaded in her refusal to have her children christened, as Dad wishes her to do, and whether she is doing herself any favors by standing firm on that issue. Back at home, Doris has had a word with young Jimmie about how he and his schoolmates interact with Paul. She begins to perceive the vicious cycle of bullying, and realizes that her own son is guilty of taunting Paul and thus fueling his little cousin's tantrums.

From Streatfeild's vantage point, giving Doris the power to address the bullying effectively cancels all the negative energy associated with Paul's obstreperous behavior, and starts moving the book to a close. Ruth and Paul will leave the studio; Paul's school, thanks to Doris, will be kinder and gentler. Noel Water's job is safe, but the reader can only speculate as to whether his time with Ruth and Paul has swayed Water's morals. Surely Water will direct another child actor in the future, and could be tempted again to broker the child's career on the whims of an adult star. On the other hand, having met Ruth, he might form a more charitable view of stage mothers. Streatfeild does not say.

The *faux* happy ending comes in the form of a party, organized by Mum, at which much glad news will be revealed. Doris will have her lads christened in the Church of England. Mum and Dad have arranged for Anna's husband to stand for Parliament: what grand "compensation" for Anna! Peter and Ruth will soon welcome a new baby: Paul will be a big brother. But as the curtain falls, issues rise. We can only conjecture about this Tring tendency to bullying, including Peter's inclination to the ice water-and-leather school of discipline. Perhaps it is part of the "Tring mold," a continuation of a long-standing pattern of abuse and control between and within generations, and currently, in 1950, firmly rooted in Mum and Dad's crafty whims. We never learn whether Doris's decision to have her children baptized constitutes her own spiritual awakening, or if Doris is savvier than Mum supposes, and willing to go for a little archaic ritual for the sake of family peace. Streatfeild does not reveal whether Anna's new status as an MP's wife is a step up, or if indebtedness to Dad's political contacts will shorten Anna's leash even further.

As to the Peter Trings, their little boy who loves to act has been ripped from a newfound opportunity, and to no apparent avail. Streatfeild leaves us wondering whether it was so wrong to allow Paul to participate in the film; if he will require deprogramming to adjust, then therapeutic intervention to deal with a rival sibling; if he will turn into a sweet, tractable brother once the schoolyard bullying abates. She leaves open the matters of whether the sphere to which he is returning is morally superior to the studio environment and whether Ruth and Peter are now, or ever have been, fit parents, committed to resolving their conflicting views on childrearing. Streatfeild does not make it clear whether Ruth was taken in by a quack, or if she will shed his influence entirely; or whether some of Ruth's adviser's teachings are sound, and other bits are just plain wrong. And she leaves open the confounding question of whether Doris, Mum, and Ruth are any more or less qualified than Spock, Gesell, Bowlby, Winnicott, Anna Freud, or other "experts" to analyze the mind of the child.

The monumental unsolved ethical problem that arcs across the novel is this: what might Streatfeild have thought of adapting *Love in a Mist* into a film? Several of her stories have been made into radio and television plays, with *Ballet Shoes* a repeat selection of producers since 1947. Streatfeild took a strong interest in the adaptations that occurred in her lifetime, writing her own radio scripts and objecting strenuously to a proposed interpretation of Posy Fossil in the 1975 television version of *Ballet Shoes*.[55] The hitch in conceiving *Love in a Mist* for the screen is that adhering faithfully to the narrative would involve employing child actors to portray six featured kiddies (Paul and his cousins), and dozens of extras, in a story that scrutinizes the use and treatment of child actors to begin with. This, however, assumes that children would be necessary to such a film. They would not. The presence of every child, including Paul, could be implied through adult dialogue or off-screen voice-overs.[56]

As Boas wrote of the Shakespeare problem plays, "the issues raised preclude a completely satisfactory outcome."[57] Streatfeild leaves us with myriad puzzlements. In her children's books, she typically blended merry storytelling with a serious message. This was a trait that endeared her to readers young and old. She does not disappoint in this problem play, cloaked in the guise of trivial adult female fare. There are many amusing passages in *Love in a Mist*, and the message is an ethical question fit to ponder: who among us has not deliberately appeared altruistic while achieving our own ends? She plants her response in Noel Water's movie title, drawn from John 8.6–7: "He who is without sin among you, let him first cast a stone… ."

More than 60 years have passed since Paul Tring's short-lived experience at Rose of England Studios as a lead character in a throwaway Susan Scarlett novel. The body of scholarly literature about stage mothers and child stars remains sparse, with a recent addition being Grace Wang's evaluation of Asian and Asian American "music moms" who, Wang believes, seek not to achieve "assimilation and inclusion" but rather to "levy the cultural capital they [and their children gain] through classical music"[58]. The quantity of published research on stage mothers may be wanting, but parenting guides and online advice sites abound. It is possible that the term "stage mother" receives less attention in studies of parenting techniques than it might, because "soccer mom" and "helicopter parent" have overtaken it in the popular press, and in mainstream self-help books and blogs of the early twenty-first century.

On 29 January 2010, Lisa Belkin, in her *New York Times Magazine* online discussion board *Motherlode*, opened a new forum, "Becoming a Stage Mother." Belkin posits that the concept of the hovering, over-involved parent descends directly from that of stage mother, and she invites other board posts on the matter. A conversation follows Linda Shuie's discussion opener, "Have I Turned into a Stage Mother?" about Shuie's daughter's fear of piano recitals. Reader responses posted in the Comments section of *Motherlode* are largely supportive of Shuie, as she tries to determine "where encouragement ends and enmeshment begins" when rearing a performing child.[59] But in the broader world of parenting forums, the conversation is not always so restrained. Posts can range from calm, to outrage, to attack, to insult, to righteously indignant defense. Bloggers and posters stand strong at their keyboards. Ready. Aim. Let the stoning begin.

A 1950s kaffee-klatsch, over-the-back-fence approach to bringing up children, and to defining the maternal role, was missing from Ruth Tring's life, but this might have been no great loss. A "yattering mob," as Doris labeled it, could have arisen from any gingham-curtained kitchen confab, even back in "comfy homsey" Illinois.[60] Ruth chose to seek out advice in her own way: To engage with the ideas of an amateur authority whose practiced, assured Word was her holy writ, at least for a while. If she developed misgivings about his ideas, Ruth could abandon *The Mind and the Child* at any time, with no bad feeling between her and the book's author—much as one might quit an online forum whose other members will not miss the absentee.

In a real community, separating from the group, or giving up on an activity that others deem promising or prestigious, can mean risking ridicule or contempt. Pulling Paul out of his contract caused Ruth to separate from the studio world and, at least temporarily, from Mum-Tring's control. (Ruth's level of continued dependency on *The Mind and The Child* could have fluctuated, though. For all we know, the book remained in her nightstand drawer, or at the back of her wardrobe, where Peter would not notice it.) Ruth perhaps risked her child's opportunity to blossom, and hobbled her relations with her in-laws and with the women in her town who might be "sniggering" at her now for having chucked Paul's career. Ruth did not pursue wealth or social rank through her son's experience in the studio, but she did seek personal "compensation" as a good mother. She does not necessarily feel either ashamed or cleansed by having accepted, and then rejected, her stage mother role. In contrast, *Bellissima*'s Maddalena withdraws her daughter from the Cinnecità film after realizing that she had been about to exploit the girl for monetary and social gain. Visconti ensures that Maddalena emerges "clean" after having tested her ambitions and then rejecting them.[61] The state of Ruth's soul is not "clean." It is murky, perplexing; it is a problem.

We may never know whether Salvo d'Angelo and Luchino Visconti had any qualms about utilizing the child actress Tina Apicella, as well as local towns-children, to disparage the same industry practices to which these young actors needed to conform in order to act in *Bellissima*. Bruno d'Angelo, Salvo's son, explains that the concept Cesare Zavattini presented to the senior d'Angelo for this film was

> one of his typical stories: cinema, which fascinates the public with its stars, spectacular compensation, and glamorous lifestyle is in reality a vacuous world where greed, indifference, deception, cynicism – as in life – are too often the rule of the game.
>
> Zavattini had no intention to show the exploitation of a child by the motion picture industry; he was rather interested in the contrast between what the public perceives as glamorous and the inner reality of the movie world.[62]

F. S. Boas commented in 1896 on Shakespeare's mood during the time in which he wrote the problem plays. Try as he might, Boas could not determine what prompted Shakespeare to enter a period in which he shifted his approach from "a sunny landscape" to a place where mountain "peaks are shrouded in thick mist," and infused his plays with societal issues that he would not resolve.[63] In the case of Streatfeild, it is somewhat easier to see why she might have chosen to write a problem novel at this point in her career. Noel Streatfeild in 1950 was completing her commitment to Hodder and Stoughton, and *Love in a Mist* was her final work as Susan Scarlett. She would soon no longer write under a pseudonym. Streatfeild had published *The Painted Garden* in 1948–9; the response was mixed. Reviewers took her to task, unjustly accusing her of rendering the "glossy" Bee Bee Studios as a happy, normal environment for children.[64] She must have been disappointed in this reaction. She was a proud and clever woman. As she rounded out her Susan Scarlett contract, she must also have seen the opportunity to respond *incognito* to her critics, and to exploit the light romance genre for her own purposes: she could hand her audience of young postwar mothers an escapist read while engaging in the rewarding intellectual exercise of weaving in a problem play that hacks away at the studio system in all its cut-rate glory. But because her identity was a secret, Noel Streatfeild's critics, and the patrons of the drugstore library of the 1950s did not know who Susan Scarlett was; or that the Susan Scarlett brand was about to die; or that Susan Scarlett was Noel Streatfeild, a woman who was versed in Shakespeare and committed to child welfare, who was attuned to human psychology, and who had the insight and foresight to broach problems of family and society that flourished in the 1950s and that continue to confound us today.

Notes

1   Noel Streatfeild, "Why Did I Ever Write a Children's Story?," *The Writer* (December 1949): 6.

2   Angela Bull, *Noel Streatfeild* (London: Collins, 1984), 118. A note on Streatfeild's papers: as of this writing, the papers of Noel Streatfeild are privately held by her family in London. The papers are housed in five records storage boxes and organized loosely into document wallets, envelopes, and binders. There exists a general box inventory, but items have been removed and replaced in other boxes. There is no archival arrangement or description. In this essay, I have thus cited the source for items from this collection simply as "Streatfeild, Papers."

3   Bull, *Noel Streatfeild*, 141.

4   Shirley Hughes, *A Life Drawing* (London: The Bodley Head, 2002), 124.

5   Streatfeild, *The Painted Garden: The Story of a Holiday in Hollywood* (London: Collins, 1949), 5.

6   Bull, *Noel Streatfeild*, 180.

7   Ibid., 176.

8   Sims, Sue Sims, Preface, *Pirouette*, by Susan Scarlett [Noel Streatfeild] (1948; reprint, Edinburgh: Greyladies, 2009), v–xi. Joy Wotton, Preface, *Poppies for England*, by Susan Scarlett [Noel Streatfeild] (1947; reprint, Edinburgh: Greyladies, 2008), v–xiv.

9   Wotton, Preface, vi. Note: The UK chain Boots the Chemist began the Boots Booklovers' Library lending service in 1898. My copy of *Love in a Mist* has the typical Boots library binding and eyelet at the top of the spine, on which are also stamped the title, author, and, at the base, Romance.

10 Streatfeild, Papers.

11 Wotton, Preface, xiv.

12 Janice Radway, *Reading the Romance: Women, Patriarchy, and Popular Literature* (Chapel Hill: University of North Carolina Press, 1984), 134.

13 Joy Wotton, Preface, *Love in a Mist*, by Susan Scarlett (Noel Streatfeild). (1951; reprint, Edinburgh: Greyladies, 2011), vii. Wotton challenges Bull's accusation that all the Scarletts "have hackneyed, sentimental plots usually built around the rivalry of two sharply contrasted girls and one desirable man." See: Bull, *Noel Streatfeild*, 176.

14 Bull, 78.

15 Ibid., 79.

16 Streatfeild, *Away from the Vicarage* (London: Collins, 1965), 173.

17 Bull, *Noel Streatfeild*, 119.

18 John Galsworthy, *The Inn of Tranquillity* (New York: Scribner, 1913), 191.

19 Streatfeild, Papers.

20 E. M. W. Tillyard, *Shakespeare's Problem Plays* (Toronto: University of Toronto Press, 1949), 5–8.

21 Streatfeild's theater background worked into her fascination with the evangelist/ media sensation Aimée Semple McPherson and McPherson's grip on her follower. See Streatfeild, *Beyond the Vicarage* (London: Collins, 1971), 99–104. The pull of McPherson can be compared to the effect that the phantasmal parenting expert has on Ruth. Streatfeild's own father was a clergyman, and sin and repentance were common themes in the household.

22 Boas, F. S., *Shakespeare and His Predecessors* (New York: Scribner, 1896), 345.

23 Ibid.

24 Ibid., 356.

25 Sally Sims Stokes, "Noel Streatfeild's Secret Gardens," in Frances Hodgson Burnett, *The Secret Garden*, Norton Critical Edition, (ed.) Gretchen Holbrook Gerzina (New York: W. W. Norton, 2006), 412.

26 W. W. Lawrence, *Shakespeare's Problem Comedies* (New York: Macmillan, 1931), 21.

27 Brian Attebery, "Elizabeth Enright and the Family Story as Genre," *Children's Literature* 37 (2009): 115, 125

28 Susan Scarlett (Noel Streatfeild), *Love in a Mist* (London: Hodder and Stoughton, 1951), 11.

29 Joy Wotton, in her 2011 preface to *Love in a Mist*, refers to Emma Tring as "an unequivocally good woman." See: Wotton, Preface, *Love in a Mist*, by Susan Scarlett [Noel Streatfeild] (1951; reprint, Edinburgh: Greyladies, 2011), viii.

30 William Shakespeare, *The Tempest*, Barbara A. Mowat and Paul Werstine (eds) (New York: Washington Square, 1994), 5:1:293.

31 Jeremy Holmes, afterword to *Saplings*, by Noel Streatfeild (1945; reprint, London: Persephone, 2002), 364, 366.

32 Bull, *Noel Streatfeild*, 124, 163, 165.

33 Nick Midgley, "Anna Freud: The Hampstead War Nurseries and the Role of the Direct Observation of Children for Psychoanalysis," *International Journal of Psychoanalysis* 88 pt. 4 (2007): 957.

34 Julia Grant, *Raising Baby by the Book: The Education of American Mothers* (New Haven: Yale University Press, 1998), 185.

35 Benjamin Spock, *Common Sense Book of Baby and Child Care* (New York: Duell, Sloan and Pearce, 1946), 211.

36 Julia Grant, *Raising Baby by the Book: The Education of American Mothers* (New Haven: Yale University Press, 1998), 238.

37 This fictitious phenomenon foretells the advice columns Dr Spock would run in women's magazines in the 1950s, and the countless letters from American mothers to Dr Spock, some of which Julia Grant analyzes in her 1998 study. See ibid., note 31.

38 Scarlett, *Love in a Mist*, 52.

39 Jane O'Connor, *The Cultural Significance of the Child Star* (New York: Routledge, 2008), 1.

40 Scarlett, *Love in a Mist*, 96, 158.

41 It appears that in England and the United States, it was not until the late 1970s that national associations of drama therapists were formed. See the website of the British Association of Dramatherapists: http://badth.org.uk/

42 *Bellissima* seems not to have reached London or New York until 1953, which argues against Streatfeild's having known of the film before she began *Love in a*

Mist. Bruno d'Angelo does not believe his father Salvo d'Angelo, or others involved with *Bellissima*, ever had contact with Streatfeild. Bruno d'Angelo, e-mail message to author, July 1, 2009.

43 E. D. Nelson, "The Things That Dreams Are Made On: Dreamwork and the Socialization of 'Stage Mothers,'" *Qualitative Sociology* 24 (2001): 454–6.

44 Margaret O'Brien, *My Diary* (Philadelphia: Lippincott, 1948), 23.

45 Joshua Gamson, *Claims to Fame: Celebrity in Contemporary America* (Berkeley: University of California Press, 1994), 29–31; Stokes, "Noel Streatfeild's Secret Gardens," 399.

46 O'Connor, *Child Star*, 66.

47 Great Britain, Departmental Committee on the Employment of Children as Film Actors, in Theatrical Work, and in Ballet, *Report* (London: HMSO, 1950), 54. Former child star Paul Petersen's foundation, A Minor Consideration, has since the 1990s promoted concern for "why things can go so completely wrong for this population of performers" [i.e. child actors]. "A Minor Consideration," http://www.minorcon.org

48 Scarlett, *Love in a Mist*, 209.

49 Ibid., 205.

50 Ibid., 207–8.

51 Ibid., 131, 143.

52 Doris can be said here to have become a figure of magic who can pass between worlds. There are many possible sources for this stratagem, of course, including Shakespeare; however, other relevant ones are C. S. Lewis's *The Lion, The Witch, and The Wardrobe* (London: Bles, 1950), which was brand-new at the time *Love in a Mist* was in process, and the work of E. Nesbit, which Streatfeild greatly admired. Streatfeild in 1958 would publish *Magic and the Magician: E. Nesbit and Her Children's Books* (London: Ernest Benn).

53 Others may find it worthwhile to apply Alexander N. Howe's *It Didn't Mean Anything: A Psychoanalytic Reading of American Detective Fiction* (Jefferson: McFarland, 2008) to *Love in a Mist*. One might approach this through the Lacanian structures Howe applies in his thesis, and begin by hypothesizing Streatfeild's book as a work of detective fiction, with Doris Tring as analyst/ detective, Ruth as hysteric/analyst/Other, and Anna and Paul as hysterics. Deciding whether Mum is the criminal or the analyst can always be folded into the rich body of unanswered matter that, to this author, helps define *Love in a Mist* as a problem play.

Another approach is to consider Anna as exhibiting the traits of histrionic personality disorder (HPD; not to be confused with hysteria), borderline personality disorder (BPD), or narcissistic personality disorder (NPD), none of which had yet been defined at the time Streatfeild was writing. See Jesse Battan, "The 'New Narcissism' in 20th-Century America: The Shadow and Substance of Social Change," *Journal of Social History* 17 (1983): 204–6. Some scholars have perceived that a diagnosis of HPD may be an example of sexism; men rarely receive this diagnosis. See Michelle Lynn Sharp, "Sex-typing and Personality Disorder Characteristics," (dissertation, Southern Illinois University at Carbondale, 1997), 2–3, 5, and 47; and Andrew Skodol et al., "Personality Types Proposed for DSM-5, *Journal of Personality Disorders* 25, no. 2 (2011): 148. Streatfeild's own treatment of her female characters' behavior does adhere to gender stereotypes.

54   Scarlett, *Love in a Mist*, 191.

55   Streatfeild, Papers.

56   "Unmemorable, characterless [children] like Geoffrey, Jimmie, and Wendy [in *Love in a Mist*] are not characteristic" of Streatfeild's novels. Wotton, Preface, v.

57   Boas, *Shakespeare and His Predecessors*, 356.

58   Grace Wang, "Interlopers in the Realm of High Culture: 'Music Moms' and the Performance of Asian and American Identities," *American Quarterly* 61 (2009): 881–903.

59   Lisa Belkin, "Becoming a Stage Mother," *Motherlode: Adventures in Parenting* (blog), *The New York Times*, January 29, 2010, http://parenting.blogs.nytimes.com

60   Scarlett, *Love in a Mist*, 8.

61   d'Angelo, e-mail message to author, July 1, 2009.

62   Ibid.

63   Boas, *Shakspere and His Predecessors*, 344–5.

64   Stokes, "Noel Streatfeild's Secret Gardens," 402.

Bibliography

A Minor Consideration. Available at http://www.minorcon.org/

d'Angelo, Bruno. E-mail message to author. July 1, 2009.

Attebery, Brian. "Elizabeth Enright and the Family Story as Genre." *Children's Literature* 37 (2009): 114–36.

Battan, Jesse. "The 'New Narcissism' in 20th-Century America: The Shadow and Substance of Social Change." *Journal of Social History* 17 (1983): 199–220.

Belkin, Lisa. *Motherlode: Adventures in Parenting* (blog). *The New York Times.* http://parenting.blogs.nytimes.com

Bellissima. Dir. Luchino Visconti. Rome: Universalia, 1951. Film.

Boas, F. S. *Shakespeare and His Predecessors.* New York: Scribner, 1896.

Bowlby, John. *Maternal Care and Mental Health: A Report Prepared on Behalf of the*

World Health Organization as a Contribution to the United Nations Programme for the Welfare of Homeless Children. Geneva: WHO, 1951.

Bull, Angela. *Noel Streatfeild.* London: Collins, 1984.

Galsworthy, John. *The Inn of Tranquillity.* New York: Scribner, 1913.

Gamson, Joshua. *Claims to Fame: Celebrity in Contemporary America.* Berkeley: University of California Press, 1994.

Gesell, Arnold. *Infant and Child in the Culture of Today: The Guidance of Development in Home and Nursery School.* New York: Harper, 1943.

Grant, Julia. *Raising Baby by the Book: The Education of American Mothers.* New Haven: Yale University Press, 1998.

Great Britain. Departmental Committee on the Employment of Children as Film Actors, in Theatrical Work, and in Ballet. *Report.* London: HMSO, 1950.

Gypsy. Dir. Mervyn LeRoy. Burbank, CA: Warner Bros., 1962. Film.

Frankel, Noralee. *Stripping Gypsy: The Life of Gypsy Rose Lee.* New York: Oxford University Press, 2009.

Holmes, Jeremy. Afterword. *Saplings,* by Noel Streatfeild, 363–7. 1945. London: Persephone, 2002.

—*John Bowlby and Attachment Theory.* London: Routledge, 1993.

Howe, Alexander N. *It Didn't Mean Anything: A Psychoanalytic Reading of American Detective Fiction.* Jefferson: McFarland, 2008.

Hughes, Shirley. *A Life Drawing.* London: The Bodley Head, 2002.

Huse, Nancy. *Noel Streatfeild.* New York: Twayne/Maxwell Macmillan International, 1994.

Laurents, Arthur. *Gypsy.* New York: Random House, 1960.

Lawrence, W. W. *Shakespeare's Problem Comedies.* New York: Macmillan, 1931.

Lewis, C. S. *The Lion, The Witch, and The Wardrobe.* London: Bles, 1950.

Midgley, Nick. "Anna Freud: The Hampstead War Nurseries and the Role of the Direct Observation of Children for Psychoanalysis." *International Journal of Psychoanalysis* 88 pt. 4 (2007): 939–59.

Nelson, E. D. "The Things That Dreams Are Made On: Dreamwork and the Socialization of 'Stage Mothers.'" *Qualitative Sociology* 24 (2001): 439–58.

O'Brien, Margaret. *My Diary.* Philadelphia: Lippincott, 1948.

O'Connor, Jane. *The Cultural Significance of the Child Star.* New York: Routledge, 2008.

Radway, Janice. *Reading the Romance: Women, Patriarchy, and Popular Literature.* Chapel Hill: University of North Carolina Press, 1984.

Ropes, Bradford. *Stage Mother.* New York: King, 1933.

Scarlett, Susan [Noel Streatfeild]. *Love in a Mist.* London: Hodder and Stoughton, 1951.

—*Pirouette.* 1948. Edinburgh: Greyladies, 2009.

Shakespeare, William. *All's Well That Ends Well.* Barbara A. Mowat and Paul Werstine (eds). New York: Washington Square, 2001.

—*Measure for Measure.* Jonathan Crewe (ed.), New York: Penguin, 2000.

—*A Midsummer Night's Dream.* Wolfgang Clemen (ed.), New York: Signet, 1998.

—*The Tempest*. Barbara A. Mowat and Paul Werstine (eds), New York: Washington Square, 1994.

—*Troilus and Cressida*. Barbara A. Mowat and Paul Werstine (eds), New York: Washington Square, 2007.

Sharp, Michelle Lynn. "Sex-typing and Personality Disorder Characteristics." Southern Illinois University at Carbondale, 1997.

Sims, Sue. Preface. *Pirouette*, by Susan Scarlett [Noel Streatfeild]. 1948. Edinburgh: Greyladies, 2009. v–xi.

Skodol, Andrew E. et al. "Personality Types Proposed for DSM-5." Journal of Personality Disorders, 25:2 (2011) 136–69.

Spock, Benjamin. *Common Sense Book of Baby and Child Care*. New York: Duell, Sloan and Pearce, 1946.

Stage Mother. Dir. Charles Brabin. Burbank, CA: MGM, 1933. Film.

Stokes, Sally Sims. "Noel Streatfeild's Secret Gardens." In Frances Hodgson Burnett, *The Secret Garden*. Norton Critical Edition. Gretchen Holbrook Gerzina (ed.), 387–422. New York: W. W. Norton, 2006.

Streatfeild, Noel. *Away from the Vicarage*. London: Collins, 1965.

—*Ballet Shoes*. London: Dent, 1936.

—*Beyond the Vicarage*. London: Collins, 1971.

—*The Circus is Coming*. London: Dent, 1938.

—*Curtain Up*. London: Dent, 1944.

—*It Pays to Be Good*. London: Heinemann, 1936.

—*Magic and the Magician: E. Nesbit and Her Children's Books*. London: Ernest Benn, 1958.

—"The Painted Garden." *Collins Magazine for Boys and Girls*, (1948): no. 7: 2–5, 45–51; no. 8: 54–7, 98–103; no. 9: 146–55; no. 10: 200–6; no. 11: 250–9; no. 12: 307–16.

—*The Painted Garden: The Story of a Holiday in Hollywood*. London: Collins, 1949.

—*The Whicharts*. London: Heinemann, 1931.

—"Why Did I Ever Write a Children's Story?" *The Writer,* December 1949: 6.

Tillyard, E. M. W. *Shakespeare's Problem Plays*. Toronto: University of Toronto Press, 1949.

The Unfinished Dance. Dir. Henry Koster. Burbank, CA: MGM, 1947. Film.

Wang, Grace. "Interlopers in the Realm of High Culture: 'Music Moms' and the Performance of Asian and American Identities." *American Quarterly* 61 (2009): 881–903.

Winnicott, Donald. *Clinical Notes on the Disorders of Childhood*. London: Heinemann, 1931.

—*Getting to Know Your Baby*. London: Heinemann, 1945.

Wotton, Joy. Preface. *Poppies for England*. By Susan Scarlett [Noel Streatfeild], v–xiv. 1947. Edinburgh: Greyladies, 2008.

—Preface. *Love in a Mist*. By Susan Scarlett [Noel Streatfeild], v–x. 1951. Edinburgh: Greyladies, 2011.

6

Building a Mystery: *Relative Fear* and the 1990s Autistic Thriller

Chris Foss

University of Mary Washington

The terrible tragedy of the mass shooting at Sandy Hook Elementary School in Newtown, Connecticut on December 14, 2012 left countless Americans (including myself) in a state of shock and sadness. For many, it seemed important to preserve a period of time devoted exclusively to grief for and remembrance of the victims, particularly the children, before turning with anger and/or resolve to address the matter of what should be done to attempt to prevent anything like this from ever happening again. Yet, quite a few members of the autistic community and their allies almost immediately were placed in a position of needing to do their best to pull themselves enough out of their mourning to defend their own from the shoddy and irresponsible initial reports suggesting that shooter Adam Lanza's likely Asperger's diagnosis was a potential explanation for such a senseless act of violence.

To cite only one example, David Halbfinger's piece for *The New York Times*, entitled "A Gunman, Recalled as Intelligent and Shy, Who Left Few Footprints in Life," carelessly encourages readers to see autism as the cause behind Lanza's heinous massacre. After noting that several former classmates mentioned Lanza had an Asperger's diagnosis, Halbfinger quotes one of these individuals "who *said* he was *familiar* with the disorder" [my emphasis] as asserting, "If you looked at him, you couldn't see any emotions going through his head."[1] Halbfinger then follows this blatant mischaracterization of autistics as unfeeling with a range of other classmate observations (that he needed "some kind of mental help," talked of "blowing things up," and seemed like "someone who was capable of that"), all of which his article thereby implicitly associates with "the disorder."[2] This gross misrepresentation of autism, which has no established connection to such violence whatsoever, shamefully contributes to the stigmatization of autistic individuals and of other persons with disabilities.

As the Autistic Self Advocacy Network asserts in an official statement on the early media reports that it felt compelled to release within hours of the shooting, "it is imperative that as we mourn the victims of this horrific tragedy that commentators and the media avoid drawing inappropriate and unfounded links between autism or other disabilities and violence."[3] Indeed, not only are "Autistic Americans and individuals with other disabilities … no more likely to commit violent crime than non-disabled people," but actually "people with disabilities of all kinds, including autism, are vastly more likely to be the victims of violent crime than the perpetrators."[4] Thus, as Priscilla Gilman observes in her *New York Times* op-ed that appeared less than a week after the tragedy, "there is a sad irony in making autism the agent or the cause rather than regarding it as the target of violence."[5] Indeed, the autistic community understands this all too well, given the multiple instances each and every year of autistic individuals (usually children) being murdered by family members and/or caregivers—which is why, even before Sandy Hook, ASAN began cosponsoring a National Day of Mourning to call attention to these (and other similar) crimes. In the end, ASAN remains adamant in its position that even if Lanza eventually is revealed to have been officially diagnosed at some point with an autism spectrum disorder, or any other disability for that matter, "the millions of Americans with disabilities should be no more implicated in his actions than the non-disabled population is responsible for those of non-disabled shooters."[6]

In one of the most compelling responses to this situation, autistic blogger Rachel Cohen-Rottenberg begins her December 15, 2012 post by reminding us of the role of scapegoating in all this. She writes, "we live in a society in which simply saying that evil is afoot doesn't cut it anymore. We want answers. We want control. We want it fixed. So we make it a sickness, because we hope that someday sickness will have a cure."[7] She goes on to note that with the Sandy Hook shooting both autism and mental illness have served as such scapegoats.[8] What is more, not only have each of these conditions been fingered as potentially responsible for Lanza's actions, but some accounts (including, again, at least implicitly, Halbfinger's) have egregiously conflated the two. As Gilman aptly reminds her readers, "Asperger's and autism are not forms of mental illness; they are neurodevelopmental disorders or disabilities. Autism is a lifelong condition that manifests before the age of 3; most mental illnesses do not appear until the teen or young adult years."[9] Obviously, blaming either one of these conditions is unacceptable, but such continuing ignorance about the nature of autism is particularly puzzling in a day and age when the latest estimates from the Centers for Disease Control and Prevention (CDC) suggest one out of every 50 school-age children is on the autism spectrum.

A related all-too-common misconception informing a number of the reactions to Newtown is the mistaken belief that "because autistic people have meltdowns, it's plausible that the shooter simply had a meltdown."[10] Cohen-Rottenberg helpfully clarifies that "Autistic people have meltdowns because their sensory systems get overloaded," and as this actually "hurts more than anyone who has never experienced it could understand," autistics may in fact "strike out in the course of a meltdown."[11] Significantly, however, more often than not "they strike out at themselves" rather than at others.[12] Yet, even in those situations when autistics might lash out violently at others (typically, in the form of screaming, hitting, and/or biting), it is crucial to bear in mind that "it's a spontaneous act," "a neurological response that is not even remotely close to premeditating a murder."[13] In other words, "People in the midst of a meltdown do not take the time and the forethought to arm themselves with a bullet-proof vest and several weapons, make their way to an elementary school, and consciously target two particular classrooms of children and the school office."[14] Rather, "most people in the midst of a meltdown just want to withdraw and get away from people and the stressors that cause overload."[15]

Given the continued misleading linkage of autism and psychopathic violence, it would seem more essential than ever to counter the damaging stereotypes that underwrite such uninformed prejudice. These stereotypes continue to abound in popular representations of autism in film and media, and of course this should come as no surprise given the long line of disabled Obsessive Avengers (as documented by Martin F. Norden,[16] and others) throughout cinema history. In this chapter, I aim to establish how in the 1990s a new subgenre I have dubbed the autistic thriller first exploited the growing dis-ease with and fear of what society perceived to be the enigma of autism as general awareness of the term (if not the condition) began to increase throughout that decade. These films constitute an important object of study because they enable us to trace a pattern of social anxiety about autism back through such cinematic representations that allow, if not encourage, the association of autism with pathological violence and preternatural evil through their foregrounding of the mysterious workings of the autistic mind in the figure of the nonverbal autistic child.

In *Cultural Locations of Disability*, Sharon L. Snyder and David T. Mitchell convincingly assert that "disability is as crucial as gender in the primal structuring fantasies" of multiple film genres.[17] They detail how "as a vehicle of sensation, disabled bodies play an important role as either the threatened producer of trauma (as in the case of the monstrous stalker) or as the threat toward the integrity of the able body (as in the case of the hereditary carrier of 'defective' genes)."[18] For Snyder and Mitchell, one must counter both these traditional constructions and offer new alternatives if culture in general and cinema in particular are to move beyond the current predominantly "debilitating narratives of dysfunction and pathology."[19] In "The Problem Body Politic," however, Ian Olney suggests that the most productive approaches to reimagining the nexus of disability and film should focus "not only on the ideological gaps, contradictions and ambiguities" within most contemporary representations, but just as crucially "on the ability of … viewers to resist or recast the 'dominant' intended meaning of these texts."[20] At bottom, it is not so much that he thinks one needs to acknowledge the ways in which conventional representations of disability are by nature "necessarily transgressive."[21] Rather, he merely believes a thorough exploration of the possibility that they may contain some "subversive potential" allows for a more sophisticated engagement with identity and difference than simply exposing problematic stereotypes.[22]

It is incumbent upon all who value cognitive and physical difference to insist upon an unflinching critique of the fundamental ableist biases of most films that depict or reference disability (à la Snyder and Mitchell).[23] At the same time, one also should attempt to remain attuned to the benefits of heeding Olney's call for broadening the bent of most disability studies critiques beyond an exclusively negative hermeneutics. Accordingly, in this essay I attempt to bring both of these emphases to bear on what I see as an important yet underexamined subtopic within disability and film, the 1990s autistic thriller.

In 1988, the commercial and critical success of *Rain Man*[24] called autism to Hollywood's attention as a largely untapped resource for future feature films. The film's sympathetic and relatively realistic, even if also ultimately more comic, portrayal of an autistic individual is deservedly noteworthy. At the same time, however, it nonetheless ultimately serves to reinforce a number of outdated assumptions about autism. Raymond Babbitt, the autistic character played by Dustin Hoffman, embodies all five traits Paul K. Longmore associates with the problematic telethon construction of individuals with disabilities: he is something of a "perpetual child"; he is "helpless, dependent, and fundamentally different from 'normal' people" who, unlike Raymond, may live in a real-world community; he is an "object of charity," both in terms of his care at Wallbrook and in terms of the emotional response his character aims to engender; he is a "vehicle of others' redemption" serving "to provide the occasion for nondisabled people to renew their humanity" (in this case, his brother Charlie, played by Hoffman's co-star Tom Cruise); and he is a figure who "touches the hearts" of viewers as yet another instance of "sentimental entertainment."[25]

While *Rain Man* certainly created its own share of unfortunate consequences for how the larger viewing public conceptualized autism, by comparison the second wave of films featuring autism in the wake of *Rain Man* unequivocally are a significant step backward from their more famous immediate predecessor. These films (which I, again, argue constitute a new subgenre I have dubbed the autistic thriller) manipulate the general public's lack of awareness and understanding of autism as a means of building a mystery upon which the plot depends both for its development and for its dramatic tension. Significantly, given the focus of this anthology, these films also typically employ an autistic child whose "pathetic" life targets and establishes a sentimental response in the viewer through the trials of bullying, the threat of institutionalization, and/ or the trauma of watching family members murdered. Some further employ that child as the vehicle of others' redemption, allowing a nondisabled main character to renew his/her humanity. Some even exploit the "otherness" of autism to suggest some sort of evil lurking behind the child's difference—and, in particular, behind the child's preternatural silence. Most substantially, however, all of these films reduce their autistic characters (even if otherwise sympathetically rendered) to a cheap plot trick rather than granting them the status of a fully developed character in a lead role. Their casting of these autistic characters as children, and as largely nonverbal children at that, plays a crucial role in their functioning as plot devices rather than as fully-drawn individuals. By portraying them either as lacking depth or as remaining trapped too far within the depths of a seemingly unknowable state of being, the filmmakers are able to position these children (and the knowledge they may possess) as the key to the mystery behind murders the nondisabled character(s) must solve.

I wish to focus primarily on one particularly illuminating example of this subgenre, *Relative Fear* (1994).[26] This Canadian Suspense/Thriller (originally released there under the title, *The Child*) was directed by George Mihalka and stars Darlanne Fluegel, Martin Neufeld, James Brolin, Denise Crosby, and M. Emmet Walsh. The film opens with the juxtaposed scenes of two mothers,

Linda Pratman (Fluegel) and Connie Madison (Crosby), giving birth at the same time in adjoining rooms. Connie has been brought over under armed guard from a federal institute for the criminally insane, and the contrast between the two mothers and the two births could not be greater. One is calm and peaceful, the other violent and out of control. When this initial chapter ends with Linda's baby scratching her on the face and drawing blood during their first night alone together, immediately after she wonders aloud who he looks like and states she just cannot figure it out, the viewer worries the world of Linda Pratman somehow has been contaminated by that of Connie Madison.

The next chapter fast forwards four years. One watches as Linda's son Adam (Matthew Dupuis) offers no resistance when his preschool classmates smear him all over with paint, apparently not for the first time. The teacher returns him to the family home, interrupting a piano lesson being given by Linda to tell her Adam needs one-on-one treatment with an autism specialist. After Linda's student, Manny Dorff (Michael Caloz), asks on his way out if Adam is always going to be retarded, we learn that Adam has not spoken at all yet, not even "Mama" or "Dada". At this point, then, Adam's character evokes our pity for him and our sympathy for his parents' distress over his disability. In the next chapter, however, when that night viewers find him watching the National Murder Network on TV and drawing a picture of bloody hands, one's worry returns. One knows something is wrong with Adam (he is not "normal"). Thus, while viewers likely immediately conclude this is not "normal" behavior for a four-year-old child, if they do not really know much about autism, they might one begin to wonder if such "unnatural" inclinations are related in any way to his disability.

Shortly thereafter, the beloved dog of Adam's maternal grandfather Earl McLuhan (Walsh), who is openly hostile to Adam, disappears—and Earl blames Adam. Then, a day or two later Manny (who has picked on Adam in another scene, forcing his mouth full of dirt) secretly takes Adam across the road to show him a gun. At the sound of gunshots, Adam's father Peter (Neufeld) rushes to the scene only to find the boy shot and Adam holding the gun. When the lead investigator, Detective Atwater (Brolin), asks to talk with Adam about the "accident," Linda tells him that is not possible, for Adam is autistic and cannot speak. Atwater murmurs to himself as he walks away, "Isn't that convenient?"[27] and viewers are tempted to concur. Pity and sympathy are replaced by mistrust and suspicion.

The audience next watches as Earl and the family housekeeper Margaret LaDelle (Linda Sorenson) both die in short succession—and in each instance we are treated to a shot of Adam staring intently at the dead body with what only can strike one as preternatural composure. The boy had established motives to wish them both dead: Earl had suggested he had photographic evidence of exactly what had transpired during the shooting incident, and Margaret was chasing Adam to deliver a spanking when she died. Viewers have not actually witnessed Adam kill anybody, but they do know that these deaths were murders and that Adam at least knows what happened in each case. Even if one does not believe a four-year-old autistic boy could be the murderer, one suspects he at least has been complicit to some degree. After all, he does not seem to be making any effort to communicate what he knows to his parents, or to the audience; Adam's eerie silence only seems to betoken his pathological evil nature (not to mention that he seems to smirk as Earl's coffin is lowered into the grave). Thus, as a vehicle of sensation in viewers, his character functions as "the threatened producer of trauma" identified by Snyder and Mitchell (even though he is only four years old).

The possibility that the film is moving toward the revelation that Adam is a "monstrous stalker"[28] is reinforced as the audience is made privy to Linda's own growing fears that something is horribly wrong with him. When she awakes to find him once again watching the National Murder Network during the middle of the very night Margaret died, she loses her temper with him. Yelling, she demands, "What is wrong with you?"[29] Then, she shakes him and screams at him, "Wake up, Adam! Wake up!!"[30] Peter intervenes, but is unable to help her chase away her feelings of desperation. She tearfully explains to Peter (in front of Adam!) that she feels so disconnected she sometimes thinks he is not even her own child. Peter's response to her hopelessness over Adam's inability to make any progress at all is to remind her (and viewers) that Adam is clearly not "stupid."[31] Far from reassuring viewers, however, this actually suggests Adam's potentially evil nature might be informed by some sort of deceptively diabolical intelligence.

Adam's character also functions as a "threat to the integrity of the able body" in the form of Snyder and Mitchell's "hereditary carrier of 'defective' genes," threatening not only the viewers but his own mother as well. The next day Linda goes to see her obstetrician about her doubts. She admits she has asked herself, "Is it just because I cannot accept that Adam is my son because he is autistic?"[32] Yet, she insists his autism is not the reason she cannot seem to fully accept he is her offspring, declaring, "From virtually the day I gave birth I've had this feeling that he wasn't mine, that he didn't belong to me, that he didn't come out of me, long before we ever learned of his condition."[33] Linda does truly love Adam, but that does not mean she is at all comfortable with the notion that this child with whom she does not seem to be able to connect came from her own body. Many parents of autistic children struggle with what they perceive as a lack of connection to their child in that they often do not have (at least early on) the conversation and eye contact and reciprocal play—much less the hugs and kisses and the "I love you"s—which are the everyday outward tokens of the parent-child bond. Initially, of course, there were those who blamed the parents for the child's autism (e.g. the pseudoscience of the refrigerator mother theory),[34] but by the '90s, autism is primarily understood to be a product of nature rather than of nurture, a result of a particular combination of genetic codes inherited from the parents. This effectively presents parents with a new and different sort of self-blame in that their own genes are the source of their child's "abnormality."

In other words, a parent cannot cordon off the otherness of the child's disability from his/her own integral Self. Autism's lineage implicates the parents. It is not then merely a matter of no longer being able to convince themselves they (and the integrity of their able bodies) are immune to the threat represented by the perceived "defectiveness" of disability, for they are the very source of contamination itself. This is a terrible possibility to face, as terrible in its own way for many parents as the refrigerator theory, for in both instances the cause of autism may be traced directly back to the parents—and in the case of the genetic etiology in particular, it is all the more terrifying in that it is not merely the disabled body which may be posited as "defective" but the able bodies of the parents as well, for the defective genes are a legacy of the parents' own biology. Of course, a disability studies perspective exposes how this is only a problem if parents and others see disability as defect rather than as natural human variation and difference, but the threat of autism as a genetic condition is a very real one regardless, not just a cinematic scare tactic (as the real-life proliferation of conspiracy theories promoting vaccines and other environmental culprits behind the surge of autism spectrum diagnoses demonstrates).

In *Relative Fear*, it is almost as if this threat is simply too overwhelming (even more so than the prospect Adam might be a murderous stalker) to be sustained for very long. Almost immediately after Linda opens up this possibility to viewers' minds, her doctor tells her about Connie's simultaneous delivery, which allows her to begin to believe their babies somehow were switched at the hospital. Surely this modern-day version of the evil changeling tradition is easier to bear, for it at least would absolve Linda (and Peter) of blame. By extension, able-bodied viewers (whom the film invites to identify with Linda) are absolved of blame. Eventually, Linda tracks down her real son at an orphanage; while very amiable and quite smart, he has never been adopted because no one has wanted him after learning who his parents were. This visit confirms for her (and the audience) that her maternal instinct was right all along—surely the evil autistic boy with whom she has been living is not her son, but instead is the monstrous offspring of serial killers. She now may see herself as completely absolved of all blame for what Adam potentially has become. He no longer contaminates her sense of herself as a mother, for Adam's evil is revealed to be fully Other to her still integral Self.

This is not only what Linda wants to believe; it is what viewers themselves need to have affirmed if their own able bodies are to be saved from the threat of a defectiveness belonging as much to the Self as to the Other. Indeed, promotional copy for the film explicitly positions Linda and Peter as "innocent": "When two babies are switched at birth, the innocent parents of a young boy with madness in his veins and violence in his heart are terrorized by a string of grisly deaths."[35] To some extent, this gestures toward an allaying of fears regarding the threat Adam represents to the integrity of the able body from a genetic standpoint. Taglines such as "Murder Is In His Blood," "Fear has a new face," and "Trusting your children can be deadly"[36] are less reassuring, however—and the Pratmans' exoneration is far from a universal absolution, for Adam still embodies the threat of genetics gone wrong. The Madison's genes, after all, remain a frightening reminder of the human face of Otherness, of evil.

One certainly may attempt to dispel the more general anxiety by insisting this is merely a case of bad genes begetting more bad genes; after all, Connie is clearly categorized as "criminally insane" for viewers from the very start. Yet was she so from birth? Her conversation with Linda suggests otherwise, that she was just a wide-eyed and lonely early teen who was seduced by the attentions of her bad-boy step-brother, her partner in procreation as well as in crime. Was he evil from birth? Were both sets of their parents? Surely one may not trace Adam Pratman's criminal tendencies all the way back to that first mythological Adam, with every single generation in-between also a serial killer who somehow managed to reproduce before being stopped. Surely at some point supposedly "good" genes begat "bad" ones. The viewer, like Linda, wants and needs to feel safe from the indictment represented by "defective" genes, but while Adam's actual lineage may disarm the most immediate danger, the threat still remains lurking below the surface, whether or not one realizes it.

In any case, the revelation of Adam's true parents does not dissolve the more immediately pressing threat of a murderous stalker within the supposedly inviolable safe space of the family home. At the very moment Linda is with Henry (her real son), Detective Atwater is paying a visit to the Pratman house because he has grown increasingly suspicious of Adam's potential involvement in all of the "accidents." With Peter outside obliviously working on a car, Atwater enters unnoticed to question Adam. Adam runs and hides, and while Atwater climbs up into the attic looking for him, we see someone putting marbles on the stairs below. Atwater, of course, slips and falls on them, as Adam watches from below.

The film cuts to follow Clive (Adam's tutor, played by Bruce Dinsmore) as he arrives at the front door to find Peter bending suspiciously over the body, now with a bloody screwdriver sticking in it. Clive calls the police and Peter is arrested for Atwater's murder, but viewers know it is the evil autistic boy who has madness in his veins and violence in his heart who in fact is responsible. Linda, returning just as the police are driving Peter away, is understandably distraught and disturbed. Alone with Adam back inside the house, she discovers that a drawing pad of Adam's contains graphic images of each death scene (including the first victim, Earl's dog Chubby). Her worst fears, and those of the audience, are confirmed.

Linda may not be to blame for Adam's evil, but that of course in no way neutralizes the threat he embodies as the all-too-lethal combination of the murderous stalker and the hereditary carrier of defective genes identified by Snyder and Mitchell as two of the most common cinematic constructions of disability. After all, wasn't she just recently shaking him and screaming at him? Moreover, may not the opening scene's scratching incident somehow suggest Adam has had it in for her from day one? Might not his evil disabled mind somehow have known all along she was not his mother and thus be motivated to punish her for this? With Peter's arrest, he now had done away with every other member of the household, even the dog. Surely she is next; surely he has been saving his best revenge for last.

Then, just as many viewers undoubtedly are urging her to get out and get out now, Adam suddenly is there, thrusting something at her. She starts—but it's just a packet of Earl's photos from the shooting. In it, she finds pictures of Clive, not Adam, shooting the boy. Linda, and the audience, breathes a big sigh of relief. The now no longer automaton-like seeming little boy-killer even tries to comfort her, and she hugs him to her, saying, "Oh baby, it wasn't you!"[37] Clive, however, arrives (of course) before she can call the police, and he discovers she now knows *he* is the murderous stalker. He reveals all to her: he actually is Adam's biological father, presumed dead in a fire that took place during the attempted capture of the couple, who has been shadowing his boy all this time, living in the attic and using the dumbwaiter to get in and out via the basement. Linda flees with Adam to the attic, but Clive breaks in and begins to strangle Linda. At this climactic moment, Adam grabs his father's gun from what he obviously knows to be its hiding place, yells out "Mommy!" (his first words, which momentarily freeze both adults), and then shoots Clive (who falls to his death).[38] The film ends with a brief scene in which Adam and Henry, now brothers, are seen out front of the house together. Henry is trying to get Adam to play a game with sticks, brandishing one himself and proclaiming himself King Arthur with Excalibur. Adam is busy digging in the ground with his own stick, seemingly completely oblivious to Henry's presence. Suddenly, though, he turns with something resembling a smile, points his stick at Henry, and says, "Bang! You're dead."[39]

I would suggest that, for most of the movie, Adam's autism serves to intensify the threat he represents, to Linda and to the viewers. As Stuart Murray has asserted in his very important article "Autism and the Contemporary Sentimental," "What we might term the 'narrative appeal' of autism in cultural texts is that it easily signifies possibly the most radical form of personal otherness."[40] For Murray, it does so because it presents one with "a person, just like you or me"—indeed, I would argue, this is intensified all the more because, unlike in the case of most physical disabilities, this person looks just like you and me—a person who nonetheless "is in fact nothing like you or me, but rather subject to a condition that supposedly defies logic and understanding."[41] "At the most extreme level of its representation then," he continues, "autism enables, because of what is seen to be its inherently unknown and ambiguous nature, the discussion of any number of issues that circulate in the popular understanding of the human condition. It is, we are led to believe, the alien within the human, … the ultimate enigma."[42]

The fact Adam is a child rather than an adult only exacerbates the viewers' discomfort. If such danger, such evil, may issue forth from a body ordinarily assumed to be so small, so innocent, so dependent, then how may one feel safe around anyone, even one's own children? Of course, one of the ways in which nondisabled individuals have relieved their discomfort with disabled adults is to see them, to treat them, as children. In *Relative Fear*, however, such infantil-ization of the disabled body is no help, for here the disabled body is already that of a child's, and yet it is still somehow a threat to the able-bodied on multiple levels. Indeed, the original Canadian title (*The Child*) actually foregrounds the disturbing possibility that viewers should regard the figure of "the child"—here not just one particular child (after all, the film is not called *Adam*) but a generalized representative of the whole category—as a menacing rather than as a sentimental entity.

But Adam didn't do it. He is not evil. This is precisely where Olney's alternative approach comes into play. *Relative Fear* shamelessly and shamefully exploits the stereotypical association of disability with evil in order to effect its surprise shocker of an ending. But, does this preclude the film from containing subversive potential where this stereotypical association is concerned? If viewers are placed in the same position as Linda, are they not (along with her) forced to confront the ways in which they allowed themselves to buy into the stereotype? What does it say about ourselves, about the "complexity of identity production," about how we conceptualize disability in general and individuals with disabilities in particular if we so readily may accept the possibility of a four-year-old autistic boy as a diabolical serial killer? Surely not all, perhaps even many, thrillers would seem to offer their audience as explicit an opportunity both to resist and, further, to recast its own stereotypical construction of disability. Olney's position suggests that even films that do not ultimately wrench their audiences out of their "debilitating narratives of dysfunction and pathology" may contain moments when the viewers find themselves rethinking representations of disability, whether or not invited to do so. How much more so, then, must a film like *Relative Fear* encourage such a response? Thus, on one level, *Relative Fear* actually serves as a particularly apt example of a film that (ultimately, at least) enlightens and instructs its audience about the all-too-common tendency to pathologize, even demonize, disability.

At the same time, however, it is important to acknowledge that the final twist and its rehabilitation of Adam in no way actually guarantees that viewers will in fact participate in such a reevaluation of their problematic presumptions about disability. Indeed, given that a self-consciously critical response is much more likely in our own day than in the first part of the '90s (when both disability awareness in general and autism awareness in particular were far less widespread), one need peruse only a few of the typical contemporary responses posted online to be reminded how for many it is the stereotype this film encourages during the vast majority of its running time that leaves the strongest impression on viewers, not the ending's deconstruction of it. One viewer, for example, writes, "The little boy who plays Adam spends the whole movie in a trance (I guess that's his autism?), and he makes you want to slap him"; or, as another insists, "creepy adam [sic] stole the show … . [I] will never look at 4 year old autistic kids the same again."[43] Clearly, resistance to or recasting of the dominant ideological message is not a given, not even after some widespread social enlightenment already has occurred, and not even when the film seems to invite it.

What is more, the ending far from unequivocally supports a more acceptable or accepting understanding of disability. For one, might not the final scene, after all, be suggesting that Adam still just might have murder in his heart? He remains the child of a pair of serial killers, after all. Even if, instead, viewers are merely supposed to see all of their formerly comfortable conceptions about childhood and disability as ultimately restored by Adam's playful "Bang! You're dead" (a completely "normal" response for many a neurotypical boy), for many disability advocates and self-advocates such a scenario is profoundly problematic in its own way. That is, even if the filmmakers intended the ending to indicate that Adam now is in fact making some progress (that he is on the road to emerging from his autism and is becoming a real boy, after all), this sort of script falls back upon a recovery story in which disability ultimately is to be eliminated instead of accommodated. Rather than prodding viewers toward an understanding of autism (and, here, nonverbal autism) as natural, normal human variation and difference (as part of a broad spectrum of neurological make-ups), it encourages them to assume autism needs to be cured or emerged from instead of accepted, respected, and valued for what it is if there is to be anything approaching even a qualified happy ending.

Thus, while *Relative Fear* does potentially allow one to become more self-aware of the cultural tendencies to sentimentalize, pathologize, and/or demonize disability, it also simultaneously—and even more forcefully—enables an uncritical absorption of these same tendencies. Still, Olney is correct to insist that acknowledging the film's subversive potential does allow for a more sophisticated approach to its representation of autism than an exclusively polemical attack with no further goal than the delineation of regressive stereotypes. A brief look at two other autistic thrillers from the '90s confirms such a position. *Silent Fall* (directed by Bruce Beresford)[44] appeared the very same year as *Relative Fear* (1994), and at first glance it seems a much more progressive film in terms of its actual engagement with autism. In *Relative Fear*, we know Adam cannot speak because he is autistic, but that is really the extent of what we learn about his disability, beyond that it might harbor diabolical evil within its silence. In *Silent Fall*, one of the film's goals appears to be to educate its viewers about autism. In numerous scenes, one is treated to mini-lessons about what autism is or is not, most substantially in the 6½-minute chapter entitled "About Autism." All of this consciousness-raising, however, while definitely taking the disability more seriously and in turn featuring it more prominently, does not necessarily translate into a less problematic appropriation of autism.

Silent Fall is the story of Dr Jake Rainer (Richard Dreyfuss), a psychiatrist who has gone into hiding from the world, his wife, and himself in the wake of the accidental drowning death of a ten-year-old autistic boy under his super-vision at the group home he used to run on his lakefront property. As the film opens, Jake's old friend Sheriff Mitch Rivers (J. T. Walsh) sends for him because nine-year-old Tim Warden (Ben Faulkner), the largely nonverbal autistic son of two incredibly wealthy locals found murdered in their bedroom, is holding the police at bay with a bloody knife at the crime scene. In part at the urgings of his wife Karen (Linda Hamilton) and Tim's sister Sylvie (Liv Tyler), and in part owing to his own disgust with the Sheriff's only other alternative, Dr Rene Harlinger (John Lithgow)—an old rival whose methods he cannot stomach—Jake decides to work with Tim.

Despite the film's good intentions, the version of autism Jake offers viewers is one that simultaneously both sentimentalizes and pathologizes Tim. According to Jake, "autism is an overpowering fear of the whole world," but "there's a boy in here, trapped behind a wall, terrified."[45] He does respect Tim's humanity—his answer for how to reach Tim is he "needs to find a way to be his friend"[46]—but his view of autism as somehow trapping the real boy inside a wall represents it as an insidious disorder/disease. The view of Tim as imprisoned by his autism renders him all the more sentimental in the viewers' eyes, even as ultimately one understands the real purpose of his character is to serve as the vehicle of Jake's redemption—working with Tim, Jake finally is able to come to terms and eventually move beyond the earlier tragedy.

Murray has fully delineated the problematic aspects of such sentimentality, though in his own admittedly brief discussion of *Silent Fall*, his emphasis on Tim as a sentimental savant overlooks the film's more significant manipulation of the dangerous side of autism's otherness. As Murray notes, *Silent Fall* does utilize the savant trope characteristic of so many cinematic portrayals of autism, but "Tim's ability as a pure mimic" does not, as he claims, actually "[lead] to the discovery of the truth of his parents' death."[47] The dialogue he eventually provides from the murder scene does not miraculously expose the perpetrator; at first, all it seems to reveal is that the intruder killed his parents while they were having sex. Then, when Sheriff Rivers discovers some soft porn pictures of Tim belonging to Tim's father, he guesses Tim was a victim of ongoing sexual abuse and thus had a motive to kill his father (and his mother, for allowing it to happen). Tim's mimicked dialogue now clearly seems to implicate himself. Sheriff Rivers's discovery forces viewers to confront the very same possibility so central to the manipulations of *Relative Fear*—that the silence, the enigma of autism cannot only potentially hide a real boy behind its wall, but can also harbor homicidal rage, even in a child.

Any initial viewer skepticism concerning Tim's ability to physically carry out this crime is immediately put to rest after Harlinger conducts a hypnotic experiment to prove Tim in fact is capable of almost superhuman strength under duress. Even though he despises Harlinger's methods, Jake accepts that Tim is guilty, and viewers accordingly conclude Tim's enigmatic disability serves as the near-perfect cloak for an obsessive avenger. As the film presents Jake both as Tim's strongest advocate (along with Sylvie) and as the true expert on autism (against Harlinger), his acknowledgment that Tim in fact committed the murder carries tremendous weight in the eyes of viewers. They are thus encouraged to recall Tim as they first encountered him, a blood-bespattered boy wildly lunging with a knife at everybody, and to admit it should have been more apparent from the start that they should be very wary, if not downright afraid, of this autistic child, whose usual blankness and silence has all along been punctuated by multiple explosive outbursts. Tim's parricidal act, be it a form of self-defense or not, positions him (like Adam) as both the producer of trauma and the hereditary carrier of "defective" genes.

Ultimately, the filmmakers reveal Tim to be innocent: the guilty party is Sylvie, who it turns out also had been abused when younger and who finally lashed out when she discovered Tim was now being subjected to the same. However, it is only after Sylvie drugs Jake and leaves him to die in icy waters— and after Tim rescues him (granted, thanks to a mimic trick)—that Jake realizes Tim didn't do it. So, while the savant ability is crucial to the plot, the viewers' willingness to see Tim's otherness as evil (to believe his autism has masked a murderer) is even more essential to its success. Indeed, the trigger for Jake's epiphany comes from finally understanding Tim's crude attempt to communicate what happened through cut-up playing cards, not from Tim's savant regurgitation of the dialogue. Overall, then, even though here the ruse lasts for 20 climactic minutes rather than virtually the whole length of the film, *Silent Fall* still testifies to the persistence of a culturally sanctioned readiness to demonize (not just pathologize and/or sentimentalize) disability. As such, it powerfully reinforces Snyder and Mitchell's point that most films work against rather than in conjunction with the goals of the disability rights advocates in general and of disability studies scholars in particular. Nevertheless, like *Relative Fear*, its eventual exoneration of its autistic subject in fact allows both current-day and then-contemporary viewers to begin to "resist or recast" the dominant impression it otherwise would leave, and this in and of itself makes its treatment of autism more complex, if not sophisticated.

Mercury Rising[48] (1998; directed by Bruce Beresford), arguably the most famous autistic thriller, never invites viewers to suspect autism is dangerous or evil. Ironically, however, without an unlooked-for reversal at the end (as in *Relative Fear* and *Silent Fall*) to encourage a final reevaluation of at least some of the otherwise most likely unexamined implications of its representation of autism, it arguably fosters a potentially more thoroughly uncritical absorption of its simultaneously sentimental and pathological representation of autism than in its pair of predecessors. The film tells the story of Art Jeffries (Bruce Willis), a demoted rogue FBI agent who stumbles upon a cover-up involving high-level National Security Agency official Nicholas Kudrow (Alec Baldwin). When nine-year-old autistic Simon Lynch (Miko Hughes) cracks a test of the NSA's new unbreakable code placed in a puzzle magazine, Kudrow decides to have Simon eliminated and only Jeffries can prevent it. Simon, of course, ends up serving as the vehicle of Jeffries's redemption; haunted by his inability to save the life of a teenage anti-government conspirator whose group he had infil-trated, Jeffries successfully protects and connects with the largely nonverbal boy who at times is portrayed as a computer and/or a robot but at others screams and tantrums at the slightest provocation. Both extremes allow for the othering of autistics, as alien or unnatural, even while the film tries to insist upon an obligatory feel-good moment at the end when Simon hugs Jeffries.

Viewers may (for example) find themselves critiquing the filmmakers' decision to dehumanize Simon's character by having him consistently deliver his lines in a robotic drone reminiscent of those incredibly unrealistic attempts at automated voicing and by having him walk around as if in the sort of deep trance usually reserved only for the somnambulist or the hypnotized—not to mention by including the ridiculous sound effects of a computer working whenever his mind (or, is the suggestion merely his eye?) is processing a puzzle.

Olney's position, then, seems further validated in that even a film which is not overtly transgressive in encouraging a critical (self-)examination of disabling assumptions about disability still may contain some subversive potential for its audience to view against the grain.

In conclusion, what a consideration of *Relative Fear* and the 1990s autistic thriller suggests is it is important to take heed of the exhortations both of Snyder and Mitchell and of Olney. These films predominantly employ disability in general and autism in particular as a vehicle of sensation that relies upon outdated stereotypes and perpetuates ableist attitudes. They abet the medical model of disability and its pathological construction of autism, and it is thus incumbent upon critical analyses to acknowledge and arraign such films' complicity in the continued widespread discrimination against individuals with disabilities. At the same time, investigating the extent to which films like these autistic thrillers allow for resistant reading/viewing offers an opportunity for a more complex, if not a more sophisticated, engagement with the critical nexus of disability and film. Given the crucial role the figure of the child has played in the cultural framing of disability from Charles Dickens's Tiny Tim on down through the American telethon industry, this sort of multi-pronged approach would seem to represent a useful means of moving beyond too simplistic an identification of the disabled child solely as a sentimental character toward a more comprehensive accounting of the truly complicated and contested nature of this figure's role in contemporary film.

Notes

1   David M. Halbfinger, "A Gunman, Recalled as Intelligent and Shy, Who Left Few Footprints in Life," *The New York Times*, December 14, 2012. http://www.nytimes. com

2   Ibid.

3   Autistic Self Advocacy Network, "ASAN Statement on Media Reports Regarding Newtown, CT Shooting," *Autistic Self Advocacy Network*, December 14, 2012. http://autisticadvocacy.org. The Autistic Self Advocacy Network (ASAN) is a highly visible and very vocal organization run by and for autistics that was co-founded by the historic first autistic presidential appointee Ari Ne'eman (currently, a member of the National Council on Disability). ASAN (like much if not most of the autistic community as a whole) advocates for acceptance and

accommodation, as opposed to the cure-based approach typical of the vast majority of autism organizations created by family members of autistics and/or professionals working in any of the numerous fields associated with autism.

4 Ibid.

5 Priscilla Gilman, "Don't Blame Autism for Newtown," *The New York Times*, December 17, 2012. http://www.nytimes.com

6 Autistic Self Advocacy Network, "ASAN Statement on Media Reports Regarding Newtown, CT Shooting."

7 Rachel Cohen-Rottenberg, "When Children Die, It's Time to Grieve and to Reflect, Not to Scapegoat," *Disability and Representation*, December 15, 2012. http://www.disabilityandrepresentation.com

8 Ibid.

9 Gilman, "Don't Blame Autism for Newtown."

10 Cohen-Rottenberg, "When Children Die, It's Time to Grieve and to Reflect, Not to Scapegoat."

11 Ibid.

12 Ibid.

13 Ibid.

14 Ibid.

15 Ibid.

16 Martin F. Norden, "The 'Uncanny' Relationship of Disability and Evil in Film and Television," in Martin F. Norton (ed.), *The Changing Face of Evil in Film and Television* (Amsterdam: Rodopi, 2007), 125–43.

17 Sharon L. Snyder and David T. Mitchell, *Cultural Locations of Disability* (Chicago: University of Chicago Press, 2006), 162.

18 Ibid., 163.

19 Ibid., 169.

20 Ian Olney, "The Problem Body Politic, or 'These Hands Have a Mind All Their Own!': Figuring Disability in the Horror Film Adaptations of Renard's *Les mains d'Orlac*," *Literature/Film Quarterly* 34, no. 4 (2006): 295.

21 Ibid.

22 Ibid.

23 *Ableist* refers to the set(s) of discriminatory assumptions that take nondisabled experience as standard and as a result typically assign (consciously or unconsciously) inferior status to individuals with disabilities. It is to disability studies as *racist* and *sexist* are to ethnic and gender studies.

24 *Rain Man*, dir. Barry Levinson (1988; Burbank, CA: MGM, 2006), DVD.

25 Paul K. Longmore, "The Cultural Framing of Disability," *PMLA* 120, no. 2 (2005): 506.

26 *Relative Fear*, dir. George Mihalka (1994; Burbank, CA: Triumph, 2005), DVD.

27 Ibid.

28 Snyder and Mitchell, *Cultural Locations of Disability*, 163.

29 *Relative Fear*.

30 Ibid.

31 Ibid.

32 Ibid.

33 Ibid.

34 This exploded theory, popularized during the 1960s by the now thoroughly discredited Bruno Bettelheim, posited that autism was caused by a cold, unloving parent's rejection of the child early in life, where such rejection would lead him or her to withdraw into a world of autistic isolation out of anger, frustration, and/or dejection.

35 *Relative Fear*.

36 "Taglines for *Relative Fear*," *IMDb*. http://www.imdb.com

37 *Relative Fear*.

38 Ibid.

39 Ibid.

40 Stuart Murray, "Autism and the Contemporary Sentimental: Fiction and the Narrative Fascination of the Present," *Literature and Medicine* 25, no. 1 (2006): 25.

41 Ibid.

42 Ibid., 25–6.

43 "Reviews & Ratings for *Relative Fear*," *IMDb*. http://www.imdb.com.

44 *Silent Fall*, dir. Bruce Beresford (1998; Burbank, CA: Warner Home Video, 2000), DVD.

45 Ibid.

46 Ibid.

47 Murray, "Autism and the Contemporary Sentimental," 31.

48 *Mercury Rising*, dir. Harold Becker (1998; Burbank, CA: Universal Home Video, 1999), DVD.

Bibliography

Autistic Self Advocacy Network. "ASAN Statement on Media Reports Regarding Newtown, CT Shooting." *Autistic Self Advocacy Network* (website). December 14, 2012. Available at http://autisticadvocacy.org

Cohen-Rottenberg, Rachel. "When Children Die, It's Time to Grieve and to Reflect, Not to Scapegoat." *Disability and Representation* (blog). December 15, 2012. Available at http://www.disabilityandrepresentation.com

Gilman, Priscilla. "Don't Blame Autism for Newtown." *The New York Times*. December 17, 2012. Available at http://www.nytimes.com

Halbfinger, David M. "A Gunman, Recalled as Intelligent and Shy, Who Left Few Footprints in Life." *The New York Times*. December 14, 2012. Available at http://www.nytimes.com

Longmore, Paul K. "The Cultural Framing of Disability." *PMLA* 120, no. 2 (2005): 502–8.

Mercury Rising. Dir. Harold Becker. 1998. Burbank, CA: Universal Home Video, 1999. DVD.

Murray, Stuart. "Autism and the Contemporary Sentimental: Fiction and the Narrative Fascination of the Present." *Literature and Medicine* 25, no. 1 (2006): 24–45.

Norden, Martin F. "The 'Uncanny' Relationship of Disability and Evil in Film and Television," in Martin F. Norton (ed.), *The Changing Face of Evil in Film and Television*, 125–43. Amsterdam: Rodopi, 2007.

Olney, Ian. "The Problem Body Politic, or 'These Hands Have a Mind All Their Own!': Figuring Disability in the Horror Film Adaptations of Renard's *Les mains d'Orlac*." *Literature/Film Quarterly* 34, no. 4 (2006): 294–302.

Rain Man. Dir. Barry Levinson. 1988. Burbank, CA: MGM, 2006. DVD.

Relative Fear. Dir. George Mihalka. 1994. Burbank, CA: Triumph, 2005. DVD.

"Reviews & Ratings for *Relative Fear*." *IMDb*. Available at http://www.imdb.com

Silent Fall. Dir. Bruce Beresford. 1994. Burbank, CA: Warner Home Video, 2000. DVD.

Snyder, Sharon L. and David T. Mitchell. *Cultural Locations of Disability*. Chicago: University of Chicago Press, 2006.

"Taglines for *Relative Fear*." *IMDb*. Available at http://www.imdb.com

7

Pundit Knows Best: The Self-Help Boom, Brand Marketing, and *The O'Reilly Factor for Kids*

Michelle Ann Abate
The Ohio State University

The more polite you are, the more responsive the other person will be. Remember that in any debate.

Bill O'Reilly, *The O'Reilly Factor for Kids*

Few other media personalities have enjoyed more success during the past decade than Bill O'Reilly. His nightly current events and political talk program *The O'Reilly Factor*, which first aired in 1996, is the most popular cable news show in the US, routinely attracting more than two million viewers.[1] Likewise, its guest list is a veritable pantheon of well-known journalists, cultural commentators, and prominent politicians. Among the figures who have made repeat appearances on *The O'Reilly Factor* since 2000 are civil rights activist Al Sharpton, Pulitzer Prize-winning journalist Bob Woodward, and politicians Newt Gingrich, Hillary Clinton, Karl Rove, Condoleezza Rice, Laura Bush, Barney Frank, John McCain, Barack Obama, and George W. Bush.

The radio version of the program—called *The Radio Factor with Bill O'Reilly*—is just as successful. According to a report about talk radio prepared by the Pew Research Center in 2007, the show enjoyed an audience of 3.25 million listeners in 2006, an increase of 1.5 million since 2003.[2] In addition, as Westwood One, the distributor for *The Radio Factor*, reveals, the program is carried on "over 390 radio stations, in 100 of the top 100 markets."[3]

Together with appearing on the show that bears his name, O'Reilly is a frequent political commentator on various television programs concerning politics and culture, as well as a regular columnist for various nationally-circulating periodicals. O'Reilly can regularly be seen as a "talking head" on current events and news analysis shows like *Hannity & Colmes*, John Gibson's *Big Story*, and segments of Fox News. Meanwhile, his weekly syndicated column appears in newspapers around the country, including the *Boston Herald*, *The Washington Times*, *The New York Post*, and *The Chicago Sun-Times*.

O'Reilly is an equally popular and prolific author. In the six years from 2000 to 2006, he released four books: *The O'Reilly Factor* (2000), *The No-Spin Zone* (2001), *Who's Looking Out for You?* (2003), and *Culture Warrior* (2006). Each of them flew off the shelves, selling millions of copies and reaching the number one spot on *The New York Times* nonfiction best-seller list.[4] In late September 2008, O'Reilly added a fifth book to his oeuvre, the memoir *A Bold Fresh Piece of Humanity*. *Bold* debuted at number 14 on *USA Today*'s best-seller list for nonfiction. Moreover, the New York *Daily News* reported that O'Reilly received an astounding $5 million advance from his publisher for the memoir; a figure that indicates his continued esteemed cultural status and strong commercial appeal in American print and visual media.[5]

In October 2004, Bill O'Reilly expanded his multimedia prowess and cultural influence into a new realm: books for young readers, with the publication of *The O'Reilly Factor for Kids*. Co-written with Charles Flowers, *Kids* is an advice and self-help text aimed at children aged 10–16. Subtitled "*A Survival Guide for America's Families*," the book is divided into four sections that address what O'Reilly feels are the most difficult personal, social, psychological, and relational issues that young people face today. The first segment, titled "People in Your Life," has chapters devoted to the subjects of friends, bullies, parents, siblings, divorce, and disagreements. The second segment, called "Your Private Life," examines the topics of money, smoking, alcohol, drugs, sex, television, music, and fun. Meanwhile, the third portion, dubbed "Your School Life," focuses on the issues of clothes, cheating, reading, self-esteem, sports, teachers, and the future. Finally, the closing section is titled "Things to Think About" and tackles issues of health, work, stereotypes, politics, death, God, and helping others.

Akin to all of O'Reilly's other media endeavors during the past few years, *The O'Reilly Factor for Kids* was a phenomenal success. The book debuted at number six on *The New York Times* best-seller list in the advice genre, and spent seven additional weeks on the chart, ultimately peaking at number four.[6] A revised paperback edition of *The O'Reilly Factor for Kids* was released in September 2005, with a new closing section on cyber-bullying.

This chapter takes its cue from the tagline for O'Reilly's popular cable program and "un-spins" the narrative content, cultural commentary, and commercial success of *The O'Reilly Factor for Kids*. In his 2004 book for young readers, the cable host brings the popular and rapidly-growing genre of advice literature to young readers, while he simultaneously replicates its many flaws. From its main title and basic premise to its literary format and specific chapter discussions, *The O'Reilly Factor for Kids* puts the self in self-help. His book may be co-written with Charles Flowers and shelved in bookstores as a nonfiction advice text for young people, but, as its title suggests, it is little more than an extension of the O'Reilly product, brand, and especially persona—a way to extend his media franchise into a new market and broaden his audience to a new demographic. During this process, *Kids* does push the boundaries of right-leaning, conservative-themed books for children into new areas. But, ultimately, even these seemingly progressive changes serve a reactionary purpose. They demonstrate that however conservatism is defined or discussed, it has commercial potential; its ideas, attitudes, and viewpoints—as O'Reilly has so successfully demonstrated on television, on the radio, and in his books for adults—can be effectively packaged and profitably sold. This time, however, the target market for these viewpoints is young people.

The doctor is in print: The growth of the self-help, personal advice and self-improvement genres

Judith Gero John has aptly noted, "There are few activities more human than the desire to offer advice."[7] Tapping into the basic human longing for knowledge and insight, books that offer help and wisdom embody one of the oldest as well as richest literary genres.

Such narratives are arguably especially popular and pervasive in the US, given the national traits of self-reliance, practicality, and self-improvement. Indeed, Arlie Russell Hochschild has written, from Cotton Mather and Benjamin Franklin to Horatio Alger and Stephen Covey, "America has been the land of self-help."[8] On subjects ranging from business success and personal growth to spiritual fulfillment and romantic relationships, "For many, the opportunity for self-improvement is regarded as a national birthright."[9] If books offering advice are one of the oldest as well as the most popular genres in the US, then those intended for child audiences would seem even more natural. Not only do boys and girls have much to learn about the world, but all self-help books—even those intended for adults—"establish a parent-child, teacher-student relationship."[10] In fact, some of the earliest books that could be placed in the advice or self-help categories—such as the medieval book of manners, *The Babees' Book*—were intended for children.[11] This legacy continues to this day. While advice books for children do not garner the same media attention as ones for adults, they remain a staple of the field, with dozens of titles released annually: *Chicken Soup for the Kid's Soul* (1997), *The Seven Habits of Highly Effective Teens* (1998), *Don't Sweat the Small Stuff for Teens* (2000), and *Unstoppable Me!: 10 Ways to Soar Through Life* (2006).

While the self-help genre has always been a fixture in American print and popular culture, it witnessed one of its biggest booms during the 1990s. Clarissa Estés's *Women Who Run with the Wolves* (1992) was a fixture on *The New York Times* nonfiction best-seller list for over 90 weeks. The following year, Deepak Chopra's *Ageless Body, Timeless Mind* rocketed to the top spot on *The New York Times* best-seller list, making its author a household name. These events paled in comparison, though, to the performance of John Gray's *Men are From Mars, Women are From Venus* (1993). As Karen S. Falling Buzzard has noted, Gray's book "quickly topped *Publisher's Weekly* charts for the next four years, with over six million copies sold, and no slow down to date. It has gone back to press every two weeks since its publication."[12]

This spike in self-help books continued into the new millennium. Some of the most commercially successful books released during the 2000s were in the self-help genre. Titles like Dr Phil McGraw's Self Matters: Creating Your Life from the Inside Out (2001), Dr Laura Schlessinger's *The Proper Care and Feeding of Husbands* (2004), Greg Behrendt and Liz Tuccillo's *He's Just Not That Into You* (2004) and Rhonda Bryne's *The Secret* (2006)—which was first released on DVD and later adapted into a book—enjoyed phenomenal popularity and prompted Inger Askehave to comment: "Never before have the bookstore shelves been so loaded with [self-help] books ... and never before have so many 'ordinary' people been consulting these books to find a way to lead a 'meaningful' life."[13] Indeed, in 2005, Anne Whitney gave the following amazing statistic: "eight of the top fifteen titles on the *Publisher's Weekly* best-seller's list for hardcover nonfiction ... are self-help books."[14] Such strong sales translated into equally strong profits. A 2006 report released by Marketdata Enterprises, an independent research publisher, found that the total self-improvement market— which included books, audiotapes, seminars, infomercials, personal coaching sessions, and support groups—exceeded $9 billion in 2005, an increase of more than 24 percent since 2003.[15] Moreover, the firm projected that sales would expand further, gaining another 11.4 percent, to rise to a total value of $13.9 billion by 2010.[16]

While self-help books may have been among the most commercially successful genres in the US, they are not universally praised. Critics of the genre say these texts do at least as much harm as good, perhaps more so. The charge most frequently levied against self-help books is that they are too simplistic. The tips, suggestions and formulas that they offer might be catchy, but they are not comprehensive. As Marcia Ford bluntly puts it, "most of life's problems cannot be solved in seven steps."[17]

Closely related to being overly simplistic, self-help books also often suffer from being formulaic. As Inger Askehave has documented, many self-help and advice books offer one basic idea which they state at the beginning and then reiterate throughout.[18] The result is that the content is quite thin. Even many of the most well-known books suffer from this flaw. As a review of Deepak Chopra's *Ageless Body, Timeless Mind* in *Publisher's Weekly* cautioned, "alert readers will finish the book with unsettling questions, the result of a book that is rife with inspirational conviction but at times thin on substance."[19]

In an even more serious problem, self-help books also largely ignore or, at least, minimize personal differences. The advice they offer is presented as universal, or "one size fits all." As Henry Giroux and Cynthia Schrager have discussed, authors address their audience as a monolithic entity, overlooking the way in which the root of many personal problems is just that, personal; they arise from the individual's particular racial, cultural, ethnic, socio-economic, familial, psychological, geographic, or generational circumstances. Henry Giroux, for instance, has written about the damaging effects that the "pull yourself up by your bootstrap" ethos has had on many minority groups because it ignores or, at least, minimizes the very real obstacles posed by race and class. "The doctrine of self-help is invariably bolstered by allusions to a few African Americans—Tiger Woods and Michael Jordan, for example—and is aimed at youth who allegedly can achieve the American dream if they quit whining and 'just do it.'"[20] On a related note, advice books also suggest that the solution to all personal and professional difficulties lie with the individual, not with larger social problems like racism, sexism, classism, or homophobia. Cynthia Schrager has commented on the gender bias that has historically permeated self-help books about commerce and enterprise. Given men's traditional place in the public sphere, the advice that these books offer is not always applicable to a businesswoman whose career difficulties may stem from gender discrimination as well as the struggles of balancing work and home life. In this way, advice books place an overemphasis on individual responsibility and personal autonomy. In the words of one critic, they "disregard the systemic social inequalities … that cause individual discontent and do not acknowledge social solutions that might actually help."[21]

At least some self-help books suffer from such societal myopia because they rely heavily on personal anecdote and individual experience rather than broad-based research. Norman Vincent Peale's *The Power of Positive Thinking* (1952)—one of the most successful titles in the modern self-help movement— has been criticized for this quality. Not only does the author base many of his points on his own subjective experiences, but much of his supporting research is taken from vague, unidentified sources: at various points, he buttresses his claims by drawing on commentary by an unnamed "famous psychologist" or a testimonial from an unidentified "prominent citizen."[22]

Equally problematic is the speed with which many self-help writers release new titles—rates that seem too swift for the book to be carefully conceived, thoughtfully constructed, and intellectually inspired. In a memorable joke from his late-night television show, for example, David Letterman satirized the frequency with which Dr Phil cranked out his best-selling texts, which totaled 13 in the eight years spanning 1999 and 2006 alone. In his typical dead-pan seriousness, the comedian held up a copy of an alleged new title by Dr Phil: *More Advice I Pulled Out of My Ass*. Finally, but not inconsequentially, self-help is often accused of being narcissistic, of promoting excessive self-interest, and of overemphasizing the individual, both on the part of the author and for its readers. As Maria Ford aptly summarized, it is "Self-help, with its perceived overemphasis on 'self.'"[23]

In light of the many ideological flaws and practical pitfalls associated with the advice movement, Micki McGee has flatly asserted that self-help books do not actually help. Instead, in the words of Stuart Ewan, "the self-help industry is an obsessional treadmill far more than a path to a better life."[24] An advice book about business and finance published in the late 1990s stated it even more bluntly. As the authors humorously but also candidly remark at multiple points in *God is My Broker* (1998): "The only way to get rich from a get-rich book is to write one."[25]

More self than help: *The O'Reilly Factor for Kids* and the promise, as well as problems, of the advice genre

The O'Reilly Factor for Kids reflects the commercial boom in self-help literature, along with its many flaws. Echoing the basic premise of the genre, O'Reilly's book purports to offer young people useful tips about life. As he says about *Kids* in the Introduction, "It will give you an edge in facing the challenges of this crazy but exciting time of your life. And that edge will make your life easier."[26] Reflecting the approach of many self-help books for adults, *The O'Reilly Factor for Kids* often outlines a series of steps for young people to follow as they confront a problem or address an issue. In the chapter dealing with parents, for example, O'Reilly walks his readers through tactics for managing disagreement more effectively. First, he suggests "In Every Argument, You Should Begin by Isolating the Conflict. What are you and your parents really disagreeing about?"[27] Then, he cautions them: "Do Not Bring Up Issues of Right and Wrong. Are your parents wrong? According to you, yes. According to them, no. So there's no going there."[28] Finally, O'Reilly advises his young readers, "Once You Understand their Reason(s), See What You Can Work Out. Safety concerns? Offer to take a safe driving course. Money? Find a job, or go for the secondhand option."[29]

Mirroring another hallmark of the self-help genre, O'Reilly stresses the need for self-reflection and self-examination. In the chapter about learning how to compromise, for instance, he includes a fill-in-the-blank worksheet for young people to complete. To aid in this process, O'Reilly offers prompts like "I've compromised/will compromise with my brother/sister by _____" and "I've compromised/will compromise with my parents by _____."[30] Later, in the chapter dedicated to the all-important topic of fun, he asks his readers to "Write down a list of the things you find the most fun to do, even stupid things."[31] He urges kids to include even those activities that are silly, embarrassing, or not very admirable because they can learn from them: "For instance, if you're a bully and you think you enjoy pantsing a kid who's younger or weaker, include that. This little list will ultimately serve as a tool for you to look at yourself and consider what your tastes in fun really say about you. So be honest."[32]

In the same way that *The O'Reilly Factor for Kids* reflects some of the most popular features of the self-help genre, it also embodies many of its problems.

Arguably the most prominent limitation is that although O'Reilly's text is ostensibly "for Kids," it becomes clear in the opening pages that it really is more focused on himself. O'Reilly begins his book by stating that he wrote the nonfiction work at least as much for his adolescent past self as for the kids of today: "I wish I'd has this book when I was a teenager because ... I had many concerns."[33] Then, in a comment that simultaneously dismisses the usefulness of the entire body of children's literature while it simultaneously places the blame for his own personal mistakes on others, he continues: "Unfortunately, no one had written a realistic book for kids. So I made dumb mistakes, got into trouble."[34]

O'Reilly goes on to openly state that his own childhood problems will not take a backseat to those faced by kids today; on the contrary, they will form the basis for his narrative: "I'm going to tell you about some of those things in this book. Maybe you'll laugh at my boneheaded behavior, but that's okay, as long as you end up smarter than I was at your age."[35] Perhaps aware that some young readers may not be persuaded by this explanation, O'Reilly adds, "What does an adult know?" and answers: "Well, I have a career that's lots of fun and makes me lots of money."[36]

Each chapter of *The O'Reilly Factor for Kids* is based on a story that the author tells about himself, usually from when he was an adolescent. These autobiographical segments are visually set off from the rest of the text in a different font. In addition, they are announced by the moniker "My Story." Moreover, they contain many self-congratulatory comments. The very first "My Story" presented in the opening chapter on friendships forms a representative example. The anecdote concludes with the following assertion: "Even though I am now famous and successful, I still keep my old friends."[37] Many similar remarks pepper later chapters. He ends a "My Story" anecdote in the chapter on alcohol, for instance, with the comment: "Given my highly-public position, I've avoided many problems by not drinking."[38] The focus here, as elsewhere, is more on applauding himself than helping young people.

While most of the personal stories that O'Reilly offers are at least tangentially related to the theme of the chapter, some seem curiously off-topic. In the chapter concerning God, O'Reilly offers a "My Story" anecdote about serving as an altar boy at St Brigid's Catholic Church. Rather than discussing how this position influenced his faith, he relays the effective method that he devised to shake down a member of a wedding party for money. O'Reilly writes:

The best man was expected to tip the boys. If the tip was not forthcoming, he and I would have the following chat:

ME: Excuse me, sir. Are you the best man?

GUY: That's me, son.

ME: Well, I just want to thank you for tipping Father Murphy so generously … but you may not know that Father does not share his good fortune with his assistants.

GUY: I didn't know that.

ME: And it's really too bad, because Richie and I will be holding the plates [with the chalice of wine and the host] during the ring ceremony … and that takes strength and stamina. *[Here I looked the guy straight in the eye]*, if you know what I mean.

GUY: *[after a slight pause]* Here's a ten for the two of you.[39]

The advice that O'Reilly culls from these anecdotes is equally problematic. Akin to many other self-help books, it is often simplistic or reductive. In the opening chapter on friendship, for instance, O'Reilly offers up such trite platitudes as "In real life, true friends stand by you when things get rough" and "If you have friends who will help you, you'll be a lot better off."[40] Similarly, he urges his readers to avoid befriending kids who are violent, do drugs, lie, cheat, get drunk, and spread "malicious gossip" (though perhaps "non-malicious gossip" is acceptable?). Echoing Inger Askehave's argument that self-help books offer one basic idea that they reiterate endlessly, he repeats these axioms in "O'Reilly's List of True Friendship Factors" near the end of the chapter.[41] Many of the other chapters likewise follow this formula. The chapter on sex, for example, ends with the direct announcement, "But I repeat my mantra … ."[42] Similarly, the section on self-esteem concludes with a recap of the points that he has already made several times: "To sum up … ."[43] Not only does this reiterative style underestimate the intellectual capacity—or, at least, attention span—of the book's young readership, but it also denies them more substantive content.

In an even more problematic feature—and one that again reflects a common flaw of the genre—*The O'Reilly Factor for Kids* places too much emphasis on individual autonomy and ignores factors like gender, race, class, and culture. Perhaps because O'Reilly is drawing on his own experiences, he seems to be addressing a largely male audience. Indeed, some of the language that he uses is sexist or at least not gender inclusive. The author frequently uses the male pronoun as universal. Discussing the importance of "dressing to impress," for example, O'Reilly writes: "There's an old saying that 'clothes make the man'. "[44]

A few pages later, addressing the existence of dress codes at many professional offices, he remarks: "Is that fair? You bet. The guy who signs the checks gets to make the rules. He wants people working for him who actually reflect the image of his company."[45] Likewise, in the chapter on self-esteem, he again fails to use gender neutral pronouns, instead often identifying authority figures—even those in traditionally female professions such as teaching—as male: "In my day, the music teacher would politely say no, as he well should, and that would be that."[46]

Other chapters contain more serious oversights. In the section on drugs, for instance, O'Reilly recounts how some of his childhood playmates became addicted to narcotics after they began appearing in their neighborhood during the late 1960s: "Right away, three of my friends got hooked on heroin. One died, two went to prison. Those two were never the same again. Their lives were ruined."[47] O'Reilly's account neglects the myriad physical, psychological, cultural, environmental, social, and even genetic factors that may lead a person to drug use. By overlooking these elements, his book offers a harsh judgment, implying that the author's childhood friends became drug users because they were weak or simply because they were bad people.

Likewise, in the chapter discussing relationships with siblings, O'Reilly ignores or, at least, minimizes many personal, psychological, and familial unknowns when he opines: "You'll forget the struggles [with your brothers and sisters] and remember the good times. It's true. You'll get together to celebrate family joys and to comfort each other in times of tragedy. You'll share the challenges of taking care of your aging parents, the delight of watching the next generation grow up, and many more."[48] This rosy picture does not hold true for many individuals, as sibling conflicts do not always reach a peaceful resolution in adulthood.

O'Reilly's minimization of outside factors is by far the most evident in the chapter on work. Echoing Horatio Alger's oft-repeated formula, he repeatedly argues that effort, education, ambition, and personal determination lead to success. To support this point, O'Reilly uses his own life story as an example: "When I was a kid, I didn't spend money foolishly for one very good reason: I didn't have any."[49] Even as a young person, O'Reilly reports, he was determined to rise above his modest origins and make something of himself. At various points throughout the book, the author tells stories about how he babysat, mowed lawns, and painted houses—jobs that earned him money but also motivated him to set higher future goals. In a comment that could have been expressed by the protagonist in a Horatio Alger novel, O'Reilly writes: "I began to contemplate the relationship between hard work and the money it earns. I also began to realize that I did not want to live the rest of my life on low wages. I began to study harder. I did not, repeat NOT, want to paint houses for the rest of my life."[50]

While the importance of hard work, the need for a good education, and the necessity of having ambition are all worthy of praise, O'Reilly ignores the many real obstacles that often interfere with an individual's ability to succeed. Indeed, the author's own success story does not take into account the many economic opportunities, educational privileges, and personal advantages that he enjoyed by the sheer virtue of his being white, male, heterosexual, and born into a family that was not living in poverty. O'Reilly concludes his chapter on work with the following naïve platitude:

> Hard work rules!
> Don't forget that.
> It's a primary rule of life.[51]

Analogous sentiments form the closing thoughts to the original version of the book. The new paperback edition of *The O'Reilly Factor for Kids* has an added new chapter on cyber bullying, but the initial hardback concludes with the following exhortation: "Just remember, life is tough, but it is also full of adventure and joy. Work hard, be honest, help others. Do those things, and you'll get the O'Reilly Guarantee: You will succeed! And I'll be happy when you do."[52] In so doing, *The O'Reilly Factor for Kids* fails to live up to its opening promise of giving young people "an edge … . An edge that will make your life easier."[53] Instead of offering them the "no-spin" truth, his advice book paints an overly rosy and ultimately distorted view of life in the US. At least some of O'Reilly's young readers, having already encountered social problems like racism, sexism, and classism firsthand, will already be sadly familiar with the inaccurate nature of this portrait.

O'Reilly, Inc.: Brand marketing and selling the self

The self-help genre was not the only publishing formula that experienced a commercial boom during the final decade of the twentieth century and the first few years of the new millennium; so did something known as brand marketing. As Karen S. Falling Buzzard explains,

> Brand names help identify the product and brands take on their own meaning
> and presence because they embody a rich configuration of symbols and
> meaning. A good brand name should appeal to its customers, be memorable, as
> well as offer a distinctive image which separates it from competing products.[54]

The most popular and successful brands, she continues, include "a wide range
of line extensions (also called sub-brands or variants). These are functionally
distinct versions of the product but trading under the same name, e.g. diet
Coke."[55]

Establishing a brand name has obvious benefits for manufacturers—
increasing public recognition, consumer purchasing frequency and, ultimately,
profits—but for buyers as well. "Buying a brand name is a matter of habit and
convenience. It is reassuring to buy consistency and known quality. It saves
the customer time, money, disappointment, and self blame."[56] Over time,
brand names come to embody much more than the products that they signify;
they also represent a personal attitude, a social image, and a cultural style.
Consumers "identify with brands and use them for self-expression. Brands
make statements to other people. They are a short-hand communication of who
you are."[57] For these reasons, brands engender communal qualities. In the words
of Karen S. Falling Buzzard once again: "Certain brands create a link with other
users: owners talk to one another, complement one another on their good taste,
and feel validated in their choices. They create social acceptance and mutual
recognition."[58]

While brand marketing has formerly been associated with industries like
clothing and car manufacturing, it has come to permeate the publishing
world during the past 20 years. Arising in part from the budget cuts at even
large publishing houses during the late 1980s and in part from the success of
Jacqueline Susann's *Valley of the Dolls*—which used a nontraditional marketing
campaign to great success—presses began releasing a smaller number of books
and promoting them in new and more aggressive ways: via media blitzes that
more closely resembled those used by Hollywood studios to promote their latest
blockbuster.[59] Publishers would saturate print, television, internet, and radio
mediums with an author's name, face, book title, jacket cover, and interview
sound-bite.

Brand marketing is an especially common feature of both contemporary
children's literature and the self-help genre. As Daniel Hade has written, "The
corporate owners of children's book publishing really aren't interested in the

business of publishing books anymore... . The business of corporate owners is developing brands."[60] He continues that if you read the annual reports from children's publishers,

> you may be surprised to learn that these brands and media assets are Madeline, Curious George, Peter Rabbit, Clifford, and the Magic School Bus. In other words, these corporations are hoping that children are attracted not to books so much as to *any* product that carries the brand's name. To the corporation, a Clifford key ring is no different from a Clifford book. Each is a 'container' for the idea of 'Clifford.' Each 'container' is simply a means for a child to experience 'Cliffordness.' In this world there is no difference between a book and a video or a CD or a T-shirt or a backpack.[61]

Operating with this new marketing ethos, "The corporation, then, seeks to expand its brand to as many aspects of a consumer's life as possible. ... The goal isn't to see as many copies of *Madeline* as possible (though that is still desirable) but to extend Madeline into as many aspects of a child's life as possible."[62] Hade uses Curious George to illustrate this phenomenon, listing the numerous toys, clothes, games, household products, electronic items, food products, dolls, videos, and school supplies available that are based on the books. But the Harry Potter series, with its massive merchandising bonanza, would serve just as well.

An analogous ethos permeates the world of self-help works for adults. Books like John Gray's *Men are from Mars, Women are from Venus* and Jack Canfield and Mark Victor Hansen's *Chicken Soup for the Soul*—to name just a few—have gone from successful single texts to commercial franchises. The books are available not only in hardback and paperback editions, but in audio formats, via CD-ROMs, on calendars, in videos, and—in the case of Gray's book—even as a Broadway show, family board game, weekend retreat, and luxury cruise seminar.[63] Both books also have numerous sequel or spin-off texts, each with slight variations on the original title so as to capitalize on its name recognition. John Gray added *Mars and Venus in the Bedroom* (1995), *Mars and Venus Together Forever* (1996), *Mars and Venus in Love* (1996), *Mars and Venus on a Date* (1997), and *Mars and Venus Starting Over* (1998) within the first five years of the publication of his original. Meanwhile, *Chicken Soup for the Soul*—which was first released in 1995—had ballooned to more than 100 spin-off titles by January 2006, including many aimed at young people: *Chicken Soup for the Teenage Soul* (1997), *Chicken Soup for the Kid's Soul* (1998), *Chicken Soup for the College Soul* (1999), *Chicken Soup for the Preteen Soul* (2000), *Chicken Soup for the Teenage Soul on Tough Stuff* (2001), *Chicken Soup for the Teenage Soul on Love and Friendship* (2002), *Chicken Soup for the Christian Teenage Soul* (2003), *Chicken Soup for the Preteen Soul II* (2004) and *Chicken Soup for the Girl's Soul* (2005), to name just a few. Some self-help authors like Dr Phil, Deepak Chopra, and Dr Laura embody their own brand. The success of their books arguably depends less on the particular title or specific content but the fact that their name and picture appear on the cover.

Since the debut of his cable news and talk commentary program in 1996, Bill O'Reilly has become an astute disciple and successful connoisseur of brand marketing. As Tom Lowry has written, "Love him or hate him, O'Reilly has done a masterful job of using the groundswell of support for his conservative views to build himself into a multimedia brand."[64] With his TV program, radio broadcast, books, newspaper columns, and the Internet, "O'Reilly generates an estimated $60 million a year for his outlets though ad and book sales, syndication fees and merchandising sales."[65] The success of these venues prompted him to expand his brand franchise into retail goods. On his official website, www.billoreilly.com, fans can purchase *The O'Reilly Factor*-themed jackets, hats, t-shirts, key chains, umbrellas, pens, flashlights, bumper stickers, mugs, car mats, lapel pins, doormats, golf balls, and children's clothing, in addition to all of his books.

The O'Reilly Factor for Kids is simply another extension of the O'Reilly brand, product, and persona. The title that he chose for the text foregrounds this element. Rather than selecting a moniker that was original, unique, and tailored specifically for this book and its subject matter, he created one that simply rehashed his already established successful one, simply tacking on "for Kids" at the end. The cover image only furthers this association. Although the author asserts in the Introduction, "*The O'Reilly Factor for Kids* is not about me. It is about you" (xiv), the book's jacket is comprised of a large photograph of the author himself. Finally, the name "O'Reilly" appears prominently not once but twice on the cover: first, in all-caps and a bold black font against a white background at the top of the page—and, incidentally, the name is much larger than any other word in the title—and then again in all-caps and fire-engine red font at the bottom.

Given the way in which *The O'Reilly Factor for Kids* is pitched and packaged, readers know what they are getting even before they examine the first page. For those who are drawn to *The O'Reilly Factor for Kids* for this exact reason, they are not disappointed. As the author reveals on the opening page of the

Introduction, the entire project began as an off-shoot of his popular cable talk program. The "Eyewitness Report" that prefaces *The O'Reilly Factor for Kids* contains the following opening quotation from a young girl identified as "Elizabeth from Ohio": "I'm 15 ½ years old. You said on your show, Mr. O'Reilly, for kids aged 10 to 16 to write in about the biggest problem in their life."[66] While the years from 10 to 16 are undoubtedly difficult ones—with the trials of puberty, peer pressure, and parental conflict—they are also a time in which young people collectively possess tremendous consumer power. As an article that appeared in *Business Week* magazine in December 2005—one year after *The O'Reilly Factor for Kids* was released—revealed, "There are nearly 21 million Tweens (ages 6–12) and young teens in the U.S. who control more than $50B in purchasing power."[67] O'Reilly is a savvy businessman who knows demographics as well as their commercial importance. As a result, it seems likely that he is aware of the tremendous purchasing potential of young people. Viewed from this perspective, his book promises to help expand his fan base at least as much as it promises to help young people navigate a difficult period in their lives.

O'Reilly's references to his popular cable show, however, are not simply confined to this opening instance. They permeate his advice book for kids, appearing roughly once per chapter, but in many cases even more frequently. O'Reilly begins the chapter on work, for instance, with the following plug: "Maybe you turn on the TV or switch on the radio and there I am, yammering away off the top of my head. I'm not looking at notes. I'm not reading questions. You don't see an aide handing me a cheat sheet (as if I were a congressman holding a hearing without a clue)."[68] Later, the final "Eyewitness Report" that precedes the chapter on politics offers the following program endorsement from "Danny," a fan of *The Factor*: "I don't understand all the political conflicts going on in the world. I like your GOOD sense of humor. You make politics easier to understand."[69] O'Reilly mentions his cable show by name later in the chapter: "If you've ever watched *The O'Reilly Factor*, you know that I spend a lot of time on political subjects."[70] For those who may not be familiar with his cable show, O'Reilly often pauses to urge young readers to contact him via the television network on which it airs: "Remember, you can always reach me via e-mail at O'Reilly@FoxNews.com."[71]

This pattern is repeated throughout the book and underscores the way in which the literary genre for *The O'Reilly Factor for Kids* may technically be self-help but the narrative format that it follows is that of his cable news show. References to his program appear in the most unexpected of places, such as during a discussion about the importance of religious tolerance and open-mindedness: "I mean, you do not want to be like one of the mean-spirited, self-righteous maniacs who attack me when I say something that sets them off. If you watch *The Factor*, you may have heard me read one of these angry letters or emails at the end of the program."[72] Moreover, in the chapter on smoking, O'Reilly does not simply mention his cable news show, he quotes himself from it: "As I said one night on *The Factor*, 'Big business sees the ordinary American as a consumer, not a fellow citizen. They want your money even if it means your life. We're there to be had.'"[73]

Perhaps the clearest example of brand marketing in *The O'Reilly Factor for Kids* appears in the final "Eyewitness Report" that prefaces the chapter on the "Dressing Game" and is attributed to "Corey in California." The youngster writes: "You should see some of the stares I get when I wear *The Factor* jacket to school!"[74] This comment combines the previous instances of cross-promotion for his cable show with product placement for his merchandizing apparel. Not surprisingly, the author also promotes the other nonfiction narratives that he has written and which are also spin-offs of the O'Reilly brand. An "Eyewitness Report" submitted by "RJ in New York" and which appears before the chapter on "Reading," for example, asserts: "Mr. O'Reilly, I am 15. My biggest problem right now is the fact that I cannot find time to go out and buy *Who's Looking Out for You?*"[75] Later, near the closing pages of *The O'Reilly Factor for Kids*, the author directly promotes this book. For kids who are wondering how to "Have a lot of fun, accomplish many things, and associate with good people," he offers the following suggestion: "My last book, *Who's Looking Out for You?*, deals with those themes. If you like this book, you might want to check out that one, too."[76]

Not surprisingly, *The O'Reilly Factor for Kids* incorporates many signature elements of his cable program. O'Reilly does not actually begin his book with the verbatim tagline, "Caution: You are Entering the No-Spin Zone" as he does nightly on the air. However, he does utter numerous variations on it. In the Introduction, for example, he writes: "You may have seen me on my daily TV program, *The O'Reilly Factor*, or heard me on the radio. If you have, you know that I tell it straight, no matter what. And I make sure my guests tell the truth, too."[77] He offers his readers a similar promise for this text: "I am as honest in this guide as I am on the air. No sugarcoating. This is straight stuff."[78] Such comments are reiterated at multiple points throughout the discussion. In one of the opening paragraphs in the chapter on teachers, for instance, O'Reilly vows: "Not all advice books will tell you the truth on this score, but I will."[79] A few pages later, in a "My Story" anecdote about the time when he was a teacher of English and history, he talks with pride about how he "dropped the truth bomb."[80]

The controversies surrounding his use of faulty or misleading information on *The O'Reilly Factor* made these assurances cause for concern. Such problems also appear in the advice book. In the chapter dedicated to the social ill of cheating, O'Reilly writes that "according to research by the Josephson Institute of Ethics ... nearly 90% of you readily admit to flat-out lying."[81] First, the Josephson Institute of Ethics publishes a report every two years, and O'Reilly does not mention the date of the specific one he is referencing. Even more problematic, the statistics from the two reports which seem the most likely for him to cite—2002 and 2004—do not match up. The data from Johnson Institute of Ethics from 2004, which is the year that O'Reilly's book was published, put the rate of lying at 64 percent.[82] Meanwhile, the figure from the 2002 report is closer—at 83 percent—but cannot be accurately called "nearly 90%" even when rounded up.[83]

Such instances of exaggeration recur. In the chapter dedicated to the subject of work, O'Reilly offers a lengthy description of a typical day on his cable and radio shows. The story presents him as not simply an exceedingly hard worker, but also seemingly a solo act, who conceives, researches, and writes his programs with little or no outside help:

> Every weekday morning I get up at 7:00 A.M. and read several newspapers so that I can absorb what's going on in the world. Then I write a TV or newspaper commentary giving my opinion on some recent event. ... After that, I start planning my radio and TV programs. I talk with my staff by phone about setting up interviews. After that I leave home for the TV studios in Manhattan, where I will write the entire script for *The O'Reilly Factor*. I'll also begin preparing my questions and approaches to the topics that will be discussed on my daily two-hour radio program. Off and on during the day, I will prepare to interview the four or five guests who will be on my nightly hour-long TV program. Some of them will be hostile, so I'll want to be sure I've anticipated every argument and have researched my points well. ... The radio program is live on the air from 12:00 P.M. to 2:00 P.M. Just before 6 P.M. I go to the TV studio to host *The Factor*. Sometime after 7:00 P.M., unless there's a special nightly program because of some breaking news, I head toward home and my family.[84]

In actuality, of course, O'Reilly has a team of script writers, researchers, and fact checkers.[85]

While the phrase "Shut up" does not appear in O'Reilly's advice book for kids, he does employ an abrupt tone which has become a hallmark of his broadcast style. In the chapter discussing the benefits and pitfalls of television, for instance, O'Reilly uses sharp language to make his points. In the space of only one page, for example, he tells his readers, "get a grip," "you've been tricked," "watch out," "you've got your priorities wrong," and "step back."[86]

The book also engages in various forms of name-calling. Discussing kids who urge their peers to "ignore their homework or cut class to 'have fun' instead," he says: "That's being a jerk."[87] Later, while addressing personal fashion choices, he partakes in dismissive labeling once again: "Sure, there are computer geniuses and authors who get respect even if they dress like geeks and bums, but they're the exception to the rule."[88] Sometimes, O'Reilly's language gets so sharp that it seems inappropriate for younger readers. In the section on sports, for instance, he tells his readers: "when you get screwed, you should use your anger to become even better at whatever it is you are doing."[89] O'Reilly goes on to discuss an experience during his teenage years when he felt that he had been unjustly cut from a local baseball team, not because he wasn't a good player but because, he says, the coach "did not like me at all."[90] In the wake of this "injustice,"[91] as O'Reilly calls it, he does not follow his own earlier advice to examine possible reasons for why the coach may have disliked his attitude so much that it caused him to disregard his baseball abilities. O'Reilly could have asked himself questions such as "Was I disrespectful to the coach?," "Did I behave inappropriately?," and "What part did I play in, or what responsibility do I have for, creating this situation?" Instead, he responds in a far different manner: "I vowed I would show that coach who cut me that he was an idiot."[92] While the author's determination and perseverance are admirable, this anecdote nonetheless embodies a missed educational opportunity: not every coach who fails to pick a young person for a sporting team is necessarily an "idiot." Here, as elsewhere, O'Reilly overlooks many possible mitigating circumstances, not the least of which is himself.

O'Reilly's favorite dismissive insult remains, of course, "Pinhead." He uses the word at various points in *The O'Reilly Factor for Kids* to describe individuals whom he feels have behaved badly, and dedicates large portions of the book to the concept. Segments called "Instant Messages" separate the book's four main sections from one another, and they consist of lengthy paragraphs describing actions and attitudes that belong to either that of a "Pinhead" or a "Smart Operator." A typical passage reads "A Pinhead is a kid who is bored … ." and "A Smart Operator is a kid who hugs his parents even at this age. …"[93] Not only are many of these examples somewhat silly, but they also bifurcate young adult behavior into a reductive and simplistic binary, for obviously not every child who experiences boredom is worthy of scorn, nor is every youngster who shows affection to his parents deserving of praise. Akin to many other passages, it simplifies a situation that is much more complex. Even here though, O'Reilly does not miss a chance for cross-marketing and self-promotion. The closing entry in the final Instant Message section reads "A Smart Operator is a kid who watches *The O'Reilly Factor*."[94] O'Reilly adds the IM-acronym "JJA"—just joking again—but the sheer number of times that he utters these comments cast doubt on that assertion.

Those who take issue with O'Reilly's broadcasting style may find the frequent references to his cable news show ironic. It is difficult not to think of O'Reilly's signature style of interrupting, talking over, and even shouting down guests and callers when reading this discussion about handling conflict with parents: "The more polite you are, the more responsive the other person will be. Remember that in any debate."[95] Similar comments can be made about the entire chapter dedicated to "Striking a Compromise"—an act for which O'Reilly is not particularly well known. The book also includes passages like "It's hard to make friends when you demand your way all the time. You know the people I mean" and "I don't interrupt in social situations, unless it is absolutely necessary—that is, when somebody is lying or spreading malicious gossip."[96]

In the same way that O'Reilly frequently mentions his cable news show in *The O'Reilly Factor for Kids*, he likewise routinely plugs his advice book for kids on his daily cable and radio shows, making repeated reference to its title, giving away free signed copies to callers, and updating fans about the text's ranking on various best-seller lists. A significant portion of references to *The O'Reilly Factor for Kids* on databases like LexisNexis, in fact, are from transcripts of *The O'Reilly Factor*. In the cross-promotional world of millennial marketing, this tendency suits his publisher just fine. "'Bill is one of our cherished marquis authors,' says Stephen Rubin, president of Doubleday Broadway Publishing Group, a unit of Random House Inc. that has published four of O'Reilly's works. 'It doesn't hurt that he shamelessly promotes his books.'"[97] These plugs have proved eminently successful. *The O'Reilly Factor for Kids* sold more than 240,000 copies within the first 18 months of its release (McEvoy). The text would go on to become the best-selling nonfiction book for juvenile readers of 2005, according to The Book Standard and Nielsen Bookscan.[98]

This astounding commercial success prompted O'Reilly to compose a follow-up text. In October 2007, he released *Kids are Americans Too*, another ostensible advice book for young readers. Demonstrating the often hastily-written nature of sequel texts, many pages in *Kids are Americans Too* contain nearly as much white space as they do text. Moreover, the book is more of an obvious spin-off of his cable news program and on-air persona than his first text. Not only is the cover image comprised of another portrait of the author, but, this time, it presents him standing beside a studio television camera. In addition, O'Reilly's name is printed in a font that is larger than the title of the book itself. Finally, the format and content of the book more closely mirrors his cable and radio program than the earlier volume. In an example that sets the tone for the entire text, *Kids are Americans Too* begins with "A Quick Bite of Reality TV" in which O'Reilly relays a story about the robbery of a single mother and then asks his readers to ponder if this was "Justice at work?" and what the occurrence says "about your rights as an American kid."[99] Throughout, O'Reilly addresses his young readers in his signature brusque style, exemplified in passages such as the following: "Let's face it. Many kids are complete morons. So are many American adults. As I say on TV, the Constitution gives all Americans the right to be a moron, and a lot of us exercise that right every day."[100]

In the Introduction to *Novel Gazing: Queer Readings of Fiction*, Eve Kosofsky Sedgwick discusses what she describes as a "paranoid" reading of texts. In this type of interpretive practice, individuals encounter ideas and information that they already know. As a result, their beliefs are not challenged, critiqued, or even broadened by the material they encounter; they are simply averred. Sedgwick asks, "What does knowledge do—the pursuit of it, the having and exposing of it, the receiving again of what one already knows?"[101]

The O'Reilly Factor for Kids participates in or, at least, encourages a paranoid reading. The messages contained in his advice book for young people simply replicate the interests, tastes, and attitudes of the adults who have purchased the text, if not the children who are intended to read it. Narratives written out of this impulse do not expand knowledge bases and change minds. Instead, they only lead to further entrenchment. Regrettably, this feature forms the true "straight talk/no spin" facet of the book.

Notes

1   Alexander Crupi, "MSNBC Closing Gap on CNN," *Mediaweek*. November 28, 2007. http://www.mediaweek.com

2   "Talk Radio Audience: 2003 and 2006 [chart]," Pew Research Center. The Project for

Excellence in Journalism. Chapter: "Talk Radio." *The State of the News Media 2007: An Annual Report on American Journalism*. http://www.stateofthenewsmedia.org

3   (Westwood) Westwood One. "The Radio Factor with Bill O'Reilly;" Program Profile Page. http://www.westwoodone.com

4   *The O'Reilly Factor* reached #1 on November 12 2000; *The No Spin Zone* attained this status on November 11, 2001; *Who's Looking Out for You?* became a *New York Times* #1 best-seller on October 13, 2003; and finally, *Culture Warrior* did so on October 16. 2006. For more information on the sales and rankings of O'Reilly's books, see the Performance Statistics analysis available through *Publisher's Weekly*: http://www.publishersweekly.com

5   Keith J. Kelly, "It's OK! And Out for Ivens." September 26, 2008. http://www.nypost.com

6   *The O'Reilly Factor for Kids* first appeared on *The New York Times* hardcover advice list on October 17, 2004. Meanwhile, it charted the paperback list on the following dates: October 23, 2004; November 6, 2004; November 27, 2004; December 4, 2005; December 11, 2005; December 18, 2005; and December 25, 2005.

7   Judith Gero John, "I Have Been Dying to Tell You: Early Advice Books for Children," *The Lion and the Unicorn* 29 (2005): 52.

8   Arlie Russell Hochschild, Book Jacket, *Self-Help, Inc.: Makeover Culture in American Life*, by Micki McGee (Oxford: Oxford University Press, 2005).

9   Stuart Ewan, Book Jacket, *Self-Help, Inc.: Makeover Culture in American Life,* by Micki McGee (Oxford: Oxford University Press, 2005).

10 John, "I Have Been Dying," 52.

11 Ibid.

12 Karen Falling Buzzard, "The Coca Cola of Self Help: The Branding of John Gray's *Men are From Mars, Women are from Venus*." *Journal of Popular Culture* 35, no. 4 (Spring 2002): 89.

13 Inger Askehave, "If Language is a Game—These Are the Rules: A Search into the Rhetoric of the Spiritual Self-Help Book *If Life is a Game—These Are the Rules*." *Discourse & Society* 15 (2004): 7.

14 Anne Whitney, "Writing by the Book: The Emergence of the Journaling Self-Help Book," *Issues in Writing* 15, no. 2 (2005): 196.

15 John LaRosa, "Self-Improvement Market in U.S. Worth $9.6 Billion," *PRWeb: Press Release Newswire*. PRWeb. September 21, 2006. www.prnewswire.com

16 Ibid.

17 Marcia Ford, "Finding Help on the Shelves," *Publisher's Weekly* (May 23, 2005): 2.

18 Askehave, "If Language is a Game," 16.

19 Molly McQuade and Sybil Steinberg, *Publisher's Weekly* 240 (June 28, 1993): 74.

20 Henry Giroux, "From *Manchild* to *Baby Boy*: Race and the Politics of Self-Help," *JAC* 22, no. 3 (2002): 529.

21 Janet Ingraham Dwyer, "Fool's Paradise: The Unreal World of Pop Psychology/ *Self-Help, Inc.: Makeover Culture in American Life*," *Library Journal* 130, no. 13 (August 15, 2005): 106.

22 Norman Vincent Peale, *The Power of Positive Thinking* (Greenwich: Fawcett, 1990), 52, 88.

23 Ford, "Finding Help on the Shelves," 2.

24 Stuart Ewan, Book Jacket, *Self-Help, Inc.: Makeover Culture in American Life*, by Micki McGee (Oxford: Oxford University Press, 2005).

25 Brother Ty, Christopher Buckley, and John Tierney, *God is My Broker: A Monk-Tycoon Reveals the 7½ Laws of Spiritual and Financial Growth* (New York: Random House, 1998), 185, 195.

26 Bill O'Reilly, *The O'Reilly Factor for Kids: A Survival Guide for America's Families* (New York: HarperCollins, 2004), xiii.

27 Ibid., 19; bold in original.

28 Ibid.; bold in original.

29 Ibid., 20; bold in original.

30 Ibid., 32–3.

31 Ibid., 90.

32 Ibid.

33 Ibid., xiii.

34 Ibid., xiii.

35 Ibid., xiii.

36 Ibid., xiii.

37 Ibid., 4.

38 Ibid., 62.

39 Ibid., 175; brackets and italics in original.

40 Ibid., 3.

41 Ibid., 7.

42 Ibid., 75.

43 Ibid., 119.

44 Ibid., 101.

45 Ibid., 103.

46 Ibid., 117.

47 Ibid., 69.

48 Ibid., 27–8.

49 Ibid., 51.

50 Ibid., 53.

51 Ibid., 155.

52 Ibid., 186.

53 Ibid., xiii.

54 Falling Buzzard, "Coca Cola of Self Help," 95.

55 Ibid., 96.

56 Ibid., 95.

57 Ibid.

58 Ibid., 96.

59 See ibid, 95–6.

60 Hade, Daniel. "Storyselling: Are Publishers Changing the Way Children Read?" *The Horn Book Magazine* (September/October 2002): 512.

61 Ibid., 512; italics in original.

62 Ibid., 512–3.

63 Toby Miller and Alec McHoul, "Helping the Self," *Social Text* 16, no. 4 (Winter 1998): 137–8.

64 Tom Lowry, "The "O'Reilly Factory: The Conservative Commentator has Spawned a $60 Million-a-Year Empire," *BusinessWeek*. March 8, 2004. http://www.businessweek.com

65 Ibid.

66 O'Reilly, *Factor for Kids*, xiii.

67 "Tween Power: Purchasing Strength of Kids," Video Report. *Business Week*. December 12, 2005. http://www.businessweek.com

68 O'Reilly, *Factor for Kids*, 151.

69 Ibid., 161; capitals in original.

70 Ibid., 164.

71 Ibid., 39.

72 Ibid., 177.

73 Ibid., 58.

74 Ibid., 98.

75 Ibid., 110.

76 Ibid., 169.

77 Ibid., xiv.

78 Ibid., xiv.

79 Ibid., 127.

80 Ibid., 131.

81 Ibid., 105.

82 Josephson Institute of Ethics, "The Ethics of American Youth: 2004 Report Card," October 2004. http://charactercounts.org

83 Josephson Institute of Ethics, "The Ethics of American Youth: 2002 Report Card," October 26, 2002. http://charactercounts.org

84 O'Reilly, *Factor for Kids*, 152–3.

85   David Sheff, "Bill O'Reilly: A Candid Conversation with TV's Most Pugnacious Newsman, about Gays and Gun Control, His War with George Clooney, Skewering the Red Cross, and that Hilary Clinton Doormat," *Playboy*. May 1, 2002: 59.

86   O'Reilly, *Factor for Kids*, 80.

87   Ibid., 91.

88   Ibid., 101.

89   Ibid., 122.

90   Ibid., 122.

91   Ibid., 122.

92   Ibid., 122.

93   Ibid., 140.

94   Ibid., 186.

95   Ibid., 19.

96   Ibid., 31, 30.

97   Lowry, "O'Reilly Factory."

98   See: "*The O'Reilly Factor for Kids*: Winner of the 2005 Juvenile Non-Fiction Bestseller Award Presented by The Book Standard and Nielsen Bookscan," *Business Wire*. September 26, 2005. LexisNexis Academic.

99   Bill O'Reilly and Charles Flowers, *Kids are Americans Too*. New York: HarperCollins, 2007), xv.

100   Ibid., xx.

101   Eve Kosofsky Sedgwick, *Novel Gazing: Queer Readings in Fiction* (Durham: Duke University Press, 1997), 4.

Bibliography

Askehave, Inger. "If Language is a Game—These Are the Rules: A Search into the Rhetoric of the Spiritual Self-Help Book *If Life is a Game—These Are the Rules*." *Discourse & Society* 15 (2004): 5–31.

Crupi, Alexander. "MSNBC Closing Gap on CNN." *Mediaweek*. November 28, 2007. Available at http://www.mediaweek.com

Dwyer, Janet Ingraham. "Fool's Paradise: The Unreal World of Pop Psychology/ *Self-Help, Inc.: Makeover Culture in American Life*." *Library Journal* 130.13 (August 15, 2005): 106–7.

Ewan, Stuart. Book Jacket. *Self-Help, Inc.: Makeover Culture in American Life*. By Micki McGee. Oxford: Oxford University Press, 2005.

Falling Buzzard, Karen S. "The Coca Cola of Self Help: The Branding of John Gray's *Men are From Mars, Women are from Venus*." *Journal of Popular Culture* 35, no. 4 (Spring 2002): 89–102.

Ford, Marcia. "Finding Help on the Shelves." *Publisher's Weekly*. May 23, 2005: 2–4.

Giroux, Henry A. "From *Manchild* to *Baby Boy*: Race and the Politics of Self-Help." *JAC* 22, no. 3 (2002): 527–60.

Hade, Daniel. "Storyselling: Are Publishers Changing the Way Children Read?" *The Horn Book Magazine*. September/October 2002: 509–17.

Hochschild, Arlie Russell. Book Jacket. *Self-Help, Inc.: Makeover Culture in American Life*. By Micki McGee. Oxford: Oxford University Press, 2005.

John, Judith Gero. "I Have Been Dying to Tell You: Early Advice Books for Children." *The Lion and the Unicorn* 29 (2005): 52–64.

Josephson Institute of Ethics. "The Ethics of American Youth: 2002 Report Card." October 26, 2002. Available at http://charactercounts.org

—"The Ethics of American Youth: 2004 Report Card." October 2004. Available at http://charactercounts.org

Kelly, Keith J. "It's OK! And Out for Ivens." September 26, 2008. Available at http://www.nypost.com

LaRosa, John. "Self-Improvement Market in U.S. Worth $9.6 Billion." *PRWeb: Press Release Newswire*. PRWeb. September 21, 2006. Available at www.prnewswire.com

Lowry, Tom. "The "O'Reilly Factory: The Conservative Commentator has Spawned a $60 Million-a-Year Empire." *BusinessWeek*. March 8, 2004. Available at http://www.businessweek.com

McEvoy, Dermot. "Something New, Something Old." *Publisher's Weekly*. March 27, 2006. Available at http://www.publishersweekly.com

McGee, Micki. *Self-Help, Inc.: Makeover Culture in American Life*. New York: Oxford University Press, 2005.

Miller, Toby and Alec McHoul. "Helping the Self." *Social Text* 16, no. 4 (Winter 1998): 127–55.

O'Reilly, Bill. *A Bold Fresh Piece of Humanity: A Memoir*. New York: Broadway, 2008.

—*Cultural Warrior*. New York: Broadway, 2006.

—*The No-Spin Zone: Confrontations with the Powerful and Famous in America*. New York: Broadway, 2001.

—*The O'Reilly Factor: The Good, the Bad, and the Completely Ridiculous in American Life*. New York: Random House, 2000.

—*Who's Looking Out for You?* New York: Bantam, 2003.

O'Reilly, Bill and Charles Flowers. *Kids are Americans Too*. New York: HarperCollins, 2007.

—*The O'Reilly Factor for Kids: A Survival Guide for America's Families*. New York: HarperCollins, 2004.

The O'Reilly Factor. Hosted by Bill O'Reilly. Fox News Network. May 17, 2002. Transcript. LexisNexis Academic.

—Hosted by Bill O'Reilly. Fox News Network. February 4, 2003. Transcript. LexisNexis Academic.

—Hosted by Bill O'Reilly. Fox News Network. March 17, 2003. Transcript. LexisNexis Academic.

—Hosted by Bill O'Reilly. Fox News Network. February 4, 2003. Transcript. LexisNexis Academic.

—Hosted by Bill O'Reilly. Fox News Network. May 5, 2003. Transcript. LexisNexis Academic.

—Hosted by Bill O'Reilly. Fox News Network. June 6, 2005. Transcript. LexisNexis Academic.

—Hosted by Bill O'Reilly. Fox News Network. February 21, 2008. Transcript. LexisNexis Academic.

"*The O'Reilly Factor for Kids*: Winner of the 2005 Juvenile Non-Fiction Bestseller Award Presented by The Book Standard and Nielsen Bookscan." *Business Wire*. September 26, 2005. LexisNexis Academic.

Peale, Norman Vincent. *The Power of Positive Thinking*. 1952. Greenwich: Fawcett, 1990.

The Radio Factor with Bill O'Reilly. Hosted by Bill O'Reilly. Westwood One. September 19, 2007. Media Matters. Available at http://mediamatters.org

—Hosted by Bill O'Reilly. Westwood One. February 19, 2008. Media Matters. Available at http://mediamatters.org

—Hosted by Bill O'Reilly. Westwood One. September 25, 2008. Media Matters. Available at http://mediamatters.org

Schrager, Cynthia D. "Questioning the Promise of Self-Help: A Reading of 'Women Who Love Too Much." *Feminist Studies* 19, no. 1 (Spring 1993): 177–192.

Sedgwick, Eve Kosofsky. *Novel Gazing: Queer Readings in Fiction*. Durham: Duke University Press, 1997.

Sheff, David. "Bill O'Reilly: A Candid Conversation with TV's Most Pugnacious Newsman, about Gays and Gun Control, His War with George Clooney, Skewering the Red Cross, and that Hilary Clinton Doormat." *Playboy*. May 1, 2002: 59.

"Talk Radio Audience: 2003 and 2006 [chart]." Pew Research Center. The Project for Excellence in Journalism. Chapter: "Talk Radio." *The State of the News Media 2007: An Annual Report on American Journalism*. Available at http://www.stateofthenewsmedia.org

"Tween Power: Purchasing Strength of Kids." Video Report. *Business Week*. December 12, 2005. Available at http://www.businessweek.com

Ty, Brother, with Christopher Buckley and John Tierney. *God is My Broker: A Monk-Tycoon Reveals the 7½ Laws of Spiritual and Financial Growth*. New York: Random House, 1998.

Westwood One. "The Radio Factor with Bill O'Reilly." Program Profile Page. Available at http://www.westwoodone.com

Whitney, Anne. "Writing by the Book: The Emergence of the Journaling Self-Help Book." *Issues in Writing* 15, no. 2 (2005): 188–214.

Part Three

Disney and Its Progeny

8

Power to the Princess: Disney and the Creation of the Twentieth-Century Princess Narrative

Bridget Whelan
SOWELA Technical Community College

> *If I WAS a princess—a REAL princess—I could scatter largess to the populace. But even if I am only a pretend princess, I can invent little things to do for people … I'll pretend that to do things like this is scattering largess. I've scattered largess.*
>
> A Little Princess (1904)

It would not be overstating things to assert that the princess narrative has been a staple throughout the body of children's literature. Even before the Grimms' initial publication of their *Kinder- und Hausmärchen* (1812), English-speaking children were enjoying translated versions of literary French fairy tales, such as Madame de Beaumont's *La Belle et la Bête* (English translation, 1757). Some of these stories were even available to English-speaking children before their direct translations. Beaumont, for example, spent much of her life as a governess in England, and it was during this time period that she published her popular *Les Magasins des enfants*, at a time when her pupils and others like them would have been expected to be able to read and write in French.[1] The prevalence of these French and German versions of fairy tales became so common that they virtually replaced the native British tales in the UK. Joseph Jacobs explains that "What Perrault began" with the 1729 English translation of *Tales of Mother Goose*, "The Grimms completed. Tom Tit Tot gave way to Rumpelstiltskin, the three Sillies to Hansel and Gretel, and the English Fairy Tale became a *mélange confus* of Perrault and the Grimms."[2] And, of course, both the Grimms' and the French storytellers' tales featured a wide variety of princess narratives. Finette in Marie-Jeanne L'Heritier's *The Discreet Princess, or the Adventures of Finette,* for example, advises her father on sociopolitical decisions, defends herself from an ardent suitor with a mallet, and tricks her own husband out of murdering her. The princess from the Grimms' "The Twelve Brothers" voluntarily secludes herself in a tree for seven years in order to save her 12 helplessly transformed brothers. Whether dutiful or rebellious, rambunctious or sweet, princesses and their narratives featured prominently in the literary lives of many nineteenth-century English and American children.

This trend in children's publishing continued with the publication of Andrew Lang's *Blue Fairy Book* in 1889, which was succeeded by a virtual parade of *Fairy Books* in the years that followed: the *Red* (1890), the *Green* (1892), the *Yellow* (1894), the *Pink* (1897), the *Grey* (1900), the *Violet* (1901), the *Crimson* (1903), the *Brown* (1904), the *Orange* (1906), the *Olive* (1907), and the *Lilac* (1910). This remarkable succession alone tells us of the continuing popularity of the fairy tale, and for our purposes, in particular, the princess narrative, at the beginning of the twentieth century.

Sandwiched within this colorful narrative display was Hodgson Burnett's *A Little Princess*, originally titled "Sara Crewe, or What Happened at Miss Minchin's."[3] It was first serialized in the popular American children's magazine *Saint Nicholas* and later published as a book in both New York and London in 1888.[4] Written by the author of the already phenomenally successful *Little Lord Fauntleroy*, the book was slated for instant success, and this would prove to be true. Burnett received $3,000 from her American publisher to reprint the book with another of her stories that very same year.[5] Later, Burnett rewrote the book as a play, titling it for the first time *A Little Princess* (the title she would again use for the revised book edition published in 1905, which is the version with which most of us are familiar today). The play ran in both London and New York, where it was more successful—so successful, in fact, that she was encouraged to republish *A Little Princess*, incorporating the additions created for the play.[6] In all versions of the story, young Sara, the protagonist, is not born a princess, nor does she ever become one. In fact, the nickname "Princess Sara" is at first mockingly given to her by some of the other girls at Miss Minchin's boarding school. Fortunately, clever and thoughtful Sara decides to appropriate her new identity, and to use it as a means to remind herself to be kind and generous towards others—in essence, to "scatter largess."

But here is the ironic thing about Sara Crewe: she was *not* a princess. Instead, she served to represent what all girls at the time were encouraged to aspire toward: ideal girlhood. When Sara, locked away with fellow servant Becky in the attic of her now hostile boarding school environment, envisioned herself a princess, she, and her young readers with her, transformed herself into a veritable Rapunzel or Sleeping Beauty in the Woods, trapped in a tower and awaiting rescue by an exotic prince from a foreign land—or, in Sara's case, an Indian lascar and his pet monkey. This image of stillness and passivity was echoed in other girls' books throughout the nineteenth and early part of the twentieth century, for "the best girls were passive, still," writes Deborah O'Keefe, "It was understood that not every girl came naturally to this exalted state but the rebellious ones were urged to emulate the saintly ones, and they usually gave in by the end of the book or at least the end of the series."[7] Sara Crewe, however, does not so much "give in" as give up—on the physical world around her, that is. Instead, she turns to the inner workings of her imagination, and in her mind's eye, this is what saves her from Miss Minchin's clutches, as she believes the gifts that Mr Carrisford and Ram Dass have lain out for herself and Becky have been produced by magic—and by her own imagination.

There is power here, however miniscule. Sara is rescued by the workings of her own imagination—something even Miss Minchin fears at times, her author pointing out the mesmerizing power of Sara's words on the woman's "narrow, unimaginative mind."[8] This imaginative power, of course, is in addition to Sara's actual physical escape, which involves her returning the lascar's monkey to Mr Carrisford's house. But it is at this point, towards the end of the novel, when Sara exclaims over her new wealth, recalling her earlier desire to "scatter largess": "Yes … and I can give buns and bread to the populace."[9] Although Sara never literally becomes a princess, she adopts the at-first unflattering appellation given to her by her schoolmates and lives her life accordingly, as if she really were a princess. As soon as she is rescued by Mr Carrisford and regains her wealth, she is more easily able to live out her "princessly" ideal by caring for the sick and the poor. For Sara, and for her author and readers, "princesshood" was not always necessarily a result of royal breeding. Instead, it could be seen as both a state of mind and an emblem of ideal girlhood which encompassed duty, compassion, and condescension towards the less fortunate. Becky the scullery maid is, after all, informed that she will now be serving the "Missee Sahib" instead of the evil Miss Minchin—a rise in circumstances if not in situation.[10]

However, even with the publication of Burnet's widely-read and beloved *A Little Princess*, the imprint the princess narrative was making on children's literature and culture was only just beginning. Most books for American children in the early part of the twentieth century featured middle-class protagonists, not wealthy heiresses like Sara Crewe, and certainly no tried and true fairy tale princesses. Books for girls in particular featured heroines who "were expected to be happy simply by virtue of their good deeds," heroines who "accurately reflect[ed] the dominant values and gender definitions of their day."[11] Princesses they may not have been, but they certainly mimicked Sara Crewe's *modus operandi* of exhibiting self-sacrifice, dutifulness, and compassion towards those less fortunate. Frank L. Baum's Dorothy from the *Oz* books stood alone as a character who "embodied both feminine virtues (compassion, kindness, acceptance of those different from herself, concern for others' feelings) and masculine attributes (rationality, assertiveness, single-mindedness, courage, perseverance)."[12] Like Sara, Dorothy is not a princess-by-birth, though she is eventually considered a sort of honorary princess by her friend, Princess Ozma.

Eventually, the mantle of princesshood was to be taken up by the Walt Disney company, which released the world's first ever feature length animated film, a groundbreaking retelling of a Grimms' fairy tale: *Snow White and the Seven Dwarfs* (1937). The film begins and ends with the opening and closing of a book, hinting at its literary origins and cleverly making the link for the audience between book and film. Interestingly, the tale loosely mimics the narrative of Burnett's *A Little Princess*: Snow White is born into wealth, loses that wealth and lives in poverty for a while, then reclaims it towards the end. However, unlike Sara, Snow White is really a princess—that is, she is the daughter of a king and queen and remains so throughout the film. Perhaps more impor-tantly, she is depicted not as a child but as a young woman, her corseted dress outlining her small but womanly curves, her face and hair made up to reflect what was considered attractive for a young woman at the time. Perhaps the most significant difference between the two lies in the fact that Snow White is thoroughly tricked by the evil female presence in the narrative and ultimately must be rescued by the prince. By depicting Snow White as less resourceful and more needy than some of her princessly predecessors, Disney was beginning to draw a line in the sand, solidifying their definition of the princess as a helpless, hyper-feminine trope.

The intention here, however, is not to draw too narrow a comparison between Burnett's and Disney's narratives, but to instead show how Disney manipulated a somewhat fluid traditional existing narrative and shaped it into its own. From that point onward, Disney staked a claim on the princess narrative. *Snow White and the Seven Dwarfs* became a formative film in the psyche of the American public. By rendering the princess and her narrative on film, and in beautiful, vivid color at that, Disney brought the princess narrative to life in a way that children had never before witnessed. Jack Zipes explains the transformation which took place in the minds of audiences when they first viewed *Snow White*, suggesting that Disney "deprive[d] the audience of viewing the production and manipulation, and in the end, audiences [could] no longer envision a fairy tale for themselves as they [could] when they read it," taking away the audience's ability to envision "their own characters, roles, and desires."[13] The film ultimately grossed some $8 million dollars internationally—a phenomenal amount of money at the tail end of the Great Depression—by the end of its first release,[14] and by the early 1980s was still categorized as "One of the top 10 box-office champs of all time."[15] Its impact was thus not to be underestimated—and not just among young girls. "Like mothers and fathers everywhere," writes Sheldon Cashdan, "my parents read *Hansel and Gretel*, *Jack and the Beanstalk*, and other popular tales to me." He continues:

> But my most vivid childhood memories of fairy tales came by way of Walt Disney. I remember sitting on the edge of my seat in a darkened movie theater watching *Snow White* and holding my breath as the gamekeeper prepared to cut out the heroine's heart. ... Today I may have trouble naming all the dwarfs, but the images of the evil queen, Snow White, and the seven dwarfs are forever emblazoned on my memory.[16]

And Cashdan agrees that the impact the film had on its audience was overwhelming, to say the least. "More than any other film," he points out, "*Snow White and the Seven Dwarfs* heralded an era of fairy-tale animation that changed the public's view of fairy tales forever."[17] And as fiction for children moved towards realism for girls—series like Laura Ingalls Wilder's *Little House on the Prairie* books (1932–2006, intermittently), *Nancy Drew* (1930–present), and *Trixie Belden* (1948–86) were the wildly popular girls books of their day—Disney continued to exert a monopoly over the princess narrative. With no other media presenting readers and viewers with alternative visions of the princess and her narrative, it was a monopoly that would swell unchecked, and one that would continue to exert its influence throughout the twentieth century and into the present.

After *Snow White*, over ten years passed before Disney released their second animated princess narrative. *Cinderella* (1950) was then followed by *Sleeping Beauty* (1959). These two films continued to conform to societal convention regarding girls and their place in society. Novels written for girls contemporary to the first "wave" of Disney princess movies suggested, says Deborah O'Keefe, that it was "desirable" for girl-heroines "to have a sweet voice so low it could hardly be heard."[18] She continues, "It was good for a girl-heroine to be misty, lisping, and inaudible, and even better for her to be dead."[19] Two of the three first-wave Disney princesses spend part of their narratives in death-like comas—each, of course, then was wakened and rescued by a male prince. Cinderella, in a sense, is also rescued from a *socially* inactive state—a state of poverty and servitude. These three films thus neatly solidified Disney's repackaging of the princess narrative, linking "princesshood" to contemporary concepts of ideal girlhood, and presenting it to the public on the big screen and in vivid color at a time when such a thing was uncommon, and hence utterly captivating to its audience.

For a while, however, the Walt Disney Company seemed content to move on and explore other narratives and mediums, leaving the princess-centered fairy tale narratives behind. But a lasting impression had been made. These three fairy tales—"Snow White," "Cinderella," and "Sleeping Beauty"—were now those most familiar to American (and perhaps other English-speaking) audiences. Early second-wave feminists like Marcia R. Lieberman became frustrated with the dichotomy between less popular, less well-known but more feminist fairy tales and those popularized by Disney. These more inherently feminist fairy tales, she wrote, "are so relatively unknown that they cannot seriously be considered in a study of the meaning of fairy tales to women."[20] Instead, most children were, of course, more familiar with the tales retold by Disney: Cinderella, Snow White, and Sleeping Beauty. "Cinderella, the Sleeping Beauty, and Snow White are mythic figures who have replaced the Old Greek and Norse gods, goddesses, and heroes for most children,"[21] she rather dismally concludes. While Lieberman was one of the first to make such a complaint, she was not the last. Karen Rowe not only agreed, but also further lamented the influence these popular fairy tales had had on fiction catered specifically to women of the '60s and '70s. She writes:

> These "domestic fictions" reduce fairy tales to sentimental clichés, while they continue to glamorize a heroine's traditional yearning for romantic love which culminates in marriage. Distinguished from the pulp magazines' blatant degradation of romance into sexual titillation, women's magazines preserve moral strictures from fairy tales, even as they rationalize the fantastic events. They render diminished counterfeits of Victorian novels of sensibility and manners.[22]

Her concerns show that while the women's movement itself had culturally outgrown Disney's version of the princess narrative, that narrative remained the only one present in the minds of American women—or at least in the minds of the editors of erotic romance novels and magazines like *Good Housekeeping* and *Redbook*. Four years previously, fellow second-wave feminist Kay Stone provided a foundation for Rowe's claims by interviewing girls and women, asking them about the impact these three films had had on their daily lives. The result, from a feminist standpoint, was rather devastating. "I thought I'd just sit around and get all this money," said one 11 year old. "I used to think 'Cinderella' should be *my* story."[23] "Well, I wouldn't really want to marry a prince like she did," admitted a nine year old. "Just somebody *like* a prince."[24]

Stone, Lieberman, and Rowe were not the only second-wave feminists to protest the influence of Disney's version of these three tales. "Ever since the late 1960s there has been a growing tendency on the part of women in England and America—and not only women—to express a non-sexist view of the world through fairy tales or through criticism about fairy tales," writes Jack Zipes.[25] "The political purpose of most of these tales is clear," he adds. "The narratives are symbolical representations of the authors' critique of the patriarchal status quo and of their desire to change the current socialization process."[26] Lieberman's suggestion that large portions of the American public remained ignorant of the existence of the more feminist tales is a telling one. Disney's monopoly—lingering evidence of this "patriarchal status quo"—over the princess narrative was nearly complete.

Frustrated with the company's appropriation and ultra-feminization of what could otherwise be seen as a powerful pro-feminist archetype, feminist critics and authors attempted to reclaim the princess narrative by either retelling those lesser known tales or putting a more feminist spin on those Disney had already retold. Jack Zipes' *Don't Bet on the Prince* (1987), which, not surprisingly, included Lieberman's essay, featured fairy tale retellings by renowned feminist authors like Angela Carter, Margaret Atwood, Jane Yolen, and Tanith Lee. One, titled "The Princess Who Stood On Her Own Two Feet," by Jeanne Desy, even features a princess who loudly declares, "A Princess says what she thinks. A Princess stands on her own two feet. A Princess stands tall."[27] "Misty," "lisping," and "inaudible" this princess is not! Outside the circle of academia, fantasists like Robin McKinley and Donna Jo Napoli continued the trend. *Beauty, A Retelling of the Story of Beauty & the Beast*, McKinley's 1978 retelling of "Beauty and the Beast," for example, featured a young heroine inaccurately named Beauty who is, by her own admission, not beautiful; Beauty is considered unusually clever by those who know her, has unfeminine aspirations to attend university, and looks askance at such "princessly" occupations as sipping tea because she fears she might break the tea cup.[28]

And then, in 1989, Disney finally returned to the princess narrative. *The Little Mermaid*, though pulled from a non-Grimms source, automatically boosted Hans Christian Andersen's tale into the fairy tale hall of fame, along with Disney's previous three retellings. The film's domestic gross was $84.4 million and stayed in theatres for some 15 weeks[29]—the "second wave" of Disney princess tales had begun. In 1991, the company turned to French tale "Beauty and the Beast"; the film (domestic gross: $145.8 million) introduced to young audiences the character of Belle, a book-loving young woman who refused the attentions of the town "hunk" in favor of continuing her reading habits and caring for her absent-minded father. In 1992, *Aladdin* ($217.3 million) had Princess Jasmine, whose only wish was to escape her father's decree that she marry a man she did not love.[30] *Mulan* ($120 million) in 1998 rounded the genre out for Disney, this time drawing from a Chinese tale and focusing on—again—a young woman who escapes the prospect of a loveless marriage, this time in favor of fighting for her father in China's war against the Mongols.[31]

All four films did well, both at the box office and in DVD and other merchandising sales. However, it was in 2000 that Disney executives (chiefly then-chairman of consumer products Andy Mooney) came up with the idea for an official "Disney Princess" brand.[32] Only one year later, the franchise netted an impressive $300 million; by 2010, that number had shot up to $4 billion.[33] The Disney Princess franchise currently offers approximately 26,000 different products on the market.[34] These products include not just media-related material, such as movie tie-in books and Disney Princess compilation CDs, but also toys, clothing, and kitchen utensils. Interestingly, one of the reasons Disney is able to offer such a variety of products is due in part to the very broadly constructed definition of "princess" that Mooney and his fellow Disney executives have put forth; heroines like Mulan and Pocahontas are not technically princesses, for instance, but simply adding them to the line-up appears to have granted them default royal status. While the motivation behind such a broad definition of "princess" is no doubt profit-oriented for Disney, it does also suggest that girlhood and princesshood still remain as tightly intertwined as they were during Sara Crewe's time—Sara Crewe, who was never born a princess and never became one, yet considered herself one all the same.

Clearly, Disney has tapped into a gold mine of marketing. Writers who have continued to return to the princess narrative throughout the century, weaving their versions in and around Disney's, seem to have realized this fact, too. But what is it about the princess narrative that has had such a lasting appeal among young readers and audiences? Marina Warner believes that "fairy tales play to the child's hankering after nobler, richer, altogether better origins, the fantasy of being a prince or a princess in disguise, the Freudian 'family romance.'"[35] Sheldon Cashdan agrees:

> Most children harbor fantasies about leading privileged lives and enjoying the liberties associated with such an existence. But the royal children in fairy tales possess neither extraordinary powers nor special skills. They are just like the other children, except for their titles. It thus is not difficult for young readers to share in the emotional travails of their royal counterparts.[36]

Children are thus invited to give in to fantasies involving mysterious royal origins by reading and viewing fanciful yet believable narratives that feature child protagonists who are much like themselves—hence their faint believability to the child audience or readership. Even Guillermo Del Toro's *Pan's Labyrinth* (2006) follows this formula, as the heroine of that film is driven to believe that she is in fact the secret daughter of the king and queen of Faerie—and, indeed, the cult popularity of Del Toro's film suggests that such fantasies may even follow us into adulthood. Second-wave Disney princess narratives have easily adapted to this formula; two of the four heroines are ordinary girls, and both Ariel's and Jasmine's greatest desire in *The Little Mermaid* and *Aladdin* is to experience life outside the sea or palace as an ordinary person.

Because of Disney's impressive ability to market and distribute their product so widely and visibly, however, it is *their* version of the princess narrative which has wormed its way into the psyche of the American public. Stone tells us that "Of the total of 210 stories in the complete edition," of the Grimms' *Kinder- und Hausmärchen*, "there are 40 heroines, not all of them passive and pretty."[37] But today, when most people think of princesses, they do not think of the wide variety of other princesses in the Grimms' or Andrew Lang's collections, such as the princess in "The Three Little Birds" who rescues and finds her two brothers as well as their long lost royal parents. Nor do they think of Del Toro's brave young Ofelia in *Pan's Labyrinth*. Neither have they likely read Robin McKinley's retelling of the Grimms' "Thousandfurs," wherein Princess Lissar saves the prince's sister from marrying Lissar's own rapist father. Instead, they may think of Ariel, who, "at first glance appears to be engaged in a struggle against parental control," writes Henry Giroux, "motivated by the desire to explore the human world and willing to take a risk in defining the subject and object of her desires."[38] These positive, even feminist-friendly character traits are, however, virtually canceled out by a film like *The Little Mermaid* (1989), where Ariel makes an unfortunate bargain with the sea-witch Ursula. Ariel's free-spiritedness is transformed into a longing to meet Prince Eric, a man she happened to see above sea one day. In order to do this, she gives up her own voice to gain admittance into the world of humans. Says Giroux, "Although girls might be delighted by Ariel's teenage rebelliousness, they are strongly positioned to believe, in the end, that desire, choice, and empowerment are closely linked to catching and loving a handsome man."[39] It may be normal, then, as both Warner and Cashdan suggest, for child readers and viewers to aspire toward prince- and princesshood, but it is Disney which has essentially taken this gender neutral aspiration and assigned specific characteristics to young male and female fantasies. Princehood remains linked with notions of power, freedom, and exploration, as exemplified by Disney heroes like Aladdin, Simba, and Tarzan, whereas princesshood is now rigidly bound to concepts like dutifulness, self-sacrifice, and desire for and subservience to males—all character traits shared by both first and second-wave Disney princesses. These Disney princesses,[40] writes Stone,

> are not only passive and pretty, but also unusually patient, obedient, industrious, and quiet. A woman who failed to be any of these could not become a heroine. Even Cinderella has to do no more than put on dirty rags to conceal herself completely. She is a heroine only when properly cleaned and dressed.[41]

Stone argues in "Things Walt Disney Never Told Us" that Disney's influence over the princess narrative is so powerful that few American women can name fairy tale heroines other than those that have been immortalized on film by Disney; furthermore, the traits listed above have become those traits now linked inexorably with princesshood.

Other critics agree that Stone is not overestimating Disney's influence; Henry Giroux also encourages us to understand that the power Disney has had in reformulating the princess narrative is thus not insignificant:

> At issue for parents, educators, and others is how culture, especially media culture, has become a substantial, if not the primary, educational force in regulating the meanings, values, and tastes that set the norms that offer up and

legitimate particular subject positions—what it means to claim an identity as a male, female, white, black, citizen, noncitizen.[42]

For generations, Disney has used the princess narrative to instill in its viewers an understanding of the position of girls and women in American society. The company's influence may not have necessarily been insidious (though many would argue that it was and is), but it has nonetheless exerted this influence on an unsuspecting populace. As second- and third-wave feminists become mothers, aunts, and grandmothers, however, awareness of Disney's (in many ways) anti-feminist presentation of the princess narrative only begins to grow. "Since when did every little girl become a princess?" wonders Peggy Orenstein. "It wasn't like this when I was a kid, and I was born back when feminism was still a mere twinkle in our mothers' eyes."[43] In *Cinderella Ate My Daughter,* new mother Orenstein recalls her frustration over her pre-school aged daughters' newfound fascination with princesses, writing, "I fretted over what playing Little Mermaid, a character who actually gives up her *voice* to get a man, was teaching her."[44]

What is it then that so many find objectionable about the traditional (i.e. Disney) princess narrative? For one, we leave girls with a very limited choice of role models when we offer them Disney princesses. O'Keefe insists that even spirited female characters, who could otherwise serve as excellent role models for young female readers and viewers, have historically "crumpled so readily under the male gaze."[45] This behavior is mimicked by all three first-wave Disney princesses and is even carried over at times into the narratives of the second-wave princesses. Jasmine's escape attempts in *Aladdin* are ultimately thwarted by her association with the title character, forcing her to return to her father's palace and ending her stint of freedom. Ariel's longing for adventure in *The Little Mermaid* is completely redirected when she first lays eyes on Prince Eric[46]—thenceforth, she can think of nothing except meeting him. When the Beast first lays eyes on Belle in *Beauty and the Beast*, she literally becomes his prisoner, exchanging her freedom for her captive father's. And in *Mulan*, the title character lives in constant fear of Shang Li's gaze; his discovery of her sex would ruin her and her entire family and could even potentially result in her execution.

The brief glimpse Disney offers into the lives of their princesses begins and ends with the princesses' romantic involvement with men. Not that Disney princes are unworthy characters—far from it. The Beast is revealed to be kind beneath his rough exterior; Shang Li is the very picture of equal parts dutifulness and compassion. But young girls do not aspire to be like Disney princes. The world around them tells them that they are princesses, and so princesses they aspire to be.[47] Deborah O'Keefe agrees: "Some readers and researchers maintain that if girls do not encounter strong female models in their reading, they can and will identify with the male models. I am skeptical of this."[48] But neither is it as simple as prescribing what Lissa Paul refers to as "hero[es] in drag"[49]—female characters who take on traditionally male characteristics in an attempt to subvert the kinds of traditional female roles the first-and second-wave Disney princesses have taken on. If that were the case, then Robert Munsch's Paper Bag Princess would have strapped on a suit of armor, taken up her sword, and defeated the dragon at the end of the book by force—but she did not. O'Keefe thus argues that if it is wrong for young female readers to be indoctrinated into a culture of submissiveness and passivity, then it is equally wrong for them to be "pointed toward the pole opposite to submissiveness, traditionally male qualities which are just as harmful—selfishness, rigidity, aggression, and the need to dominate."[50] She furthermore reminds us that there are still positive traditionally feminine traits to be considered, such as "sympathy, cooperation, flexibility."[51] Therefore, "Instead of engaging in such simplistic stereotype switching," suggests Roberta Trites, "feminist characters use a variety of means, notably employing their imaginations and trickery, to enact a transcendence of gender roles."[52]

If such feminist characters really do exist in children's literature, where then do they fit in within the princess narrative—or can they fit in at all? Has Disney's influence been so overarching that the princess narrative has been forever branded as anti-feminist? Yes—and no. Can the princess narrative then be reformed, so to speak, and is this a desirable reformation? This time the answer is certainly yes. Attempts at reformation are always possible, and in this case change is certainly desirable by many who object to Disney's version of what it means to be a princess. Thus, not surprisingly, around the turn of the twenty-first century, a new brand of princess narrative is beginning to be written and marketed to young female readers: what I will refer to from here on out as the "third wave" (i.e. contemporary feminist) princess narrative.

In *Waking Sleeping Beauty*, Trites essentially gives a perfect definition for what I consider to be the feminist or "third wave," if you will, princess narrative. She writes that "Many feminist children's novels seem to be direct revisions of earlier images of passive femininity in children's literature."[53] Although Trites is here speaking of children's books in general, her theory of intertextuality amongst feminist children's book authors is rather uniquely suited to fairy tale and princess narrative revisions and can easily be applied to these twenty-first century revisions of the Disney-defined princess narrative. She rightfully points out that feminist authors who do revise fairy tales "often rewrite these tales to suit their own ideological purposes."[54] Naturally, "the form these ideological revisions usually take is to depict how much more aware of her agency the protagonist is than are the characters in the tale the author is revising."[55] Trites continues: "Although these revisions take a variety of forms, most of them rely on a character who rejects stereotypical behavior to balance assertiveness with compassion."[56] The third-wave princess is a princess who "rejects stereotypical behavior" from the past, behavior that was perpetuated by the Disney princesses. This behavior was also often echoed by the majority of girl characters in books published for children up through the '60s, '70s, and '80s, or, right up to the beginning of the "second wave" of Disney Princess films (i.e. the films of the '90s). The images from many of these picture books, writes Leslie Paris, often "showed boys on adventure or climbing trees, while girls were often homebound, watching admiringly from the porch as the boys played and explored."[57] "Watching admiringly from the porch" is very nearly a prerequisite for a Disney Princess; think of Cinderella gazing out at the world from her tower, or Ariel peeking up through the waves to spy on Eric's ship. And although most first Disney princesses do manage to escape the confines of domestic solitude to carve out the semblance of adventure, that "adventure" often still revolves solely around marriage and romance. Like the girls in the children's books previously mentioned, Disney princesses thus typically exhibit behavior that includes characteristics considered to be unpalatable to contemporary feminists, such as passivity, dutifulness, and subservience to male characters. But today's "third-wave" princess moves beyond simple rejection; she must "balance assertiveness"—a new assertiveness not previously seen in first- and second-wave Disney princess narratives, and one that might initially be more traditionally associated with male characters—with "compassion." In other words, these third-wave princesses exchange negative, traditionally feminine characteristics (i.e. passivity) for more positive, traditionally masculine traits, such as assertiveness and rebelliousness. However, they retain those traditionally feminine characteristics which are still considered positive by contemporary feminists (i.e. compassion). The resulting character is not a "hero in drag" but a new kind of heroine, and for the princess narrative specifically, a new kind of princess: the third-wave princess. Contemporary examples include works by bestselling authors like Shannon Hale, Gail Carson Levine, and Meg Cabot. Cabot's *The Princess Diaries* (2000), for example, stars Princess Mia Thermopolis, a lanky, unpopular high school student who resists her grandmother's attempt to turn her into a more traditional princess figure. Mia's journey from awkward nobody to "self-actualized" (but somehow still not popular) student council president is the focal point of the series, not her on again/off again relationship with boyfriend Michael Moscovitz. In Levine's *Ella Enchanted* (1998) and *Fairest* (2006), princesses Ella and Aza rely on sheer wit and determination to defeat the villains in their respective narratives and win the respect of those around them; romance for these princesses is, again, secondary to the overall plot of each novel. And in Hale's *Princess Academy* (2006), Miri teaches herself and her fellow academy students a unique form of magic and ultimately uses that magic to help defend her village from a deadly group of bandits. All of these princess protagonists exhibit the above stated character traits; they are assertive, clever, and rebellious in a way that many Disney Princesses are not, and yet they remain compassionate towards those they love and wish to protect.

But how successful have these and other so-called third-wave princess narratives truly been? I have said that the answer to the Disney question—that is, has Disney's influence on the princess narrative been truly overpowering?—is both yes and no. Why?

First, we have to acknowledge that the response against Disney by feminist storytellers has been strong and, in many ways, both a critical and marketing success. Feminist fairy tale authors like Levine and Hale have received Newbery Honor awards for their efforts (*Ella Enchanted* and *Princess Academy*, respectively). Both Levine and Cabot have had their own widely popular feminist princess narratives turned into movies (*Ella Enchanted* in 2004 and *The Princess Diaries* in 2001). These authors also market themselves rigorously; they blog, tweet, and participate in book signings throughout the year. Either as a response to their own success or simply as a continued reaction to Disney, many, *many* princess-themed narratives have emerged in the past ten years. Many YA and intermediate authors have even hit the ground running, so to speak, by making their first publication a princess narrative: see E. D. Baker (*The Frog Princess*, 2002), Julie Berry (*The Amaranth Enchantment*, 2009), and even the three above mentioned authors. Publishing houses cannot seem to get enough of this new wily but still royal heroine. In essence, princesses have become good for business.

And they are not alone in their crusade against (or rather, their reformation of) the more traditional Disney princesses. They have a surprising and perhaps not entirely welcome new ally: the Walt Disney company.

In 2009, Disney released its latest princess-themed film, an adaptation of E. D. Baker's *The Frog Princess*. *The Princess and the Frog* arrived with much fanfare just before the holiday season. Disney marketed the film almost to distraction, and the media was abuzz over the company's first black princess. Not surprisingly, *The Princess and the Frog* also garnered some immediate criticism; some claimed Tiana's love interest, Prince Naveen, was not black enough.[58] Disney's response: Well, he's not white.[59] In "Her Prince Has Come. Critics, Too," Brooks Barnes was one of the first to point out something problematic about the narrative involving Disney's first black princess: "We finally get a black princess and she spends the majority of her time on screen as a frog?"[60] Then again, some of the criticism was misplaced. Neal A. Lester notes that "the first and only African-American princess, unlike other Disney princesses, is not a princess by birth but rather becomes a princess through marriage to a prince,"[61] which is, of course, untrue. Neither Cinderella, Belle, nor Mulan were born to royal parents, yet all have been welcomed into the Disney Princess pantheon.

These criticisms aside, however, *The Princess and the Frog* became the first Disney princess film to feature a heroine who aspired for something more than romance throughout the film's narrative. Tiana is introduced to us as a young woman whose greatest goal in life is to own her own restaurant—that goal does not change, not when she first meets Prince Naveen, not when she realizes she loves him, and not even after she marries him. While some of her predecessors do have dreams and aspirations, they all involve, in some way or another, marriage to a man. Mulan, for example, despairs over having to marry in order to make her family happy; presumably, she would rather marry to please herself—which she does at the film's conclusion by falling in love with Shang Li, agreeing to a match that ends up pleasing all parties involved. Jasmine's goal in *Aladdin* is similar; she wishes to escape her life as a sultan's daughter and her father's decree that she marry a prince. In fact, romance often completely drives the plot forward in earlier Disney Princess films—consider, for example, Cinderella's desire to dance with Prince Charming at the ball, or Ariel's desire to become human and meet Prince Eric. Previous Disney Princess films also always inevitably conclude with either a wedding or a declaration of love. But Tiana's desire to own her own restaurant literally has nothing to do with marriage; presumably, she can accomplish this goal through hard work and with time.[62] Furthermore, Tiana is the first princess whose narrative does not end with marriage (or romance in general): the narrative concludes with her finally building and operating her dream restaurant.

Tiana is a third-wave princess because she exhibits both positive traditionally feminine traits (compassion, understanding) and positive traditionally masculine traits (enterprise, cleverness, assertiveness) while eschewing those negative traits that have been traditionally associated with femininity and (so-called "first- and second-wave") Disney Princesses. It is Tiana who finds the path through the swamp; it is she who keeps herself and Naveen safe and well fed throughout their journey. She purchases her business with her own money and at no point requires rescuing—save, perhaps, for the kiss at the end with Naveen, though, to be fair, he needs it just as much as she does.

Much to Disney's dismay, however, *The Princess and the Frog* did not do as well at the box office as they might have hoped—a dismal $104 million domestic gross.[63] This had surprisingly dramatic consequences for Disney's next and perhaps last (so they claim) princess film: *Tangled* (2010). "Disney is wringing the pink out of its princess movies," write Dawn C. Chmielewski and Claudia Eller in the LA Times.[64] The company went so far as to completely alter the storyline; the title of the film was changed from "Rapunzel" to "Tangled," and the film's director, Glen Keane, who had previously worked on Disney princess films like *Beauty and the Beast* and *The Little Mermaid*, stepped aside, allowing Ron Clements and John Musker to eventually take over at the helm. Pixar and Disney Animation Studios president Ed Catmull claims that they "did not want to be put into a box" and that Disney wanted to produce "movies to be appreciated and loved by everybody"—not just girls.[65] "Young boys won't go to girl movies," agrees film analyst Paul Dergarabedian.[66] Essentially, since *The Princess and the Frog* did not garner as much income as Disney might have hoped, this perceived failure was placed at the feet of America's boys, who had suddenly refused to stop seeing princess-themed films—or rather, had begun to respond to Disney's aggressive marketing scheme that began in 2000, linking all things "princess" with girls.[67]

Since movies for girls—i.e. princess movies—were no longer deemed marketably salient, Rapunzel's story underwent a transformation that no other Disney princess has yet had to endure: she was forced to share the lead with her male love interest.[68] Even more grating perhaps is the fact that Rapunzel does not even have control over her own story. Flynn Rider narrates the story, though his narrative presence all but disappears for most of the film; he mostly bookends the narrative, introducing us to himself and Rapunzel, and concluding the story by telling the audience that he eventually asked Rapunzel to marry him, and she accepted. Despite this, however, Rapunzel's narrative seems to have a more satisfactory beginning. Feminist heads likely nodded as we saw Rapunzel sing about the creative accomplishments she had been forced to perfect over the years in her tower. It is virtually impossible not to compare a young girl who spends her days baking, painting, and dancing to those feminine "accomplishments" that were so scathingly mocked by ironists like Jane Austen and deconstructed by critics like Virginia Wolfe. Throughout the montage of artistic endeavors, we see Rapunzel struggling to find new surfaces to paint on and despairing over having to read the same books again and again. This is clearly a non-traditional princess trapped in an all too traditional setting, and she aches to escape. And she is clever enough to orchestrate her own escape, too, convincing the wily Flynn Rider to lead her to the site of the floating lanterns; her desire to see them in person is for all intents and purposes her life's ambition.

But floating lanterns do not exactly compare to owning one's own business—let alone saving all of China. And like Mulan and Belle, Jasmine and Ariel, Rapunzel's story ends with romance. The culmination of her narrative is not the fulfillment of her life's dream but her marriage to Flynn Rider. Clearly, her feminist tendencies have been diminished so that additional focus can be placed on Flynn. As the narrator, he exerts definitive control over the story. He is Rapunzel's guide, for he is older, wiser, and worldlier than she. Rapunzel may be clever in the beginning, but she is consistently easily duped by her mother, whereas Flynn never loses sight of what he wants and desires.

Today, any girl who wants to be a princess can become one. She can drag her parents or guardians to the store and purchase a princess costume. She can purchase princess school supplies, princess socks, dresses, and hair ribbons. She can play with princess dolls, swim in princess plastic pools, and ride her princess bike. And millions of other girls can do the same.

It is too early to tell how the creation and popularity of the Disney Princess franchise will affect American girls as they become teenagers and adults. Its effect on literature has already begun, however. Shannon Hale relates on her blog the shock she felt upon hearing her four-year-old daughter claim that "Princesses aren't strong." When Hale disagreed, her daughter wisely "pointed to a picture of Disney['s] Cinderella, Sleeping Beauty, etc., and said, 'But these princesses aren't strong.'"[69]

Disney has spent the past 100 years or so defining "princess" for American consumers. In 2000, they began marketing their version of "princess"; the result was so cataclysmically successful in the eyes of feminist parents and guardians that it spawned a wave of anti-Disney sentiment. Authors like Hale wrote novels that featured princesses as unlike their Disney predecessors as possible: clever princesses, strong princesses, princesses whose lives do not revolve around romance and subservience to a prince. Hale admits to being directly inspired to write by feminist fairy tale rewriters like Robin McKinley.[70] Will she and other children's and YA authors continue to revisit and revise the princess narrative? It seems likely. The sequel to *Princess Academy*, *Palace of Stone*, recently topped out at #8 on the New York Times Bestseller List. New YA authors like Jessica Day George and Marissa Meyer are continuing to help swell bookstore shelves with twenty-first-century princess narrative retellings. Of course, trends in children's publishing do tend to come and go. Stephanie Meyer's wildly popular *Twilight* series has rocketed the paranormal romance to the spotlight, while Suzanne Collins' equally popular *The Hunger Games* has done the same for teen dystopias. But where *Twilight*'s Bella Swan is often lambasted for being weak-willed and apathetic, *The Hunger Games*' tough-talking, bow-wielding Katniss Everdeen is lauded as a "radical female hero."[71] It seems readers are thirsty for young female protagonists who break the mold—a mold that has to some degree been created and packaged by Disney.

Even Disney is finding it hard to break free from this same mold. In late 2010, the company declared that it would no longer be producing fairytale-inspired animated films. The poorly producing *The Princess and the Frog* was to blame, as "Disney discovered too late that 'Princess and the Frog' appealed to too narrow an audience: little girls."[72] The following year's *Tangled* was meant to hopefully "draw boys, teenagers and adults to the theater, succeeding where its frog-prince saga failed."[73] But while Disney has yet to renege on its promise to cease producing fairytale-inspired animated films, it *has* managed to produce yet another princess narrative.

Brave was released in the summer of 2012; the film was produced by Pixar Studios but distributed by Disney. However, it is safe to say that the two companies are one in the same—Walt Disney Studios bought Pixar in 2006. *Brave* was a tremendous success; it ranked #1 at the box office and earned $66.7 million during its opening weekend.[74] Its producer, Katherine Sarafian, was quick to declare the film's protagonist, Princess Merida, as very separate and distinct from her Disney Princess predecessors: "There's a grand tradition of Disney princesses," she claims. "[Merida] is a Pixar hero. It is completely different from a Disney princess."[75] Sarafian is obviously trying to draw a line in the sand between *Brave*'s definition of what it means to be a princess (and, by association, a girl) and the pink and sparkly assault on American girls—not to mention the "assault" on their parents' wallets—that is the Disney Princess franchise. Even the dialogue between Merida and her mother seems to be written in an attempt to draw a distinction between these old and new definitions of "princess"—"I suppose a princess just does what she's told!" Merida says at one point in the film. "A princess does not raise her voice!" replies her mother. The exchange is not so much meant to label Merida as "feminist" and Elinor as "anti-feminist," however; rather, it serves to show how the film itself no longer expects its viewers to buy into the traditional femininity as represented by the Disney Princesses. Merida does *not* have to be submissive and silent because she is a princess—and a girl. Certainly, no one in the audience is meant to believe that Merida must give up her autonomy because she is a princess. But her mother's response makes it clear that, princess or not, Merida is still a teenager and must do as her parents dictate.

But is Merida really all that different from her non-Pixar predecessors? Like Mulan, she chaffs under the strict rules enforced by her culture, rules that dictate how she must act and dress simply because she is female. In one memorable scene, Merida purposefully rips her ceremonial dress so that she can more properly aim her bow. Like Belle and Mulan both, she is an accomplished horsewoman. And like some of her later Disney predecessors, she has no desire to be wed to a man not of her choosing. Merida's storyline skips rather chaotically between the crisis she creates with her mother, whom she inadvertently turns into a bear, and her desire to escape the arranged marriage her parents are attempting to set up for her. Ultimately, where *Brave*'s narrative differs from previous Disney Princess narratives is in its ending. The film does not end with a romance; Merida does not fall in love, though she does allow that she may one day have to do the responsible thing and marry.

The fact that the film's producers are quick to distance themselves from the Disney Princess franchise certainly suggests that effort has been made by the company to divorce itself from a franchise with an increasingly shrinking demographic. Merida also has yet to be accepted into the Disney Princess pantheon, although visitors to Walt Disney World in Orlando, Florida can expect to visit with her, as with all the other Disney Princesses. While Disney's concerns are monetary, however, the public seems more keen on seeing films and reading books that feature strong, active, and thoughtful female protagonists—protagonists like Merida.

It seems likely, then, that the princess narrative will continue to evolve. We have already begun to see princesses who resemble the wide swath of readers their narratives are capable of attracting when they are no longer forced to conform to Disney's ideals regarding femininity and sexuality. Marissa Meyer has already introduced us to Cinder, a differently abled princess who is missing a foot, an arm, and more internal organs than even she is aware of. And Malinda Lo has already given us her novel *Ash*, another loose retelling of "Cinderella" which features a romantic relationship between its female protagonist and a female fairy. Novels like Meyer's and Lo's prove to us that the princess narrative is capable of evolving and yet still continuing to enchant readers and viewers as much as the original tales themselves once did and continue to do. For now, Disney is trying desperately to continue its multi-billion dollar Disney Princess franchise without turning off potential consumers. It is fair to suggest, then, that we can expect to see more princesses like Merida, Cinder, and maybe even Ash in the company's future. It may even be that the meaning behind my term "anti-Disney" will become muddled, that princesses like Merida and the ones in the contemporary novels like *Ash*, *Cinder*, and *The Frog Princess* will come to truly redefine "princess" in the minds of the American public. Still, critics like Peggy Orenstein continue to rebel against the princess narrative and seem entirely unaware of its more recently feminist evolutions. The power of the Disney Princesses looms large over the princess narrative—even to the point that Disney's own efforts to conform to a seemingly more feminist-friendly audience sometimes fail. Perhaps only time will tell whether Disney's decision to stop making fairy tale animated films altogether will signal the end to their dominance over the princess narrative.[76] All that can be certain is that so long as there is a market for the ever evolving princess narrative, Disney will continue to sell it.

Notes

1 Jean Bloch, "The eighteenth century: women writing, women learning," in Sonya Stephens (ed.), *A History of Women's Writing in France* (New York: Cambridge University Press, 2000), 89.

2 Joseph Jacobs, *English Fairy Tales* (London: David Nutt, 1890), 229.

3 Gretchen Holbrook Gerzina, *Frances Hodgson Burnett: The Unexpected Life of the Author of* The Secret Garden (New Brunswick: Rutgers University Press, 2004), 117.

4   Ibid., 119.

5   Ibid., 119.

6   Ibid., 235.

7   Deborah J. O'Keefe, *Good Girl Messages* (New York: Continuum International Publishing Group Inc., 2000), 12.

8   Burnett, *A Little Princess*, 176.

9   Ibid., 308.

10 Ibid., 301.

11 Gail Schmunk Murray, *American Children's Literature and the Construction of Childhood* (New York: Twayne Publishers, 1998), 90.

12 Ibid., 104.

13 Jack Zipes, "Breaking the Disney Spell," in Elizabeth Bell, Lynda Haas, and Laura Sells (eds), *From Mouse to Mermaid: the politics of film, gender, and culture* (Bloomington, IN: Indiana University Press, 1995), 33.

14 Leonard Maltin, *Of Mice and Magic: a history of American animated cartoons* (New York: Plume, 1980), 57.

15 CP, "Snow White to be released for the sixth time: The voice behind the fairy tale," *The Globe and Mail*, July 5, 1983, LexisNexis Academic.

16 Sheldon Cashdan, *The Witch Must Die: The Hidden Meaning of Fairy Tales* (New York: Basic Books, 1999), 1.

17 Ibid., 40.

18 O'Keefe, *Good Girl Messages*, 164.

19 Ibid., 164.

20 Marcia R. Lieberman, "One Day My Prince Will Come: Female Acculturation through the Fairy Tale," *College English* 34, no. 3 (1972): 384.

21 Ibid., 384.

22 Karen Rowe, "Feminism and Fairy Tales." *Women's Studies: A inter-disciplinary journal* 6, no. 3 (1979), 238.

23 Kay Stone, "Things Walt Disney Never Told Us," *The Journal of American Folklore* 88, no. 347 (January–March 1975): 48.

24 Ibid., 48.

25 Jack Zipes, "Preface," *Don't Bet on the Prince: Contemporary Feminist Fairy Tales in North America and England* (New York: Methuen, 1986), xi.

26 Ibid., xi–xii.

27 Jeanne Desy, "The Princess Who Stood On Her Own Two Feet," in Jack Zipes, (ed.), *Don't Bet On The Prince: Contemporary Feminist Fairy Tales in North America and England* (New York: Methuen, Inc., 1986), 46.

28 Robin McKinley, *Beauty: A Retelling of the Story of Beauty and the Beast* (New York: HarperCollins Publishers, Inc., 1978), 6–8.

29 John Brodie and Jay Greene, "Dwarfs Tell Disney: Draw!; Rival studios get serious about animation," *Variety*, July 11–July 17, 1994, News: 1, LexusNexus Academic.

30 Ibid.

31 Eileen Fitzpatrick, "Mulan, Dalmations, and Winnie-The-Pooh Due in '99," *Billboard*, November 2, 1998, Shelf Talk: 1, LexusNexus Academic.

32 Peggy Orenstein, *Cinderella Ate My Daughter: Dispatches from the Front Lines of the New Girlie-Girl Culture* (New York: Harper, 2011), 13.

33 Ibid., 14.

34 Ibid., 16.

35 Marina Warner, *From the Beast to the Blonde: On Fairy Tales and Their Tellers* (London: Chatto & Windus, 1994), 210.

36 Cashdan, 30.

37 Kay Stone, "Fairytales for Adults: Walt Disney's Americanization of the Märchen," in Burlakoff and Lindahl (eds), *Folklore on Two Continents: Essays in Honor of Linda Dégh* (Bloomington, IN: Trickster Press, 1980), 42.

38 Henry Giroux, *The Mouse That Roared* (Lanham, MD: Rowman & Littlefield Publishers Inc., 1999), 98.

39 Ibid., 99.

40 Stone was exclusively referring to the first-wave Disney princesses in her article: Snow White, Cinderella, and Aurora.

41 Stone, "Fairytales for Adults," 43.

42 Giroux, *Mouse that Roared*, 2–3.

43 Orenstein, *Cinderella Ate My Daughter*, 4.

44 Ibid., 4.

45 O'Keefe, *Good Girl Messages*, 169.

46 It is important to note that Eric does not see her at this point—he first sees her when she rescues him from the shipwreck. At that point, it's over for the both of them. They can think of nothing but one another.

47 Orenstein, *Cinderella Ate My Daughter*, 3.

48 O'Keefe, *Good Girl Messages*, 13.

49 Lissa Paul, "Enigma Variations: What Feminist Theory Knows About Children's Literature," *Signal* 54 (September 1987), 199.

50 O'Keefe, *Good Girl Messages*, 22.

51 Ibid., 22.

52 Roberta Seelinger Trites, *Waking Sleeping Beauty* (Iowa: University of Iowa Press, 1997), 5.

53 Ibid., 11.

54 Ibid., 40.

55   Ibid.

56   Ibid., 12.

57   Leslie Paris, "Happily Ever After: *Free to Be ... You and Me*, Second-wave Feminism, and 1970s American Children's Culture," in Julia L. Mickenberg and Lynne Vallone (eds), *The Oxford Handbook of Children's Literature* (New York: Oxford University Press, 2011), 525.

58   Brooks Barnes, "Her Prince Has Come. Critics, Too," *The New York Times*, May 21, 2009. http://www.nytimes.com

59   Ibid.

60   Ibid.

61   Neal A. Lester, "Disney's *The Princess and the Frog*: The Pride, the Pressure, and the Politics of Being First," *The Journal of American Culture* 33, no. 4 (December 2010): 299.

62   Tiana's difficulties regarding her desire to own her own restaurant are mostly related to her race and gender, and what it means to be a black woman living in 1950s' New Orleans. Prince Naveen is strategically poor and can offer her no rise in circumstances.

63   Box Office Report, *Variety*, March 19–April 4, 2010, Film, 10.

64   Dawn C. Chmielewski and Claudia Eller, "Disney restyles 'Rapunzel' to appeal to boys," *Los Angeles Times*, March 9, 2010. http://latimes.com

65   Ibid.

66   Gloria Goodale, "How 'Tangled' topped 'Harry Potter' at the box office," *The Christian Science Monitor*, December 6, 2010. http://www.lexisnexis.com

67   Of course, it remains to be seen whether the Disney Princesses were indeed wholeheartedly rejected by boys—or by their parents.

68   To be fair, Jasmine in *Aladdin* does not even share the lead with Aladdin. He is the hero, and she is merely the love interest.

69   Shannon Hale, "Wonder Woman is a princess too," *Squeetus Blog: Official Blog of Shannon Hale*, January 31, 2011. http://www.squeetus.com/stage/main.html

70   Shannon Hale, "Books: the goose girl," *Squeetus Blog: Official Blog of Shannon Hale*. http://www.squeetus.com/stage/main.html

71   A. O. Scott and Manohla Dargis, "A Radical Female Hero from Dystopia." *The New York Times*, April 4, 2012. http://www.nytimes.com/

72   Dawn C. Chmielewski and Claudia Eller, "Disney Animation is closing the book on fairy tales," *Los Angeles Times*, November 21, 2010. http://latimes.com

73   Ibid.

74   Meriah Doty, "Brave ushers in a different kind of Disney princess: Merida the tomboy," *Yahoo!Movies*, June 25, 2012. www.movies.yahoo.com

75   Ibid.

76   Chmielewski and Eller, "Disney Animation."

Bibliography

Barnes, Brooks. "Her Prince Has Come. Critics, Too." *The New York Times*, May 29, 2013. Available at http://www.nytimes.com

Bloch, Jean. "The eighteenth century: women writing, women learning," in Sonya Stevens (ed.), *A History of Women's Writing in France*, 84–101. New York: Cambridge University Press, 2000.

Box Office Report. *Variety*, March 29–April 4, 2010, Film, 10.

Brodie, John and Jay Greene. "Dwarfs Tell Disney: Draw!; Rival studios get serious about animation." *Variety*, July 11, 1994–July 17, 1994, News, 1. Available at http://www.lexisnexis.com

Cashdan, Sheldon. *The Witch Must Die: The Hidden Meaning of Fairy Tales*. New York: Basic Books, 1999.

Chmielewski, Dawn C. and Claudia Eller. "Disney restyles 'Rapunzel' to appeal to boys." *Los Angeles Times*, March 9, 2010. Available at http://articles.latimes.com

—"Disney Animation is closing the book on fairy tales." *Los Angeles Times*, 21 November 2010. Available at http://articles.latimes.com

CP. "Snow White to be released for the sixth time: The voice behind the fairy tale." *The Globe and Mail* (Toronto, ON), July 5, 1983. www.lexisnexis.com

Desy, Jeanne. "The Princess Who Stood On Her Own Two Feet, " in Jack Zipes (ed.), *Don't Bet On The Prince: Contemporary Feminist Fairy Tales in North America and England*, edited by Jack Zipes, 39–47. New York: Methuen Inc., 1986.

Doty, Meriah. "Brave ushers in a different kind of Disney princess: Merida the tomboy." *Yahoo!Movies*, June 25, 2012. Available at http://movies.yahoo.com

Fitzpatrick, Eileen. "Mulan, Dalmations, and Winnie-The-Pooh Due in '99." *Billboard*, November 2, 1998. Available at www.lexisnexis.com/hottopics/lnacademic

Gerzina, Gretchen Holbrook. *Frances Hodgson Burnett: The Unexpected Life of the Author of* The Secret Garden. New Brunswick: Rutgers University Press, 2004.

Giroux, Henry. *The Mouse That Roared*. Lanham, Maryland: Rowman & Littlefield Publishers Inc., 1999.

Gloria Goodale. "How 'Tangled' topped 'Harry Potter' at the box office." *The Christian Science Monitor*, December 6, 2010. Available at www.lexisnexis.com/hottopics/lnacademic

Hale, Shannon. "Books: the goose girl." *Squeetus Blog: Official Blog of Shannon Hale*. Available at http://www.squeetus.com/stage/main.html

—"Wonder Woman is a princess too." *Squeetus Blog: Official Blog of Shannon Hale*. Available at http://www.squeetus.com/stage/main.html

Hodgson Burnett, Francis. *A Little Princess*. New York: Simon & Schuster, 2001.

Jacobs, Joseph. *English Fairy Tales*. London: David Nutt, 1890.

Lester, Neal A. "Disney's *The Princess and the Frog*: The Pride, the Pressure, and the

Politics of Being First." *The Journal of American Culture* 33, no. 4 (December 2010): 294–308.

Lieberman, Marcia R. "One Day My Prince Will Come: Female Acculturation through the Fairy Tale." *College English* 34, no. 3 (1972): 383–95.

Maltin, Leonard. *Of Mice and Magic: a history of American animated cartoons.* New York: Plume, 1980.

McKinley, Robin. *Beauty: A Retelling of the Story of Beauty and the Beast.* New York: HarperCollins Publishers Inc., 1978.

Murray, Gail Schmunk. *American Children's Literature and the Construction of Childhood.* New York: Twayne Publishers, 1998.

O'Keefe, Deborah J. *Good Girl Messages.* New York: Continuum International Publishing Group Inc., 2000.

Orenstein, Peggy. *Cinderella Ate My Daughter.* New York: HarperCollins, 2011.

Paris, Leslie. "Happily Ever After: *Free to Be … You and Me*, Second-wave Feminism, and 1970s American Children's Culture," in Julia L. Mickenberg and Lynne Vallone (eds), *The Oxford Handbook of Children's Literature*, 519–38. New York: Oxford University Press, 2011.

Paul, Lissa. "Enigma Variations: What Feminist Theory Knows About Children's Literature." *Signal* 54 (September 1987): 186–201.

Rowe, Karen. "Feminism and Fairy Tales." *Women's Studies: A inter-disciplinary journal* 6, no. 3 (1979): 237–57.

Scott, A. O. and Manohla Dargis. "A Radical Female Hero from Dystopia." *The New York Times*, April 4, 2012. Available at http://www.nytimes.com

Stone, Kay. "Fairytales for Adults: Walt Disney's Americanization of the Märchen," in Burlakoff and Lindahl (eds), *Folklore on Two Continents: Essays in Honor of Linda Dégh*, 40–67. Bloomington, IN: Trickster Press, 1980.

Trites, Roberta Seelinger. *Waking Sleeping Beauty.* Iowa City, Iowa: University of Iowa Press, 1997.

Warner, Marina. *From the Beast to the Blonde: On Fairy Tales and Their Tellers.* London: Chatto & Windus, 1994.

Zipes, Jack. "Breaking the Disney Spell," in Elizabeth Bell, Lynda Haas, and Laura Sells (eds), *From Mouse to Mermaid: The Politics of Film, Gender, and Culture*, 21–42. Bloomington, IN: Indiana University Press, 1995.

—"Preface." *Don't Bet on the Prince: Contemporary Feminist Fairy Tales in North America and England.* New York: Methuen, 1986.

9

Surreal Estate: Building Self-Identity in *Monster House*

Michael Howarth
Missouri Southern State University

I'm currently house-sitting for a fellow professor, shacked up in a two-story Victorian house built in 1898, musty and expansive with black widows roaming the basement and a cross breeze rustling through the loose floorboards. As a single man I feel dwarfed and insignificant, intimidated by over 3,000 square feet. The gothic atmosphere is intense and stifling, and wandering through the house on a nightly basis, listening to the attic sputter its creaks and groans, I tend to double-check dark corners and tiptoe down the stairs in hesitation.

Ensconced in this nineteenth-century house, I seem to remember my own childhood fears, namely the monster in the closet and the zombies in the backyard. I'm remembering strange neighbors and dense woods prone to afternoon explorations. I find myself constantly reflecting on spooky archetypes, specifically that infamous childhood image of an eerie, mysterious house waiting somewhere down the road, the front lawn overgrown with weeds, and cracked windows caked with dirt and grime. Most children recognize such a house in their neighborhood. They create stories about its history and inhabitants, daring each other to run up to the front steps and ring the doorbell, and watching broken windows for signs of movement as they run past on the opposite side of the road. For most children, that dark, mysterious house represents the unknown. And in both literature and film, it often represents psychological fears and anxieties that stem from the natural process of moving past childhood and progressing into adolescence.

During childhood, many children constantly feel on the verge of something frightening and fantastic. The future is menacing and mystifying, oppressive and startling, and so what better way to express the terrors of childhood, and the transition into adolescence, than by setting such crises and conflicts inside of a horror film. At any age, gothic stories can trigger our own personal memories and experiences, often stirring up so many emotions, anxieties, and desires that they allow us to consider how we would react if placed in similar circumstances involving death, betrayal, suffering, or loneliness. It is understandable that we might want to escape from all the anger, fear, and hate that infuse many gothic stories. Yet, at the same time, we are still captivated and entranced by the morbid details, grotesque characters, and disturbing plots. It is human nature to develop a fascination with darkness and negativity, to question how suffering plays a role in shaping someone else's life.

And it feels good to have an outlet for the emotions we experience in our own lives, emotions we might want to repress or deny. Gothic stories are crucial to our development because "understanding what pleases or frightens us the most is absolutely key to understanding what it means to be human and how human beings relate to and treat one another."[1] Gothic stories also entertain because they allow us the opportunity to lose ourselves in another character's anguish and distress; at the same time, they produce *Schadenfreude*, creating a sense of comfort and pleasure by reminding us that, at least for the moment, we ourselves might be free of such pain and emotional duress. Such stories provide an unconscious outlet for our own pain rather than force us to acknowledge our own personal feelings of anger, aggression, hate, etc.

And this is precisely why the gothic becomes a necessary element in helping to shape our lives: it assures us that while struggling with difficult events is an unavoidable part of human existence, the journey it provides will only strengthen our growth, thus helping us advance to yet another mature stage in the long cycle of life. On a simpler level, Gothicism allows us to realize that we will not be crushed by our own emotions, but will, instead, survive and prevail. At some point in our lives we will all encounter the Big Bad Wolf, but how we manage the fears he elicits will depend on our psychological development and the lessons we have already learned. As well, such encounters can provide a potential opportunity to relearn those lessons that we once learned wrong, but now have another opportunity to correct.

While many parents might wish to shield their children from negative emotions and scary stories, it is this introduction to natural and supernatural fears that helps guide children toward resolving those distressing emotions within themselves, thus pushing them on toward a greater sense of independence. The reason fear is so effective—as presented in the gothic—in helping children come to terms with their anxieties is because children are vulnerable and helpless, already experiencing intense fear at the thoughts of being abandoned, or even viewed as worthless and insignificant by parents and peers. These scary moments, whether they are experienced in books, films, or reality, have lasting impressions on a child's psyche and can assist him or her in not only understanding his or her limits, both emotionally and physically, but also the methods that others employ (and these "others" can be either the child's own parents or the characters in a book or a film) to overcome fear and apprehension. Only after we are able to control our fears can we then use the experience to help resolve certain crises and thus progress toward future stages of psychosocial development.

In children, this thought process and self-reflection often occurs on a subconscious level because children are not able to understand fully their own feelings or the different ways in which the greater world functions. Without this introduction to fear, children may enter adolescence unprepared to resolve intrapersonal and interpersonal conflicts, such as issues like puberty, sex, relationships, peer pressure, etc. So Gothicism in children's literature and film, besides being a source of entertainment, thus achieves a didactic purpose by supplying the emotional training wheels that we all must acquire so as to navigate through life's many pitfalls and setbacks.

Gil Kenan's *Monster House* is an animated film bursting with gothic imagery and intense situations, an adventure story loaded with creepy images and scary scenes that centers on a trio of school-age children (DJ, Chowder, and Jenny) who battle an angry, possessed house that eats trespassers. The house, which is owned by a cantankerous old man named Mr Nebbercracker, comes alive with the spirit of his dead wife, and the children must battle the house to save themselves and their neighborhood. Clearly, the house metaphor in films is not unique to children's movies, or even children's literature, but *Monster House* is different from other stories in that it contextualizes the angst and frustrations so often associated with adolescence, where "the goal is ecstasy, but the path to luminosity often winds through dark streets filled with gloom and terror."[2] The monster house itself, in fact, is a dominating reminder of the trials and tribulations that are necessary for successful growth and development. *Monster House* succeeds in delivering an important message for pre-teens because it explores the transition children make as they move into teenage years typically fraught with identity conflict and role confusion.

The director, Gil Kenan, uses mise-en-scène and cinematography to portray gothic elements (specifically the monster house) as an externalization of the psychological. These film techniques, coupled with the story's gothic elements, remind viewers that adolescence is a period of transition dotted with many struggles and hardships. These struggles "are unavoidable and an intrinsic part of human existence," and "if one does not shy away … one masters all obstacles and at the end emerges victorious."[3] To mature, DJ and his friends must not only interact with the film's gothic elements, but triumph over them as well. As the film progresses, the monster house becomes a metaphor for thinking about the various crises and conflicts that plague children as they move from childhood into adolescence.

We must remember, however, that there are many ways to define adolescence. Some educators, doctors, and psychologists believe it begins with the first signs of puberty; others designate adolescence as lasting only during the teenage years. And some psychologists contend that "adolescence is not a period between childhood and adulthood since that implies a recognizable point at either end" and, instead, regard it "as a continually shifting situation because adolescents occasionally have child status and occasionally have adult status."[4] This last definition seems to make the most sense, as it allows children the freedom of balancing between two worlds, either consciously or subconsciously. And since children are often confused about their identities, eager to become adults but scared to leave behind the safety net of childhood, this last definition also emphasizes the idea that adolescence occurs at different ages for each child, contingent on both their surrounding environment and their relation to family and peer groups. Therefore, it will be this less concrete definition of adolescence to which I will refer throughout the course of this essay.

Monster House opens with an establishing shot of a quiet suburban neighborhood. The scene pulsates with an exaggerated sense of innocence as orange leaves swirl through the air and a little girl in pigtails rides her tricycle down the street, singing "la, la, la" and saying hello to a fence, random leaves, and the blue sky. The camera tracks alongside the little girl, providing viewers with the same sense of movement and freedom. But when her tricycle runs off the pavement and onto a patch of grass, she becomes stuck in front of the monster house. Kenan introduces the monster house in a low-angle shot that emphasizes its gloominess and dominating presence. With windows in place of eyes, and porch railings substituting for teeth, the monster house certainly seems alive and menacing. Bare, gnarled trees line the house on either side of the yard, and their twisted branches stretch beyond the boundaries of the screen at odd angles, providing the scene with a surreal and unsettling atmosphere reminiscent of the German Expressionistic style of the silent era. The obscure camera angles also suggest a distorted reality, one that will reflect DJ's emotions as he battles the monster house with his two friends and attempt to form his own identity separate from that of parents and peers.

These wide, expansive shots of the monster house and the surrounding yard are then contrasted with close-ups of Mr Nebbercracker, the old man who lives in the house and screams at children whenever they venture onto his property. In a typically gothic shot, the first image of Nebbercracker is an extreme close-up of his eyes peeking out of a darkened doorway, an extension of the monster house that seems to loom over the neighborhood with its piercing features. Mr Nebbercracker comes running out of his house, hands raised in the air, and screaming, "Get off my lawn! Do you want to be eaten alive?" In a series of shots that parallel those same ones used to introduce the monster house, Kenan shoots Mr Nebbercracker from a low angle, not only emphasizing his dominance over the neighborhood children, but also linking him further with a house that he is connected to spiritually as well as physically.

As the scene ends, the little girl runs screaming down the street while Mr Nebbercracker rips the front wheel off of her bike. She has lost her tricycle, itself a symbol of childhood and playtime, and this loss of innocence during the opening scene of the film is an ominous foreshadowing of the conflicts that will soon arise when the three main characters, themselves innocent and naïve, collide with the film's gothic elements and begin to experience the adult world. Kenan seems to be emphasizing that innocence and danger do not exist in separate worlds. In fact, they often coexist, one influencing the other, and this is especially true during the various stages of childhood when children crave independence from their parents and often make foolish and dangerous mistakes in order to prove their autonomy and self worth.

Clenching pieces of the broken tricycle in both his fists, Mr Nebbercracker walks up his front steps. As he does so, the colors become muted and hazy, and the camera jostles up and down and from side to side. It soon becomes apparent that someone is watching Mr Nebbercracker through a telescope. He turns around and Kenan frames his angry face in an extreme close-up, whereupon we hear the sudden click of a camera. In a brilliant reverse shot, Kenan then switches point of view to reveal DJ, the main character, who is watching Nebbercracker through a telescope in his upstairs bedroom across the street. By zooming rapidly from Nebbercracker's yard directly into DJ's bedroom, Kenan suggests an existing connection between the two characters, one that will develop over the course of the film and aid DJ in his attempts to move beyond childhood and into adolescence.

Our first glimpse of DJ is an extreme close-up of his eye as the camera zooms through the entire length of the telescope. Typically, in both cinema and literature, a shot of an eye symbolizes a new angle or perspective; it alerts the viewer that he or she (or even one of the characters) will soon change his or her perspective and begin to see the world in a new light. And as the film unfolds, DJ moves from seeing the world through a child's eyes to understanding the world from a more grown-up point of view. In the opening scenes of *Monster House*, DJ seems to be looking into a world that scares him, but one that he still wants to join, and this conflicted feeling certainly mirrors the trepidation exhibited by most adolescents.

In his landmark text, *Identity: Youth and Crisis*, renowned psychologist Erik Erikson defines the adolescent stage as "Identity versus Role Confusion," and he argues that, "The greatest problem we encounter is who we think we are versus who others may think we are or are trying to be."[5] During this tumultuous period of growth, the child searches for social ideas, cliques, fashion styles, or places that will allow him to establish a sense of trust with others, and also to prove himself capable of being viewed as a trustworthy person who is ready to be initiated into adulthood.

At the beginning of the film, DJ is clearly in the final stages of childhood and attempting to cross the border into adolescence. His voice cracks when he speaks, and when his friend, Chowder, asks why he doesn't want to go trick or treating, DJ says, "Maybe I'm getting too grown up." Later, when asked why he is acting so weird, DJ tells Elizabeth, his babysitter, that he's "having lots of puberty." During these scenes, Kenan employs wide shots to show multiple characters in the same frame, thus illustrating DJs dependence on adults and peers. His parents ignore his comments about the monster house across the street, interpreting his spying and observations as pubescent whims. These early scenes reflect the way many children feel at being ignored or misunderstood by adults. And by continually placing DJ and his parents in the same shot, Kenan suggests that DJ has not yet achieved the sense of autonomy that adolescents typically desire. This idea is reinforced later when DJ gets mad at Elizabeth and shouts, "Don't talk to me like I'm a baby, okay? I'm practically a grown up."

Yet, amid all the raging hormones, DJ still clings to childish traits. He has a stuffed animal, a rabbit, which he keeps on his bed. This rabbit is a symbol of his childhood innocence, and when Bones, Elizabeth's boyfriend, rips it apart with his bare hands, we sense an ending to DJ's childhood that will resonate throughout the film as he assumes such adolescent qualities as flirting with girls, taking charge in moments of crisis, and even showing compassion and understanding for Mr Nebbercracker when it becomes apparent that the neighborhood rumors surrounding his life are untrue.

In addition to fraternizing with stuffed animals, DJ hangs out with his best friend, Chowder. Chowder, who is less mature than DJ, wears a red cape around his neck, begs his friend to go trick or treating, and when his basketball bounces into Nebbercracker's yard, he cries and whines until DJ ventures toward the monster house to retrieve it. Chowder is important, however, because he acts as a foil character to DJ; he mirrors DJ's own immaturity while also reminding DJ that such behavior does not reflect the attitudes and personality traits of a mature adolescent. When DJ agrees to venture onto Nebbercracker's lawn to retrieve Chowder's basketball, Chowder shoves him closer to the house and says, "Hurry up!" Here, Chowder acts like a child, wanting the reward, but refusing to put forth the effort to achieve it. And when Nebbercracker catches DJ and drags him toward the monster house, Chowder still refuses to leave the safety of the sidewalk to help his friend. Instead, he looks around the neighborhood and begins shouting for help. These scenes illustrate that while he is still just a child, DJ is clearly more mature than Chowder.

Another example occurs after Mr Nebbercracker has suffered a heart attack and been taken away by the paramedics. The mood is somber and serious, but Kenan injects a touching moment into the scene when Nebbercracker's hand trails across the lawn and one of the blades grips his finger, like a grieving lover, and then refuses to let go. Not only does this scene continue to emphasize the special relationship between Mr Nebbercracker and the monster house, but it also presents Nebbercracker in a more sympathetic light, casting him as more of an irritated elderly man and less of a maniacal killer who hates children. This sympathy translates to the viewer, but also to DJ, who begins to show the first signs of concern and sadness for a man he previously hated and feared. As the ambulance drives away, Chowder nudges DJ in the ribs, laughs, and says, "Whoa!" DJ then looks at Chowder and shakes his head in disapproval, disgusted that his friend is unable to see the tragedy in the situation. In this shot, Kenan places DJ in the foreground, thereby diminishing Chowder and stressing the point that, unlike Chowder, DJ is beginning to respond more seriously to adult issues.

It is also important to note that Mr Nebbercracker's apparent death is the catalyst that fuels the monster house's vengeance. And it is this vengeance that initiates DJ's loss of innocence and his subsequent journey into adolescence. When Nebbercracker collapses on the front lawn, Kenan immediately pans right to a medium shot that shows the monster house slamming shut its front door. This shot is then followed by a quick cut that reveals a sudden spark, flames erupting in the fireplace, and thick, black smoke billowing out of the chimney. Clearly these intense flames, which are matched by a deafening roar, are symbolic of the house's anger at losing Mr Nebbercracker. But they also symbolize DJ's own emotions, both his fear and anxiety at watching Mr Nebbercracker collapse right in front of him, as well as his own raging hormones and feelings of confusion.

For DJ, the turning point in his maturation process occurs after he falls asleep and dreams about the monster house. In one of the film's scarier scenes, the shadow of the monster house creeps into his bedroom through the window, growing larger and larger as the screen becomes saturated in a deep red. As the shadow forms on his bedroom floor, complete with bright yellow eyes and a gaping mouth, a large black hand rises up and snatches DJ while he sleeps. Upon waking from this nightmare, DJ immediately clutches his stuffed bunny as an act of protection. If we understand the monster house to symbolize the conflicts and crises that plague children as they move from childhood into adolescence, then clearly this scene illustrates the moment when DJ moves beyond his own childhood and begins his adolescence.

Bettelheim would remind us that "objects such as dolls and toy animals are used to embody various aspects of the child's personality which are too complex, unacceptable, and contradictory for him to handle."[6] While the stuffed bunny certainly functions as an extension of DJ's personality, the monster house represents another side of his personality that is now struggling to break free from the grip of childhood. The gigantic hand that snatches DJ, and the overwhelming sense of helplessness that consumes him, certainly mirror those same feelings often experienced by children on the threshold of puberty: scared and anxious about the changes occurring inside their own bodies, moving toward an unknown future that seems incomprehensible, and feeling as if they have no control over the events in their own lives.

And it is immediately after this terrifying nightmare that Bones runs into DJ's bedroom and rips apart the stuffed bunny, a last link to DJ's childhood that he clings to in moments of terror and confusion. Following this gothic scene involving the nightmare and the loss of his treasured rabbit, DJ does seem to exhibit more adolescent characteristics. These changes coincide with Erikson's belief that we shed childhood labels and identifications in favor of new ones that society accepts as representative of an adult personality. As Erikson explains, "These new identifications are no longer characterized by the playfulness of childhood ... with dire urgency they force the young individual into choices and decisions which will, with increasing immediacy, lead to commitments 'for life.'"[7] One of these decisions will typically involve a heightened interest in the opposite sex, and DJ acts on these impulses when he meets Jenny and later saves her from the monster house.

Jenny is a self-described "two term class president at Westbrook prep" who roams suburban streets to sell candy, and in her introductory scene, she bargains with DJ's babysitter to sell her some peanut clusters and a licorice whip. In bargaining successfully with someone much older, Jenny shows herself to be cunning and intelligent. This contrast between Jenny and the two boys is made clear as Kenan then cuts to a shot of DJ and Chowder running reconnaissance in an upstairs bedroom, the floor littered with urine filled soda bottles and the boys completely exhausted as they keep watch on the monster house and scribble down notes. Jenny's introduction at this point in the film also parallels an emphasis on mixed sex groups during adolescence. Whereas children will typically associate with members of the same sex, a physical and emotional change during puberty will shift attention to members of the opposite sex. Given the intense moments DJ has endured up to this point in the film (involving his parents, his babysitter, and the monster house), it makes sense that he is now ready to interact with girls and handle the possibility of a romantic relationship.

In fact, the boys' first glimpse of Jenny is through the telescope, and there is a comic tone to the scene as DJ and Chowder fight for control of the telescope. This scene suggests themes of voyeurism and reminds viewers of the obligatory manner in which young boys often spy on girls. In film terms, scholars often refer to this act as scopophilia, which occurs in spectators when they watch films; often associated with the male gaze of Hollywood, scopophilia relates to the manner in which men (and the camera) objectify women into sexual beings. Laura Mulvey, however, reminds us that Sigmund Freud "associated scopophilia with ... a controlling and curious gaze. His particular examples center around the voyeuristic activities of children."[8] Because children are naturally curious of the world around them, they often mimic and imitate the people and events surrounding them. DJ's constant looks through the telescope signify his growing interest in the adult world, with which he seems ready to interact; and his gazing at Jenny through the telescope marks the beginning of his growing interest in the female body, one that seems natural given previous remarks in the film concerning puberty and hormones.

And since part of being an adolescent certainly means gaining an under-standing of gender roles and their accompanying characteristics, as well as feeling confident and mature in the presence of the opposite sex, it makes sense, then, that the monster house is labeled as a female. In battling the possessed house, DJ combats his own fears about girls and relationships, and his physical confrontation with the monster house symbolizes the emotional turmoil erupting inside of him. It is only while fighting the monster house and risking his life that DJ appreciates not only the innocence of being a child, from which he is so eager to escape, but also the intelligence and perseverance that one needs to become a mature and responsible adult.

When the monster house tries to eat Jenny, both DJ and Chowder save her, and in a comical scene they each grab one of her arms and pull her like a wishbone, fighting over her as if she is a prize. What follows is a series of scenes in which both boys attempt to impress Jenny with machismo and sophistication. Chowder tells her how he hates the government and adult authority. And when Jenny comments on the posters in his room, DJ says, "Posters are stupid. I was going to tear them down and put up some art." These dialogue scenes comprise the second act of the film, which, from a narrative standpoint, provides a needed lull from the action-packed first third. But the second act also builds on DJ's interest in girls and his thinking more like an adult to solve adult problems. He deduces that the smoke erupting from the monster house's chimney symbolizes some form of life residing inside the house; and he concocts a detailed plan, using technology and a prop dummy fashioned out of a vacuum cleaner, to deliver cold medicine into the monster house so it will fall asleep, whereupon the three children can sneak inside and put out the fire by extinguishing the heart. And it does not escape a child viewer's attention that DJ, Chowder, and Jenny survive their ordeal while the two police officers, who symbolize adult protection and authority, fall victim to the monster house and are promptly devoured.

The children's journey through the monster house represents a tonal shift in the film. Prior to this point, Kenan employs an equal mixture of gothic and comedic moments, fills the screen with vibrant colors, and presents most of these scenes in wide-angle shots that reveal a quiet and quaint suburban neigh-borhood. These picturesque images of an autumn day also provide the audience with a false sense of comfort and security. Even though the children experience danger, they can still search out the protection of adults or retreat to the safety of their own homes. But up until now, none of the adults has been able to offer these children the protection they need. DJ's parents have left for a conference, his babysitter is mean and indifferent, and the police officers are bumbling stooges. Having been let down for the first half of the film, especially by the two officers, the children must learn to make their own decisions and combat their fears. When the children enter the monster house they are alone in unfamiliar surroundings, and they must act resourcefully if they wish to survive.

Once the children become trapped inside the monster house, Kenan fills his scenes with close-up shots that reflect the mounting panic and claustrophobia as experienced by the children; and these scenes also create anxiety within the audience by limiting what it, too, can see inside of each shot. Yet this sequence of tight, individual shots, taken together, also reveals the enormity of the monster house. By illustrating the vastness of the house, which is then paralleled with the children's reactions to its sublime atmosphere, Kenan illustrates the naivety of the children and suggests how all children sometimes feel while living in an adult world that they don't always understand, and that, at times, seems overbearing and dominating.

To further emphasize these themes and ideas, Kenan darkens the palette of the film by saturating each scene with varying shades of gray and black. He reveals long, gloomy shadows punctuated by slivers of light that emanate from the children's flashlights. Wandering through the house, the children can barely see in front of them, and they become fearful of strange noises that surround them from all directions. As stated before, the darkness represents the unknown, those hidden parts of our identities that we have yet to discover; and it is only by venturing into the darkness, and experiencing those gothic moments, that we can allow the unknown to create the necessary anxiety and terror that form the basis for our learning experiences. These strong emotions then spark reflection and observation in the minds of children and adults, whether consciously or subconsciously, and thus allow for a deeper understanding of how the greater world functions.

Inside the monster house, the children's lives are changed forever, much like our entrance into young adulthood. The gothic moments they encounter while roaming the inside of the house help them to realize the absurdity of their childish ideas. And Kenan makes it clear through his handling of cinematography and mise-en-scène that these scary moments inside of the monster house provide clarity for DJ and help him transition from childhood into adolescence. Such a moment occurs when DJ finds assorted pictures of Mr Nebbercracker and his wife, Constance. The children huddle next to each other, and the shots are close-ups that reflect their tension and anxiety. These shots add to the sense of claustrophobia and also remind us that DJ and his friends are venturing into unfamiliar territory, not just physically, but emotionally, too. For years, DJ has believed the rumors that Mr Nebbercracker killed and ate his wife. But now, as he examines their wedding picture, he begins to doubt the neighborhood fables concerning the mysterious couple. The look of comprehension that spreads across DJ's face implies that he is beginning to understand that there might be a different version of the story. To emphasize this point, Kenan uses the yellow glare from the flashlight to frame DJ's face in a tight close-up, thus symbolizing the importance of this moment in DJ's growth and development.

Another moment occurs when DJ explores the basement and discovers Constance buried in cement and surrounded by a shrine of flowers, pictures, and cards. The atmosphere is gothic and menacing. The frame is filled with hundreds of toys; the ceiling is low and shadows slash across the characters' faces. In an especially scary moment DJ falls on top of the tomb, whereupon the cement breaks open to reveal her skeleton. This scary moment is symbolic of DJ's own realization that Mr Nebbercracker loved his wife, and that he did not, in fact, kill and eat her. For child viewers experiencing role confusion, this scene especially resonates. Every child, at some point in his or her life, has been the focus of bullying and false rumors. Every child has been shunned and misunderstood. In some ways, DJ's validation of Mr Nebbercracker provides home and comfort for any child who feels ignored and abandoned.

This scene is also important because it arrives at a point in the film when DJ is beginning to experience his own feelings of love, namely for Jenny. One gets the sense that by navigating through the monster house, and discovering the truth about Constance, DJ has now gained a deeper appreciation of love and caring that he might be able to exhibit in his own personal relationships. This burgeoning relationship between DJ and Jenny, as well as DJ's epiphanies inside the monster house, now allow him to shun his childhood fear of Mr Nebbercracker and initiate a friendly relationship with him, too. And it is during this part of the film that we really begin to see the balance of power shift as DJ acts more like a grown-up and less like a child.

When Mr Nebbercracker arrives back at the monster house, his arm in a sling and wearing a hospital gown, he becomes angry at DJ for snooping around inside his home while he was away. In the past, DJ would have screamed and run back home to the comfort of his stuffed bunny. Now, however, he puts his hands out, halts Nebbercracker, and says, "You didn't kill her, did you?" Here DJ attempts to relate to Nebbercracker and to show that he understands the old man's situation. He no longer sees Nebbercracker as a threat. He realizes that the old man's crazy actions were not spiteful or malicious, but performed to protect neighborhood children from the monster house, whose anger stems from Constance having died as a result of a confrontation with children when the house was being constructed. Just as DJ learned that Mr Nebbercracker was not the person everyone assumed him to be, so might children understand that even though they do not always understand their parents' actions, those actions might be intended to keep children from physical and emotional harm, and to help them remain safe.

To emphasize this newfound closeness and adult connection, Kenan combines DJ and Nebbercracker in a tight close-up. In a role reversal, DJ then runs after Nebbercracker and tells him, "Now it's our turn to protect you. Let her go." When Nebbercracker says, "But I'll have no one," DJ takes his hand and says, "That's not true." Clearly, in this scene, DJ has assumed a parental role and taken responsibility for the old man's safety. This scene is crucial in the evolution of DJ's development because all children want to feel important and needed. They are so used to being controlled by adults that they relish the opportunity to live vicariously through a character that not only earns an adult's respect, but also plays a vital role in ensuring that adult's survival.

Having convinced Mr Nebbercracker that remaining with the monster house might not be the smartest decision, the children and the old man flee through the neighborhood as the monster house suddenly uproots itself and chases them down the street and into a construction site. Kenan uses many low-angle shots to show the monster house as it lumbers down the street, with its gnarled tree hands reaching for the children, and its porch railings jagged and broken like fangs. This obligatory chase scene is punctuated with dramatic moments as DJ stops to help a tiring Mr Nebbercracker and, later, Nebbercracker himself tries to distract the monster house so the children can escape harm. There is even a touching scene where Nebbercracker reaches out and strokes the front porch step as if he is caressing his wife's cheek.

And while the monster house is too large to fit entirely in the same shot as Mr Nebbercracker, Kenan executes a brilliant shot that finds Nebbercracker reflected in one of the upstairs windows. Thus, even in the midst of screaming and destruction, the director still manages to remind us of the personal relationship between Constance and Mr Nebbercracker. Trembling, he tells her, "We've always known this day would come." Then, striking a match, Mr Nebbercracker assumes adult responsibility, lights three sticks of dynamite, and attempts to destroy the monster house so no one else will get hurt. These dramatic scenes add poignancy to the story, and they also remind the audience that happiness and sadness exist together, that gothic elements and suffering are a necessary part of life. There are many events in life that people might find terrifying (such as going through puberty, being bullied at school, or getting married), but understanding our emotions and then braving our way forward is what allows us to mature, to find purpose and meaning in our lives, and to develop a sense of our own identities.

But Mr Nebbercracker is unable to blow up the house. And in another role reversal, he hands DJ the sticks of dynamite with which to destroy the monster house. He says, "You have to help me, please. I know you can do it." This exchange is crucial in DJ's growth process because an adult's validation is what children oftentimes crave, and such support will help them to mature, and also to develop their self-confidence. With Nebbercracker's encouragement, DJ risks his life to save his friend. During the climactic battle, he climbs to the top of a crane, swings from a metal cable, and manages to throw the dynamite into the chimney, all of which are dangerous activities not typically associated with children.

These surges of confidence translate to other characters, as well. For example, Chowder illustrates his courage and bravery by operating a bulldozer to fight the monster house, and when the house splinters into a million pieces, he shouts, "Look who just won? It's me, the screw-up!" In a symbolic moment at the end of the film he unties his cape, which suggests that he, like DJ, is also moving away from childhood and venturing into the adolescent landscape. Jenny, too, climbs to the top of the crane with DJ and throws him the sticks of dynamite; and, of course, it was her quick thinking that, earlier in the film, freed them from the monster house when they were about to be swallowed up.

Clearly, these moments are more embedded in fantasy than in reality. After all, I don't know too many adults who would climb to the top of a crane or play with sticks of dynamite, but these moments still reveal hidden truths that children will understand and appreciate. As stated before, in attempting to complete their own identity, many adolescents will often mirror the actions and behaviors of others. This trial and error process is important because, as children, "we play roles and try out for parts we wish we could play for real, especially as we explore in adolescence."[9] In *Monster House*, DJ attempts to play many different roles. He tries to impress Jenny with his fake bravado and problem-solving skills, and he moves from being a terrified child, who constantly flees from Nebbercracker, to a resilient adolescent who protects and saves the old man from the very thing he loves most in this world, namely his departed wife now embodied in the monster house.

It is important to remember, however, that the transition from childhood to adolescence is not sudden; it is gradual and often disrupted with spurts of doubt and helplessness. *Monster House* is effective because it allows the children to doubt; it allows them to experience pain. In doing so, the film tells child viewers that these are normal emotions which are representative of the human condition. Certainly DJ exhibits moments of uncertainty, as illustrated toward the end of the film when he becomes frustrated and yells, "We are babies. What were we thinking?" And even at the end of the film, having saved an adult from almost certain death, and having won the affection of a pretty girl, DJ agrees to go trick or treating with Chowder, saying, "We've been working all night." This final scene is effective because it illustrates that DJ and Chowder are still children, albeit more mature and aware than they were at the beginning of the film. True, they are progressing into adolescence, but they have not yet shed all of their childish thoughts and ideas.

Thus, DJ's eventual conquering of the monster house reflects a newfound strength and confidence in dealing with girls, especially during the climactic battle when Jenny hugs DJ and then kisses him on the lips, which prompts DJ to say, "I kissed a girl! I kissed a girl on the lips!" We must also remember that Nebbercracker's wife (the fat lady in the circus who at one point is referred to as "The Lady as Big as a House") suffered her gruesome death as a result of childish pranks. So the monster house's vengeance is also adult anger directed at children, and we know how children often complain that adults do not under-stand or respect them.

By helping to defeat the monster house at the end of the film, DJ not only proves himself capable of handling adult pressures, but he also earns the respect and friendship of Mr Nebbercracker. In defeating the monster house, the children are not simply illustrating the old cliché that good triumphs over evil, but, instead, combating those conflicted emotions inside themselves which they must conquer in order to move beyond childhood and begin the long march toward adulthood. And by battling the monster house, which symbolizes the angst and frustrations of adolescence, the children are, in some ways, fighting themselves. This intense battle emphasizes the insecurities that often arise during the tumultuous stage of identity and role confusion.

When the monster house finally explodes at the end of the film, the implication is that all the characters have moved on to higher stages of self-development in their lives. Certainly Mr Nebbercracker is now freed from protecting the neighborhood against the monster house, and he is also able to travel and live his own life; Constance's soul is freed from her gruesome ties to the house, and her spirit is no longer angry and vengeful; and the three children, having now adopted different roles and freed themselves from a constant dependence on adult protection, are ready to use this scary experience as a stepping stone into their adolescence. The destruction of the monster house does suggest an approaching end to their childhood, but it also suggests a new beginning in which they can practice many other identities that will assist them on their path toward establishing a personal identity, securing a sense of independence, and moving successfully through adulthood.

Notes

1   Carrie Hintz and Eric L. Tribunella, *Reading Children's Literature: A Critical Introduction* (Boston: Bedford St. Martin's, 2013), 11.

2   Maria Tatar, *Enchanted Hunters: The Power of Stories in Childhood* (New York: W. W. Norton, 2009), 12.

3   Bruno Bettelheim, *The Uses of Enchantment* (New York: Vintage Books, 1989), 8.

4   Ruth Cline and William McBride, *A Guide to Literature for Young Adults* (Glenview, IL: Scott Foresman & Co., 1983), 3.

5   Erik Erikson, *Identity: Youth and Crisis* (New York: W. W. Norton, 1994), 110.

6   Bettelheim, *The Uses of Enchantment*, 55.

7   Erikson, *Identity*, 155.

8   Laura Mulvey, "Visual Pleasure and Narrative Cinema," in Leo Braudy and Marshall Cohen (eds), *Film Theory and Criticism* (New York: Oxford University Press, 1999), 835.

9   Erikson, *Identity*, 110.

Bibliography

Bettelheim, Bruno. *The Uses of Enchantment*. New York: Vintage Books, 1989.

Cline, Ruth and William McBride. *A Guide to Literature for Young Adults*. Glenview, IL: Scott Foresman & Co., 1983.

Erikson, Erik. *Identity: Youth and Crisis.* New York: W. W. Norton, 1994.

Hintz, Carrie and Eric L. Tribunella. *Reading Children's Literature: A Critical Introduction.* Boston: Bedford St. Martin's, 2013.

Monster House. Dir. Gil Kenan. 2006. Culver City, CA: Sony Pictures Home Entertainment, 2006. DVD.

Mulvey, Laura. "Visual Pleasure and Narrative Cinema." In Leo Braudy and Marshall Cohen (eds), *Film Theory and Criticism*, 833–44. New York: Oxford University Press, 1999.

Tatar, Maria. *Enchanted Hunters: The Power of Stories in Childhood.* New York: W. W. Norton, 2009.

10

The Wild and the Cute: Disney Animation and Environmental Awareness

David Whitley
Cambridge University

A number of important recent animated films have focused thoughtfully on images of how human experience intersects with different elements of the natural order. Pixar's *Wall-E* imagines an earth where natural life forms have been all but eliminated in an apocalypse of trash, while, slightly earlier, *Finding Nemo* recreated a world of breathtaking beauty under the oceans to stage a drama that registered human interactions with the sea environment in probing forms. Warner Brothers' *Happy Feet* blends a narrative about a penguin, who does not fit into his avian community, with images of the human drive for progress, increasingly threatening natural diversity in the hitherto pristine environment of the Antarctic. Dreamwork's *The Bee Movie* is a bee's eye view of human needs and consumption. The film explores its central conceit of a bee crossing over into human society through a string of gags and comic twists that play on differences between the social order of bee and human communities. And the films that have emanated from the extraordinarily creative Ghibli Studio in Japan have long been preoccupied with issues that connect the human protagonists of its movies in profound and challenging ways with the natural environment. Given the wealth of high quality animated productions that have recently focused on environmentally sensitive issues, then, it is worth asking whether there may be a tradition within popular, mainstream feature animation that such films are able to draw on in selective and distinctive ways. This chapter will argue that such a tradition does indeed exist and that its origins (perhaps rather surprisingly given the benighted status that is often accorded to Disney's ideological credentials in recent writing) lie in the experiments that Disney undertook with the animated feature form in the classic period of its development.

Before we look at what qualities might constitute this tradition, we should examine briefly a few of the core ideas of environmental criticism that may be relevant in assessing the credentials of these films. There are, I think, two notions that are especially important here. The first of these is the concept of "androcentrism," which defines a set of unexamined assumptions that many writers of environmental criticism who focus particularly on the role of the arts have seen it as their task to challenge or displace. "Androcentrism" is a broad term drawing together ways of looking at the world that place human concerns and interests at their centre. To a certain degree, of course, androcentrism is inevitable, since we cannot acquire a disembodied perspective that views the world with divine omniscience and detachment. But the term, as it is commonly deployed, foregrounds and critiques the way post-enlightenment assumptions about human prerogatives have tended to marginalize other—often older— views, in which humans were seen attempting to maintain a more harmonious and integrated relationship with other life forms. Post-enlightenment philoso- phies have rather, it is asserted, underpinned an implicit project of mastery of the natural world.

The second term often invoked to support the critique of androcentric ideas is a more loosely defined concept of "wildness." "Wildness" is not just a particular kind of landscape or space in nature that has managed to preserve a degree of separateness from human civilization. It is also a process, the complex, apparently unregulated interaction of all life forms in a given area that consti- tutes in totality the form of the natural world. "Wildness," as Patrick Murphy has defined it, is profoundly antithetical to the aesthetic Disney evolved in its feature films:

> Disney's full-length animated feature films reveal a consistent, although incoherent, worldview on nature and women that is escapist and andro- centric. The escapism is based on denying wild nature as an integral part of the biosphere at the world level and as part of individual character at the personal level. The denial of wild nature serves the fabrication of a timeless, universal and unchanging order articulated in part by means of cultural values and generalizations.[1]

Murphy brings the concepts of "androcentrism" and "wildness" together in his critique of Disney films. The use of archetypes and fables to affirm apparently universal (but actually culturally imbued) human values within Disney films, it is argued, is effectively a denial of wild nature. Images of wild animals are subsumed within the human personalities that are superimposed on them, while human affinities with the wild are erased in plots that assert the essential timelessness of the qualities that define human character. Even the landscape is transformed in the rampant androcenticism that drives the representation of the world in Disney movies. Murphy accords with Richard Schickel's view that, just as the "creative will" inherent in anthropomorphizing fantasy denies real animal nature in Disney, so too "all inner conflicts about the nature of the land" are "similarly resolved … he always and only showed us a clean land. Indeed the whole wide world was scrubbed clean when we saw it through his eyes."[2]

This is a memorable phrase and the twin concepts of wildness and andro-centrism open up critical perspectives on Disney animation that could enable us to see the films with new eyes. But these concepts have tended to be deployed in the critical literature from a rather narrow perspective thus far, and it seems to me that they do not tell the whole story. My main objection to them is that the judgments inherent in the use of these terms have been based to far too great an extent within a paradigm of "realism" that is only partially applicable to the kinds of film narratives that Disney—and indeed other major animators—have developed. Such criticism has tended to treat the realistic portrayal of the world as the ideal Disney films are striving for, in other words, and to see the play of fantasy elements within this realism as a distortion that falsifies and imposes the human-centred values of the "creative will." Without denying the importance of the realistic texture with which Disney managed to imbue the animated medium, or the commercial appeal that this quality successfully embodied, it seems to me that realism is only one of the aesthetic principles driving the Disney project. To elevate realism to the status of standard-bearer of truth is rather to put the cart before the horse. Animated movies were founded on the freedom they encapsulated to play with "natural" form and space. Disney may have repositioned that freedom closer to the realism of mainstream cinema, but he never abandoned the aesthetic licence bestowed by images that were drawn. We are in danger of misunderstanding the nature of animated art, if we invoke too narrow a criterion for representational truth in relation to the films.

I would like to propose what I think is a better way of understanding films in the classic Disney canon, before reaching any judgment about the quality of environmental consciousness the films may render. There are, I think, three major elements in the Disney aesthetic, and it is the interrelationship of these elements, as much as the subordination of one to the other, that is key to understanding fully the films' impact. I shall call these three elements the "poetic," the "fabular," and the "realistic".

The poetic element involves using images whose primary function is emotive, metaphorical, or symbolic. Such elements do not necessarily undermine the realistic texture of the film, but their principal effect is not naturalistic. In the deftly orchestrated scene when Baloo appears to have died in *The Jungle Book*, for instance, the tropical landscape is transformed by rain falling. The persistent heavy shower that continues until Baloo is understood by all the protagonists to be still alive is not imposed in a jarringly unnatural way—indeed it is prepared for by the rolling thunder and forks of lightning that punctuate the epic struggle with the tiger, Shere Kahn, in the preceding scene. But the effect of the rain—which is gentle and persistent rather than torrential—is to draw a misty veil over the landscape that provides a backdrop to the theatrical circle within which Baloo's body is displayed. This, combined with suggestive lighting, produces an image of a contained space that imbues Baloo's body with a special aura, a natural equivalent for the ritual space of the funeral service, perhaps. The musical accompaniment of church organ music and the conventional linking of rain with tears complete this chain of associations. While, in one sense, this poetic use of natural imagery could be seen as clearly "androcentric," in that it stages natural processes to evoke emotions in relation to what is essentially a human drama, there is no reason why such poetic techniques should, in themselves, induce a false consciousness or lack of imaginative connection with the environment. Indeed poetry, in its wider domain, has long been thought of as an art form whose roots and inspiration are closely entwined with the natural world. I will come back to this issue when discussing *Bambi* later.

The fable element in animation is clearly equally important. Very few of Disney's animated films are constructed around an even remotely realistic plotline, and those involving animals almost invariably make use of the classic fable convention that allows animals to talk. The fable, in all its many variants, is essentially a reductive narrative form, and its association with memorable, often epigrammatic, kinds of moralizing might appear to lend credence to Murphy's claim that Disney's fable-like narratives tend to erase difference in their assertion of universal traits in human character and moral constants. However the fable is also a highly flexible narrative form, whose implications and meanings can vary greatly according to the intentions of its author, the culturally attuned predispositions of its readers and the visual images with which it is often accompanied. Although the animals in traditional fables are more emblematic than realistic, and often serve as thinly disguised substitutes for human dilemmas and understandings, their animal nature remains important. Aesop's fables, in particular, tend to focus on strategies for survival in a harsh world, as much on conventional human ethics, and they foreground the implacable cruelty, or amorality, of the natural order. In more extended versions of the fable, such as the narratives produced by Chaucer and Henryson in the Middle Ages, realistic observation of animals' habits and behavior was built into the spare outlines of the traditional story. And everywhere in the domain of the fable one finds opportunities exploited for (often playful or ironic) reflection on differences between human culture and the natural order, as well as parallels used to highlight ethical points in memorable form. Hence, narratives whose form is similar to that of the fable may not be wholly or uniformly androcentric. Elements of wildness are often present as a counterpoint to human aspirations and concerns, offering a corrective to the idea that human culture is either autonomous or self-sufficient. The fable is also a provocation to thought and, although Disney films may be conceived as more founded on sentiment, the films may still include spaces for reflection. Some of these are more obvious and conventional perhaps—*The Lion King*'s framing of its dynastic narrative with the ecologically grounded trope of the "circle of life," for instance. Some can be more quirky and offhand. When the apes encounter the humans' camp for the first time in Disney's *Tarzan*, for instance, they exclaim "The horror!"—a deliberate echoing and pastiche of Conrad's famous use of the phrase in *Heart of Darkness*. This self-consciously contrived allusion is one of a series of devices in the film that play on differences between human culture and the natural world.

The realistic dimension of animation has certainly become a crucial element within films that engage with environmental issues, even though, as I am arguing, too exclusive a critical concern with this dimension may be limiting. It is clear, nevertheless, that the creative and technological resources brought to bear on achieving a realistic texture for images can be a way of honouring the distinctive qualities of the natural forms depicted and of giving more emotional weight to the theme of nature.

There is a world of difference between the *Mickey Mouse* shorts and *Bambi*, for instance. *Bambi*, indeed, would not have achieved the depth of its emotional alignment with conservation issues without the care that was taken to render animal movement and environmental detail with accuracy as well as poetic grace. Even in the first Disney feature film *Snow White*, where the fairy tale source provides a narrative structure closer to fable than in *Bambi*, individual animal species and movements are far more carefully differentiated than in any earlier animation. As a result, the playful and joyous pastoral elements that are used to amplify the heroine's innocent alignment with nature in the forest scenes acquire more emotional weight and become integral to the film as a whole. As the latter example makes apparent though, it is the interrelationship of the realistic dimension with the fable and poetic modes that produces the film's full emotional effect and range of meanings. It is all too easy, as many commentators have done, to see nature in *Snow White* simply as subsumed into the heroine's project of domesticating her feral dwarves and animal friends, without acknowledging sufficiently the emotional weight of the larger themes that are bound up with the heroine's plight.[3] *Snow White* embodies an ideal of harmonious integration between the human and natural orders, manifested with playful, comic élan in the housework scenes within the dwarves' cottage. But the animals' lives remain rooted in the forest rather than the house, to which they are drawn through kinship with Snow White's natural innocence. When humans other than Snow White enter the cottage, the animals withdraw shyly back into their natural forest domain. The realism in the film, which reproduces animal movements and different species' characteristics with care, also acknowledges implicitly the animals' independence and the essential separateness of the realm of nature.

The full potential of this animated realism for creating an emotive quality of environmental consciousness could not be achieved, however, without experimenting further and developing a different kind of film idiom. This second stage of development can be seen most clearly in *Bambi*, which, from the period of its re-release in the 1950s, has consistently been amongst the most popular of all Disney's feature animations.[4] As a project, *Bambi* also posed some of the most fundamental challenges for the animation team amongst all the early classic features. Disney had worked on *Bambi*, "in fits and starts" from early in 1935,[5] and he detailed some of his best staff to develop the project with urgency from late 1938, wanting to build on the phenomenal success of *Snow White* with an equally prestigious, though in many ways quite different, film. When the first formal story conference for *Bambi* was convened in September 1938, Disney's executive producer, Dave Hand, announced that the storyline would be sufficiently developed for the animation process to begin on 1 December and that the film would be scheduled for release a year later. In fact, however, the film took a further four years before it could be brought to the screen, and even then required some quite severe, last minute editing because there was not time to complete some longer sequences that were planned for the middle section. A variety of factors contributed to this massively extended production period, but perhaps the most important of these was a growing awareness that the animators needed to discover a new visual idiom for the film to be able to realize its potential and do justice to its underlying themes. The realism, that had been such a distinctive element within *Snow White*, needed to be taken a stage further and combined sensitively with the poetic element for the images to be adequately responsive to the theme of nature at the film's heart. Two of the film's leading animators, Ollie Johnstone and Mark Thomas, put it like this in retrospect:

> Walt was demanding eloquence from images that he hadn't even imagined before. He was no longer pushing for extra characters, comic situations, and funny attitudes as much as feelings and sensations we each carry away from visiting the deep woods.[6]

The "new eloquence" that Johnstone and Thomas refer to here was required in order to make the sensuous experience of nature ("the feelings and sensations" of "the deep woods") palpable for viewers. But this eloquence goes beyond the care, research, and technical development undertaken in capturing the movement and forms of wildlife with a verisimilitude not previously seen in the animated medium. Indeed, one of the breakthroughs along the road to discovering an idiom within which the animators could respond to the demands of the films' action with assurance was the inclusion of a less detailed, more fluid visual style that owed something to the poetic technique of oriental painting and was pioneered by the Chinese born illustrator Ty Wong. When it was discovered that the drive for increasing realistic detail was producing images with a surface texture that was too densely cluttered to be truly evocative, Wong showed the other animators how the natural environment could be rendered with fewer brushstrokes, in a still careful but freer style, that better captured the feeling and mood of the scene.[7]

How then did this new animated idiom work in practice, and to what extent was it successful in embedding a genuine environmental awareness within a commercial, child-oriented aesthetic, that made animals as cute as possible to secure young viewers' identification with them? To assess this crucial critical question, I shall examine in some detail one of the most iconic and moving scenes in the film, the death of Bambi's mother. Here, the case for an "androcentric" drama designed to generate exclusively human sentiment from a scene invoking merely the trappings of "the wild" would seem to be at its strongest. A large part of the emotional power of this scene clearly derives from the way that it deals so sensitively, yet feelingly, with one of the most primary fears of childhood, the loss of one's mother. And yet, as I hope to show, this highly charged human theme does not, in fact, erase environmental awareness. Rather it acts to deepen the emotional resonance of that awareness through the multi-faceted modes of identification that it makes available.

What kinds of environmental awareness thread through the poignant drama of the mother's death in *Bambi* then? The most obvious and powerful of these is the way the whole of the action is premised on the animals' need to find food resources in periods of intense scarcity, if they are to survive. The reason Bambi and his mother are in the meadow when the hunters open fire on them is because they are desperate to taste the first new grass of spring. They have been presented, realistically, as half starved towards the end of the winter season. "I'm hungry, Mother," says the young Bambi plaintively at the end of the preceding scene; and shots of the deer stripping the bark from trees earlier on, when the frozen ground will yield no other sustenance, make it clear to the child viewer why this should be. There is a strong sense then, as in tragedy, of a predeter-mined set of forces and contingencies that are driving the action in this scene.

The fundamental law of the natural world that this exemplifies–that wild creatures are forced to take more risks as their food resources dwindle–is rendered in more subtle forms than are perhaps immediately obvious, however. The scene in which Bambi and his mother begin eating the new grass in the middle of the meadow, for instance, is intercut with a high-angle shot that is, I think, unique in the film. For almost the whole of the rest of the film the camera remains closely aligned to the animal protagonists, usually in medium range or close up, and consistently from an angle level with their bodies. The effect of this stylistic constraint is to align the viewer emotionally and in terms of point of view with the detail of the small creatures' lives. Here in the meadow sequence, though, the camera suddenly cuts back and upwards, enacting the equivalent of a crane shot in live action cinema. The deer are now seen from a greater distance and from above, with the large open expanse of the meadow environment showcased around them. Why this shift of cinematic perspective? What are its effects? One notable effect, I think, is to isolate the clump of new grass within the still snow-covered terrain of the rest of the meadow, emphasizing how scarce the food still is at this early stage of spring. Another equally important effect, perhaps initially even more striking, is to emphasize how exposed the deer's bodies are within the open expanse of whiteness that surrounds them. This sense of exposure, rendered with more graphic intensity by the high-angle shot, alerts the viewer to incipient danger, while the accompanying soundtrack and the alert, nervous movement of the deer as they raise their heads from eating reinforce this. In a sense, then, the whole drama is played out with a hyper-keen visual and aural awareness of the relationship between the animals and their environment, displayed with a strong emotional charge for the audience. This awareness shifts in terms of meaning and perspective when the deer flee, after the hunters' first shot is fired. The detail of the meadow scene is now dramatically recast as a more uniform white background blur: the fleeing deer focus solely on obstacles, such as rocks and breaks in the terrain in front of them, negotiating these at speed as they attempt to reach the safety of the forest. The viewers' gaze is forced to prioritize only what is meaningful in the environment from the point of view of the deer's escape. Finally, as the tracking camera follows the lone form of Bambi back into the thicket that is his safe "home" in the middle of the forest, the snow begins to fall again.

The snow falling at the end of this scene plays a vital role in securing its affective power and it would be easy to read this as a poetic device that essentially restores a human-centered perspective to the drama, securing identification with the protagonist's pained bewilderment at his mother's death. Even if we take this view, however, it is worth saying that the symbolic associations of the snow, here, work with a wonderfully delicate, evocative power. The purity of the snow's form seems to chime with the sense of innocent nature that is at the film's heart, even as its coldness serves as a reminder of death. Indeed, although in many ways of a different order, the artistry of the scene is reminiscent of the way James Joyce uses the image of snow at the end of his great short story, *The Dead*. There too, a sense of loss and emptiness is tempered with the apprehension of something larger and more all encompassing which, if not exactly consolatory, seems momentarily to lift and purify the spirit. Yet there is another dimension to the emotive power of the snow in *Bambi* that is easily overlooked. In a more prosaic, literally "down to earth" way, the snow links to the images of physical hardship that have preceded the meadow scene and driven the animals' need to take risks. Thus a harder edged, environmental perspective remains thoroughly rooted in the poetic texture of the films' most effective imagery.

I have dwelt on the multifaceted nature of this iconic scene in *Bambi* at some length because it seems to me exemplary of early Disney animators' discovery that images within a sentimental, comic art form could be charged with meanings connecting potently with a particular kind of environmental vision. Since the plotline of *Bambi* is more oriented towards natural history than fable (though there is certainly no shortage of fantastical elements), it is through the mode of the "poetic" that these meanings are largely drawn into effective focus. In other plots, such as *The Jungle Book* or *The Lion King*, where a fable element is more predominant, the poetic mode tends to be less strongly developed. But the potential for combining any of these modes to forge connections with environmental themes was realized in early Disney films in ways that seem to me to provide a legacy in the realm of popular art which later animators have been able to draw on and redefine. To demonstrate this link to contemporary animation I would like to conclude with a few comments about Pixar's *Finding Nemo*.

Although in some ways they are very different kinds of film, there are some marked similarities between *Finding Nemo* and *Bambi* in terms of both structure and visual texture. In both films the plotline involves a young animal losing its mother in a violent scene at an early stage of the creature's development (whilst still an egg, in fact, in Nemo's case). Both films display a sustained and detailed interest in the flora and fauna of the particular kind of natural environment within which the action takes place (although the underwater world of the ocean in *Finding Nemo* obviously exhibits very different qualities to the forest environment in *Bambi*). Both films also shape key elements of their dramatic narratives around images depicting human interventions within the natural environment. As I have argued elsewhere, *Finding Nemo* is less single-mindedly focused than *Bambi* on the destructive effects of human interactions with nature.[8] But the central motif of the film—a wild fish being taken into captivity in a marine aquarium to serve human aesthetic needs—generates satire and moral opprobrium to some degree. And other images—such as the detritus of war evinced in unexploded mines and the intensive, industrial-scale fishing depicted at the end—connect to potent environmental themes of our age. Perhaps the most interesting line of connection between the two films, however, resides in the quality of the images, rather than more directly in their meaning. The animation team on *Finding Nemo* were quite explicit in acknowledging their debt to *Bambi* and the sense that they were trying to create a film in the same tradition. An immense amount of creative and technical energy was deployed in trying to get the underwater environment to look and feel as realistic as possible, but this look was also stylized—given a "poetic" dimension—by drawing on the visual texture of *Bambi* for inspiration. As Sharon Calahan, director of photography put it:

For us, in addition to defining the elements that tell the brain "this is water", we wanted to create a visual style that evoked the soft quality that made *Bambi* so beautiful … We knew we were getting there when an art director, who was seeing our work for the first time, reacted by using the "Bambi" word. We consider that to be the highest of compliments.[9]

The poetic "softness" and beauty of this visual style is capable of creating a sense of awe in the viewer in relation to the natural world depicted. The realism of the film, which is also a way of honouring the claims of that world on our attention, is thus harnessed to a potentially more profound set of feelings. Not all recent animations achieve (or indeed necessarily attempt) to embody such profound undertones for their comic and sentimental plots. But *Finding Nemo* shows what animation can do at its best, and the combination of fable, realism, and poetic forms that Disney pioneered in relation to the natural world is proving to be an immensely versatile and probing territory for contemporary animators to develop.

Notes

1   Patrick Murphy, "'The Whole Wide World was Scrubbed Clean': the Androcentric Animation of Denatured Disney," in Elizabeth Bell, Lynda Haas and Laura Sells (eds), *From Mouse to Mermaid: the Politics of Film, Gender, and Culture* (Bloomington: Indiana University Press, 1995), 126.

2   Richard Schickel, *The Disney Version: the Life, Times, Art and Commerce of Walt Disney* (London: Pavilion Books, 1968), 53.

3   Eleanor Byrne and Martin McQuillan, *Deconstructing Disney* (London: Pluto Press, 1999).

4   Janet Wasko, *Understanding Disney: The Manufacture of Fantasy* (Cambridge: Polity Press, 2001).

5   Neal Gabler, *Walt Disney: the Triumph of the American Imagination* (New York: Vintage Books, 2006).

6   Ollie Johnston and Frank Thomas, *Walt Disney's 'Bambi': the Story and the Film* (New York: Stewart, Tabori and Chang, 1990), 143.

7   Gabler, *Walt Disney*, 302.

8   David Whitley, *The Idea of Nature in Disney Animation: from Snow White to WALL·E.* (Aldershot and Burlington: Ashgate, 2012).

9   Mark Cotta Vaz, *The Art of Finding Nemo* (San Francisco: Chronicle Books, 2003), 21.

Bibliography

Bambi. Dir. James Alger, et al. Burbank, CA: Walt Disney Productions, 1942. Film

The Bee Movie. Dir. Steve Hickner and Simon Smith. Glendale, CA: Dreamworks, 2007. Film.

Byrne, Eleanor and Martin McQuillan. *Deconstructing Disney*. London: Pluto Press, 1999.

Conrad, Joseph. *Heart of Darkness*. 1900. Harmondsworth: Penguin, 1995.

Cotta Vaz, Mark. *The Art of Finding Nemo*. San Francisco: Chronicle Books, 2003.

Finding Nemo. Dir. Andrew Stanton and Lee Unrich. Emeryville, CA: Pixar, 2003. Film.

Gabler, Neal. *Walt Disney: the Triumph of the American Imagination*. New York: Vintage Books, 2006.

Happy Feet. Dir. George Miller and Warren Coleman. Burbank, CA: Warner Brothers, 2006. Film.

Johnstone, Ollie and Frank Thomas. *Walt Disney's 'Bambi': the Story and the Film*. New York: Stewart, Tabori and Chang, 1990.

Joyce, James. "The Dead," in *Dubliners*. 1914. Harmondsworth: Penguin, 1972.

The Jungle Book. Dir. Wolfgang Reitherman. Burbank, CA: Disney Studios, 1967. Film.

The Lion King. Dir. Roger Allers and Rob Minkoff. CA: Disney Studios, 1994. Film.

Murphy, Patrick "'The Whole Wide World was Scrubbed Clean': the Androcentric Animation of Denatured Disney," in Elizabeth Bell, Lynda Haas, and Laura Sells (eds), *From Mouse to Mermaid: the Politics of Film, Gender, and Culture*, 125–34. Bloomington: Indiana University Press, 1995.

Schickel, Richard. *The Disney Version: the Life, Times, Art and Commerce of Walt Disney*. London: Pavilion Books, 1986.

Snow White and the Seven Dwarves. Dir. William Cottrell et al. Burbank, CA: Disney Studios, 1937. Film.

Tarzan. Dir. Chris Buck and Kevin Lima. Burbank, CA: Disney Studios, 1999. Film.

Wall·E. Dir. Andrew Stanton. Emeryville, CA: Pixar, 2008. Film.

Wasko, Janet. *Understanding Disney: The Manufacture of Fantasy* Cambridge: Polity Press, 2001.

Whitley, David. *The Idea of Nature in Disney Animation: from Snow White to WALL·E*. Aldershot and Burlington: Ashgate, 2012.

Conclusion: Criticism and Multicultural Children's Films

Iris Shepard and Ian Wojcik-Andrews

St. Gregory University and Eastern Michigan University

Based upon the 2008 Washington D.C. conference of the same name, the anthology *Kidding Around: The Child in Film and Media* provides valuable insights into the intersections between children's media, the child spectator, literary and electronic media criticism, and history. Organized into three fascinating main sections—Rites of Passage and Impasse, Childhood as Text, and Disney and Its Progeny—*Kidding Around* uses environmentalist, autist, ageist, psychoanalytic, historical, and ideological forms of criticism to examine literary texts and self-help manuals such as Noel Streatfeild's *Love in a Mist* and Bill O'Reilly's *The O'Reilly Factor for Kids* as well as the kinds of physical spaces children occupy such as playgrounds. Primarily though, *Kidding Around* examines representations of the child in Hollywood centric films such as *Bambi, Monster House, Finding Nemo, The Sixth Sense, Mercury Rising, Lolita,* and *Happiness.* This conclusion first makes some general comments about the importance of *Kidding Around* in the history of children's film criticism. We then want to suggest some of the political and textual directions future critics of children's films might take.

In terms of the history of children's film criticism, *Kidding Around* is an important anthology as it stands at the head of a long line of important works of criticism that stretch back to the revolutionary years of 1917 when *The Cinema: Its Present Position and Future Possibilities* was published. That colossal book emerged as a response to the fear that spectators in general and young viewers especially would be adversely affected by film's ability to reflect the social, political, and moral unrest of the time. Over the course of the twentieth century, children's film criticism underwent several broad developments. In the 1950s, for example, cultural anthropological forms of criticism as practiced by Margaret Mead and Martha Wolfenstein influenced the study of children's films. Unsurprisingly, feminist studies were brought to bear on children's films in the 1960s. This changed by the 1970s and 1980s when left-oriented critics such as Jack Zipes looked at the commercialization of fairy tales and fairy tale films and progressive-thinking organizations such as the Children's Literature Association emerged as the champion of children's literature and media. Back in 2000, the question was asked: how will children's film criticism develop in the twenty-first century?[1] An exemplary anthology of critical essays, *Kidding Around* clearly answers that question and thus when future scholars look back at these twentieth- and early twenty-first century developments, *Kidding Around* will appear on the critical horizon as a significant landmark, a major contributor to the history of children's film criticism.

What new directions might children's film criticism take after *Kidding Around*? What pressing areas of investigation jostle for attention, demanding a say in the conversations about children's films? One such area for children's cinema and film critics to explore further is "A radical, polycentric multiculturalism … [that] … cannot simply be nice, like a suburban barbecue to which a few people of color have been invited."[2] In the book from which this quote comes, *Unthinking Eurocentrism: Multiculturalism and the Media*, Ella Shohat and Robert Stam unpack the legacies of colonialism, especially in relation to film. Though not condemning Hollywood completely, they nonetheless argue that First World cinemas historically and currently deploy metaphors of conquest, narratives of discovery, and images of animalization and infantilization that reinforce Eurocentrist ideologies in contemporary mass media. Simply identifying and critiquing cultural stereotypes is insufficient, they argue, if we are to evolve toward a "polycentric multiculturalism" that includes Thirdist cinemas and a radical pedagogy, a "kind of pedagogic jujitsu in the form of the classroom hijacking of media texts."[3] For Shohat and Stam, thinking about the polycentrist, multicultural classrooms of tomorrow requires unthinking the Eurocentrist classrooms of today. We argue that studying multicultural children's films from critical perspectives that challenge hegemonic notions of childhood, the child, and their relation to history, class, race, gender, and age, is both a small step on the path toward a liberatory pedagogy of multicultural children's films and a giant step toward the kind of "polycentric multiculturalism" envisaged by Shohat and Stam.

To that end, we would call upon future children's film critics to continue talking about all things multicultural, especially as they relate to the relationship between multicultural children's films and history. The tendency, in relation to multicultural children's literature, is to write about the different cultural groups in the US as though they were separate historic and historical categories—African American, Asian American, Latino American, and Jewish-American—each with its own set of concerns. On the one hand, this approach to the writing of history is consistent with the need to highlight lost, forgotten, or underprivileged authors, critics, writers, and texts of all kinds that have been otherwise buried beneath the rubble of mainstream, dominant culture. Unearthing and bringing back to life these otherwise long dead and forgotten texts that echo the trials and tribulations of a culture's rich but otherwise dormant past is central to a progressive politics of diversity. On the other hand, isolating the various histories of minority cultures, highlighting their most traumatic as well as uplifting and inspiring moments, canonizing a few of their chosen literary, philosophical, and filmic texts, and producing a linear, teleological history of that culture surely homogenizes real cultural difference. Similarly in film studies: periodizing the incredible diversity of cinematic history, searching for broad trends among film producing nations, and canonizing a few exemplary movies from a range of cultures tends to elide the enormous contributions of others, whose efforts are typically lost in the historical record, and privileges the contributions of the few. It seems to us that the relationship between children's film criticism, multicultural children's films, and historiography is one pressing area that critics might to explore.

Several essays in *Kidding Around* tantalizingly provide a glimpse at an important aspect of children's films that we think needs bringing into full focus: endings. To highlight how mainstream Hollywood films have such different endings than many international films, we will briefly compare and contrast *Harry Potter and the Deathly Hallows 2* with a Thirdist film such as *Osama*. *Harry Potter and the Deathly Hallows 2* is what Richard Neupert, in *The End: Narration and Closure in the Cinema* calls a "closed" film.[4] Neupert goes on to say that

> The Closed Text film has the most secure ending of the four groups and satisfies conventional demands for unity and resolution. Closed Text films are historically dominant because their narrative modes derive from classical traditions [and] they have proven commercially successful. [Their] resolution, with an epilogue as a closure device, returns the viewer to a pleasurable spectator position.[5]

Neupert's discussion of closed text films is clearly relevant to a discussion of *Harry Potter and the Deathly Hallows Part 2*. At the conclusion of *Harry Potter and the Deathly Hallows 2* Harry defeats Voldemort. Harry marries Ginny

Weasly. Ron, her brother, marries Hermione. Both couples have children who attend Hogwarts. Though the children's presence suggests a new beginning—the trope of the child here signifying a fresh start in the ceaseless struggle of good over evil—the married couples are really the focus of the end, not the children. Overall, at the end of the movie, conventional, Aristotelian demands for unity and resolution are satisfied.

But, to borrow Frank Kermode's phrase, our sense of this type of ending is problematic for a number of reasons. These reasons include the perpetuation of hegemonic views of the family and the erasure of race and other differences. The timeless image of familial harmony is surely contradicted by the historical reality from which that image of the family emerged. Certainly in Marxist-feminist terms, the nuclear family has played a less than progressive role throughout history and yet is offered to audiences at the end of *Harry Potter and the Deathly Hallows 2*, as it is in many other corporate movies directed toward the young, as a sanctuary, a hiding place from which to avoid all that is wrong in the world today. These days blended families, grand parenting, gay marriage and families, television shows and movies about changing parental roles, and the like, all seem to suggest a new beginning in familial configurations and social relations to which the world's most popular movie franchise and its concluding image of a traditional nuclear family under siege but alive and well nonetheless seems breathtakingly indifferent.

Endings as exemplified by *Harry Potter and the Deathly Hallows 2* are important to discuss for other reasons. The closed ending silences discussions of ethnicity and race. Many First World children's films simply skirt both issues. True, in a response to criticism about its seemingly racist scenes in films like *Dumbo* and *The Jungle Book*, Disney acknowledges other cultures through films like *Pocahontas*, *Aladdin*, and *Mulan*. But Disney continues to narrate history from a white, mainstream, centrist position; multicultural characters are Westernized and "whitened" or portrayed in animal form. In Disney's recent *Princess and the Frog*, we see the first African-American princess, but the treatment of race here is problematic because Tiana spends over two-thirds of the film as a frog. Thus the Harry Potter series' representation of racial tension in a culture that likes to deny the continued existence of racism and treat it as a relic last seen in the 1960s Civil Rights Movement might be seen as a bold choice, one that allows readers, viewers, and critics ample opportunities to discuss a pressing social issue. Several grassroots organizations are formed to fight discrimination in the series including the Society for Elfish Welfare and the Order of the Phoenix. However, the all-important ending of *Harry Potter and the Deathly Hallows 2* asserts a racial hierarchy that privileges whiteness and minimizes the racial diversity for which the main characters fought so hard. To state the obvious: Harry, Ron, Hermione, and their children are the triumphant victors who survive the apocalypse.

The issue of social class is relevant here too. A further area where the ending of *HPDH2* serves to perpetuate the dominant ideology is in shifting all attention away from marginalized populations such as the house elves and the Giants that throughout the series have held prominent positions. John Fiske in *Television Culture* explores the role representations of grotesque bodies serve in opposing the dominant ideology: "The grotesque realism of the ugly, distorted body is therefore opposed semiotically and politically to the dominant. It is an appropriate means of articulating the social experience of many subordinated and oppressed groups in capitalism."[6] In other words, the inclusion of grotesquely shaped bodies and distorted forms of speech is an attempt to reflect the experiences of powerless groups, including their abuse by the dominant class. But again, despite the uprisings of the social classes represented by the nonhuman groups who populate Hogwarts, it is the upright, normal bodies of white, healthy, human characters to which spectators are asked to bear witness at the narrative's end.

Third World, or Thirdist, films such as *Osama, Turtles Can Fly, A Time For Drunken Horses,* and the like, are what Neupert calls Open Text films, those which "spring from aesthetic and political traditions that evade dominant ideological forms of the narrative film just as the closed text could be argued to reinforce dominant aesthetic and ideological modes of representation."[7] Kurdish cinema, of which *Osama* and *Turtles Can Fly* are representative examples, are multicultural children's films that not only challenge traditional ideas about film aesthetics, narrative teleology, and spectatorship (how we think children should feel at the end) but film making itself. Unlike their First World counterparts, Thirdist films directed toward the young recognize that they are always already, as Althusser would say, caught up in the ideological nature of the camera as an instrument of bourgeois ideology. In short, Third films aesthetically and politically destabilize the norms and conventions associated with film such as the function of the happy ending and the role of the child spectator and in doing so create a space for more open-ended discussions about children's cinema that suggest the new directions it might take in the twenty-first century.

Siddiq Barmak's 2003 *Osama*, starring Marina Golbahari in the title role, illustrates many of these points. Set in Afghanistan during the Taliban rule,

Osama is a 12-year-old Afghan girl whose hair is cut by her mother so that she looks like a boy and thus can survive under the misogynistic policies of the Taliban. Originally, Barmak produced a relatively happy ending in which Osama escapes the clutches of the elderly Mullah to whom she is forcibly wedded at the end of the movie. Barmak changed the film's ending though feeling that ironically an unhappy ending would be more consistent with the reality of Osama and her mother's life under Taliban rule. The revised ending has Osama alive but trapped in the Mullah's home with his three other wives. In the penultimate scene, we see the Mullah washing and bathing, a sign that the brutal marriage between him and the 12-year-old Osama has been consummated against her will. Barmak's unhappy ending of course is not merely supposed to make us angry but move us to outrage and, thus, action. In this regard, the unhappy albeit culturally and historically accurate conclusion is, in Neupert's terms, open: no heroic prince storming the castle to free the trapped Osama is provided for young audiences.

In First World children's films, happy endings resolve most if not all of a film's thematic conflicts and in the process reifies the dominant ideologies of the era and the historical conditions within which the film was produced. Blockbusters such as *Harry Potter and the Deathly Hallows 2* try to subvert society's normative values in regards to race, class, gender, and age but still inexorably move toward centrist endings that, ironically enough, support the very status quos they try to challenge: the inclusion of characters of color is mitigated by the film's whitest conclusion. Multicultural children's films, from within the US and from overseas, end less neatly. They leave open the possibility of the young spectator's resistance to what might be called the politics of the middle ground. Thus, whereas Hollywood centric films champion centrist positions through the erasure of the extremes of age (young and old) and the sketching in of the powerful symbol of the nuclear family, Thirdist films for the young such as *Osama* and *Turtles Can Fly* offer open endings consistent with their own cultural context and thus challenge not just the idea of a happy ending but Western views and beliefs of agency, subjectivity, and freedom therein implied.

The endings of movies, especially those related to children's films, are far from simple, convenient methods for concluding a narrative. Like children, endings are complex. It is not difficult to see how the happy endings of most mainstream movies from studios such as Disney, Pixar, DreamWorks, and so forth are intimately tied to capitalism, ideology, and psychoanalysis: fairy tale endings are commercially successful, emotionally cathartic, and wedded to traditional morals, gender relations, and core humanist values. But not all movies have conventional, fairy tale endings. The end of a Hollywood-type movie, populated by stars, grand sets, dazzling special effects, and the like, frequently confirms what we thought might happen (given the beginning, the ending can be guessed) but multicultural movies for the young such as *The Secret of Roan Inish*, that in ways tend more toward the casually lyrical rather than the carefully scripted, the thoughtful vignette rather than the focused scene, close with open-ended questions rather than neat answers. In other words, American, independent, and foreign multicultural children's movies, especially those focused on age, class, race, and gender themes, certainly conclude (the lights and credits come up and we leave) but not necessarily by bringing full circle the ever-popular, monomythic narrative typically used to structure the trajectory of most mainstream American children's films such as *Harry Potter and the Deathly Hallows 2*. Countercultural children's movies tend toward open-endedness, incompleteness. Mainstream children's films tend toward closure, regardless of the fissures and cracks—the structuring absences that nonetheless call to us from deep within the film's collective unconscious—that struggle for equality within the movie itself. In this regard, mainstream Western movies, as a reflection of late capitalism, ruthlessly destroy the radical, volatile, subversive elements—the movie's political unconscious in Jameson's words—that, id-like, have otherwise clung to life within the reel world of the filmic narrative, albeit at the margins. At the end of such movies, all the marginalized characters who have spent the life of the movie struggling for their identity—the very old and the very young, the inhumanly grotesque and the impossibly attractive, for example—are erased, eliminated, banished, and exiled from the cinematic world they have fought so hard to defend and replaced by the image of the middle aged, married couple and their children.

We have been suggesting that multicultural children's film, however they may be defined, is an important area of discussion future critics might have as part of a broader conversation about children's media or children's visual culture. We have also suggested that there is a pedagogical component to multicultural children's films. In the final chapter of *Unthinking Eurocentrism*, Shohat and Stam call for a "radical pedagogy of the mass media … [that] … would heighten awareness of all the cultural voices they relay."[8] As a way of suggesting what role scholars of children's films might play in the development and implementation of this radical pedagogy, imagine, if you will, the following MLA job posting:

A tenure track position at a mid-western university is available starting Fall 2025 in Children's Film Studies subject to university and department funding and Personnel Committee approval. A PhD in children's cinema and film is required with primary/secondary research areas in globalization, hybridity, mass media, diversity, and technology studies. Prospective candidates teach First, Second, Third, and Fourth World children's films at undergraduate and graduate levels supervise MA thesis and PhD dissertations, and propose special topics such as Gerontology, Aging Studies, and Films starring Children or Children's Bodies, the Imperial Imaginary, and Films from Iran, Iraq, and Afghanistan. Most significantly is the required outreach/community service. Prospective candidates will take children's films to children's classrooms and produce a radical pedagogy of the mass media. In subsequent interviews, prospective candidates must be able to articulate their vision of a future world in which children around the world use images of the child as created by children themselves.

We are not kidding around!

Notes

1 Ian Wojcik-Andrews, *Children's Films: History, Ideology, Pedagogy, Theory* (New York: Garland, 2000), 47.
2 Ella Shohat and Robert Stam, *Unthinking Eurocentrism: Multiculturalism and the Media* (New York: Routledge, 1994), 358.
3 Ibid., 357.
4 Richard Neupert, *The End: Narration and Closure in the Cinema* (Detroit: Wayne State University Press, 1995), 35.
5 Ibid., 41.
6 John Fiske, *Television Culture* (London: Metheun and Co., 1987), 249.
7 Nupert, *Narration and Closure*, 136.
8 Shohat and Stam, *Unthinking Eurocentrism*, 356.

Bibliography

Fiske, John. *Television Culture*. London: Metheun and Co., 1987.
Harry Potter and the Deathly Hallows 2. Dir. David Yates. Burbank, CA: Warner Bros., 2011. Film.
Kermode, Frank. *The Sense of an Ending: Studies in the Theory of Fiction*. Oxford: Oxford University Press, 1966.

National Council of Public Morals. *The Cinema: Its Present Position and Future Possibilities Being the Report of and Chief Evidence Taken by the Cinema Commission of Inquiry Instituted by the National Council of Public Morals.* New York: Arno Press and New York Times, 1917.

Neupert, Richard. *The End: Narration and Closure in the Cinema.* Detroit: Wayne State University Press, 1995.

Osama. Dir. Siddiq Barmak. Afghanistan: Barmak Film, 2003. Film.

The Princess and the Frog. Dir. Ron Clements and John Musker. Burbank, CA: Walt Disney Studios, 2009. Film.

The Secret of Roan Inish. Dir. John Sayles, 1994. Culver City, CA: Tristar Home Video, 1995. DVD.

Shohat, Ella and Robert Stam. *Unthinking Eurocentrism: Multiculturalism and the Media.* New York: Routledge, 1994.

Turtles Can Fly. Dir. Bahman Ghobadi. Iran: Mij Film Company, 2004. Film.

Wojcik-Andrews, Ian. *Children's Films: History, Ideology, Pedagogy, Theory.* New York: Garland, 2000.

Wolfenstein, Martha. "The Image of the Child in Contemporary Films," in Margaret Mead and Martha Wolfenstein (eds), *Childhood in Contemporary Cultures,* 277–93. Chicago: University of Chicago Press, 1955.

Zipes, Jack. *Breaking the Magic Spell: Radical Theories of Folk and Fairy Tales.* New York: Metheun, 1979.

Notes on Contributors

Michelle Ann Abate is an associate professor of literature for children and young adults at The Ohio State University. She is the author of three books of literary criticism: *Bloody Murder: The Homicide Tradition in Children's Literature* (Johns Hopkins University Press, 2013), *Raising Your Kids Right: Children's Literature and American Political Conservatism* (Rutgers University Press, 2010), and *Tomboys: A Literary and Cultural History* (Temple University Press, 2008).

Michelle Beissel Heath is an assistant professor of English at the University of Nebraska, Kearney, where she specializes in children's literature and nineteenth-century British literature. She has articles on nineteenth- and early twentieth-century children's play and literary texts that appear in *Childhood in Edwardian Fiction: Worlds Enough and Time* (Palgrave, 2008), *Oceania and the Victorian Imagination* (Ashgate, 2013), *Critical Survey*, and *Jeunesse: Young People, Texts, Cultures*.

Chris Foss is professor of English at the University of Mary Washington in Fredericksburg, Virginia, where he teaches a first-year seminar on representations of autism in literature and film and an upper-level course on disability and literature, in addition to courses in his primary area of specialization, Nineteenth-Century British Literature. His work has appeared in a variety of edited book collections and in journals such as *Disability Studies Quarterly*, *European Romantic Review*, *LIT: Literature Interpretation Theory*, *Literature/Film Quarterly*, and *Prism(s): Essays in Romanticism*.

Michael Howarth grew up in Falmouth, Massachusetts. After earning his BA in English at James Madison University, he entered the MFA Program in Writing at the University of Alaska Anchorage where he studied the novel and short story. Following his MFA, he attended the University of Louisiana where he earned his PhD in children's literature. He currently teaches children's literature and film studies at Missouri Southern State University, where he also directs the Honors Program. His work has appeared in such publications as *The*

Southwestern Review, Flashquake, Farmhouse Magazine, DASH Literary Journal, Mud Luscious, Jura Gentium Cinema, and *Interdisciplinary Humanities.*

Alexander N. Howe is an associate professor of English at the University of the District of Columbia where he teaches courses on American literature, literary theory, and film. He is the author of *It Didn't Mean Anything: A Psychoanalytic Reading of American Detective Fiction* (McFarland, 2008) and the co-editor of *Marcia Muller and the Female Private Eye: Essays on the Novels that Defined a Subgenre* (McFarland, 2008). He is currently completing a volume on female investigators in noir and neo-noir films.

Iris Shepard is an assistant professor at St Gregory University in Shawnee, Oklahoma. Her primary research interests include children's film and young adult literature. Her scholarly work has been published in *JAELP* and *Signal,* as well as in several essay collections. She is currently writing a YA dystopian novel.

Sally Sims Stokes is a librarian and social and cultural historian whose published work ranges from a study of the bicycle as an instrument for nineteenth-century dress reform to an analysis of religion as a factor in tenant selection in the New Deal town of Greenbelt, Maryland. Since 2004, she has been writing about the novels of Noel Streatfeild, focusing on Streatfeild's presentation of child performers in film, and on her perceptions of human behavior and family dynamics. Sally Stokes teaches in the Cultural Heritage Information Management program at the Catholic University of America.

Adam Wadenius earned his Master's degree in Film Studies at San Francisco State University, and he currently teaches Film, Media Studies, and Production for several colleges in the Bay Area. His research interests include the work of Julia Kristeva, horror and the abject, postmodern theory, cultural studies, and American independent cinema. He is currently working on a project entitled, "I Know Definitely You Are the Middle Piece," which examines the monstrous representation of bisexuality in Tom Six's *The Human Centipede.*

Brian Walter is associate professor of English and Director of Convocations at the St Louis College of Pharmacy. His scholarly and professional work has appeared in (among others) *Boulevard, The Southern Quarterly, Nabokov*

Studies, Music, Sound, and the Moving Image, and *CineAction*; authors, figures, and topics covered include Nabokov, Harington, Wharton, political dystopias on film, and tropes of American innocence. His areas of scholarly and professional interest include modern English and American literature, the novel, film and literature, and children's film and literature.

Bridget Whelan was born and raised in Lake Charles, LA. She graduated from McNeese State University in 2002, earning her Bachelor of Arts in English, and again in 2005, earning her Master of Arts in English. A lifelong love for the fantastic and the whimsical led her to pursue a PhD in English with a concentration in the field of children's literature. In 2012, she earned her Doctorate in English at the University of Louisiana at Lafayette and today continues to write and publish in her field. She currently teaches English at SOWELA Technical Community College.

David Whitley is on the faculty of Education at the University of Cambridge where he lectures on poetry, film, and children's literature. He is the co-editor, along with Morag Styles and Louise Joy, of *Poetry and Childhood* (Trentham, 2010) and author of *The Idea of Nature in Disney* (Ashgate, 2008). He is currently involved in a research project studying the benefits and possibilities of teaching poetry to students from elementary school through post-secondary education.

Kevin A. Wisniewski is a PhD candidate in Literacy, Language, and Culture at the University of Maryland Baltimore County. He is the editor of *The Comedy of Dave Chappelle: Critical Essays* (McFarland, 2009), and his essays and reviews have most recently appeared in *Genre, The Maryland Historical Magazine, Alphaville: Journal of Film and Screen Media, Southern Historian, RainTaxi: Review of Books*, and the anthology *The Stewart/Colbert Effect: Essays on the Real Impacts of Fake News* (McFarland, 2011). His poetry and poetry translations have been published in *The Chiron Review, The Sierra Nevada Review, basalt*, and *The Chariton Review*, among others. His current interests include print and digital culture, the history of publishing and social reading, and he teaches Public History at Stevenson University in Baltimore.

Ian Wojcik-Andrews teaches children's literature and children's film classes at Eastern Michigan University. He has just finished teaching a graduate class in Multicultural Children's Films (Winter 2013). Previous articles and books include "A History of Children's Cinema and Film: The Case of Multicultural Films" (2009) and *Children's Films: History, Ideology, Pedagogy, Theory* (2000). Other forthcoming articles are "A Multicultural History of Children's Films " (2013) and "Elder Quests and Kid Ventures Equals Kid Quests" (2013). He is a member of the ChLA.

Wynn Yarbrough teaches children's literature and media, English literature, and creative writing at the University of the District of Columbia. His research interests include anthropomorphic tales, gender, African-American children's poetry, and Edwardian literature. His book of poetry, *A Boy's Dream*, was published by Pessoa Press in 2011 and his *Masculinity in Children's Animal Stories, 1888–1928: A Critical Study of Anthropomorphic Tales by Wilde, Kipling, Potter, Grahame and Milne* is available from McFarland Press. He serves as Book Reviews Editor for Interdisciplinary Humanities and is a current board member of the Humanities Education and Research Association.

Index

abjection (Kristevean concept) 3, 14, 33–5, 37, 39–47
able bodies 126, 127
ableism 136n. 23
adolescence 5, 34, 46, 76, 193, 194, 196, 200, 208
  identity construction 196, 199, 200, 206, 207, 208
  role confusion 5, 195, 198, 204, 207
adult world 66, 75, 177, 197, 201, 203, 205
adulthood 21, 148, 175, 196, 198, 202, 203, 207, 208
advice literature 141 *see also* self help genre
Aesop's Fables 215
Afghanistan 227, 230
ageism 228, 229
ageist criticism 224
aggression 18, 37, 39, 178, 194
Aladdin, film 174–7,181, 226
alienation 15, 18
Althusser, Louis 227
Andersen, Hans Christian 82, 174
androcentrism 212–13, 217
anxiety 18, 35, 77, 195, 200, 203, 204
Aristotelianism 226
Asperger's Syndrome 4, 119, 120
Atwood, Margaret 173
Austen, Jane 183
autism 2, 4, 120, 121, 123, 126, 132, 134, 135–6n. 3
autist criticism 223
autistic children 120, 123, 133
Autistic Self Advocacy Network 120, 135–6n. 3
autistic thriller 121, 122, 123, 134, 135

Bambi film 6, 214, 215, 216, 218, 219, 220
Barmak, Siddiq 227, 228
Bee Movie, The 211
Bettelheim, Bruno 137n. 34, 200

branding
  marketing and consumption 150–2, 154
  cross-promotion 154, 157
bullying 101, 107, 108, 123, 140, 149, 204

Cabot, Meg 180
capitalism 6, 227, 228, 229
Chaucer 215
child
  audiences 141
  image of 12, 13, 14, 52, 53, 54, 55, 61, 64, 65, 66, 193, 224
  spectator 223
Child, The, film 130 *see Relative Fear*
childhood 3–7, 14, 16, 19, 21, 27, 34, 52, 54, 58, 61, 65, 66, 72, 75, 77, 81, 85–7, 131, 196, 200, 203, 204, 207, 224
  anxieties 193–5, 202
children's film and cinema 3, 6, 195, 224–30
children's film criticism 223–5
children's literature 1, 2, 3, 5, 84, 146, 150, 167, 169, 178, 195, 224
Children's Literature Association 1, 224
children's media 1, 2, 3, 5, 6, 223, 299
cinematography 195, 203
citizenship 4, 71, 72, 73, 75, 76, 78–80, 83, 86, 87, 97, 100, 101, 104, 106
Civil Rights Movement 226
class 6, 73, 74, 76, 77, 83, 101, 143, 147, 149, 169, 224, 227, 228, 229, 230
cliques 198
colonialism 224
Conrad, Joseph 215
Creed, Barbara 34–5, 39, 41, 45, 46

disability 120, 122, 124, 126, 128, 130–5
disabled bodies 129
Disney 5, 6, 84, 170–86, 211–17, 219, 220, 221, 223, 226, 228

Disney Princess brand (media and toy
    franchise) 174–5
Disney Princesses
    first wave 172, 177
    second wave 175–9, 182
    third wave 177, 179, 180, 182
Dream Works Studios 228
drugs 140, 147, 148
Dumbo, film 226

Ella Enchanted, film 180
endings (open and closed narratives) 228–9
environmental criticism 6, 212, 213, 223
environmentalism 211, 218
Erikson, Erik 198, 200–1
erotic images 51, 52, 56, 59, 61, 62, 64,
    65, 173

fairy tales 12, 83, 84, 167–8, 170–6, 179,
    180, 184, 186, 224
family (changing structure of) 98, 99, 100,
    108, 111, 149, 175, 196, 226, 228
family romance (Freudian concept) 175
father 20–7, 34–47, 60, 82, 102, 105, 124,
    129, 133, 168, 171, 174, 175, 177, 181
    law of 34, 35
    symbolic 20, 21
fatherhood 43, 45
feminine 3, 33–5, 41–4, 170, 174, 178,
    179, 182, 183
feminist criticism 5, 21, 172, 173, 176,
    172, 178, 180, 183, 184, 185, 186,
    220–1, 228
film studies 225, 230
Finding Nemo, film 6, 211, 220, 221, 223
First World children's film 226, 227, 229
First World cinema 224, 227
Fiske, John 227
folklore 12, 13, 24, 31
Foucault, Michel 14, 16, 20, 22, 25
Fourth World children's film 230
Freud, Anna 100, 101, 108
Freud, Sigmund 61, 75, 201

Geertz, Clifford 22
gender 1, 6, 39, 73, 83, 122, 123, 143, 144,
    147, 148, 149, 170, 176, 178, 202,
    224, 228, 229, 228

normative expectations 35, 37, 44, 74
German Expressionistic style 197
gothic imagery 193, 194, 195–6, 202, 206
Gothicism 195
Great Depression 171
Grimms' Fairy Tales 83, 167, 168, 170,
    174, 175
grotesque bodies 227
grotesque characters 194

Happiness, film 3, 33–47, 223
Happy Feet, film 211
Harry Potter and the Deathly Hallows 2,
    film 6, 224, 226, 227, 228, 229
Heart of Darkness 215
Henryson, Robert 215
heroes 106, 172, 176, 178, 184
heroines 97, 170–6, 179–81, 216
Hollywood film 6, 55, 104, 122, 150,
    223–5, 228, 229
Horatio Alger, character 141, 148
horror films 2, 3, 36, 39, 41, 194

identity (construction) 5, 26, 33, 40, 41,
    54, 71, 97, 11, 122, 130, 168, 195,
    197, 198, 206, 207, 208, 229
ideological criticism 4, 6, 13, 14, 34, 122,
    131, 144, 179, 211, 223, 226, 227,
    228
independence (child's quest for) 3, 5, 58,
    62, 71, 194, 197, 208
innocence 5, 11, 25, 55–9, 61, 63, 64, 65,
    196, 197, 198, 200, 202, 216

Jameson, Fredric 229
Joyce, James 219
Jungle Book, The, film 214, 220, 226

Kenan, Gil 5, 195, 197, 199, 200, 201, 203,
    205
Kermode, Frank 226
Kids are Americans Too 157–8
Kristeva, Julia 3, 14, 33, 34, 40–5
Kubrick, Stanley 3, 4, 54–6, 59–61, 64–7

Lacan, Jacques 21, 114n. 53
Lady in the Water film 11, 16, 27
Lebeau, Vicky 4, 24, 54, 55, 61, 66

liminal 3, 15, 18
Lion King, The, film 215, 220
Little House on the Prairie 171
Lolita, film (Kubrick) 3, 54, 55, 56, 58–60, 65, 66, 223
Lolita, film (Lyne) 3, 54, 55, 60–6, 223
Lolita, novel 51, 53, 54
Love in a Mist 97–100, 103–5, 108, 109, 111, 223
Lyne, Adrian 3, 15, 18

male gaze 52, 177, 201
marketing 1, 4, 5, 55, 149–54, 157, 175 *see also* branding
marketing (millennial) 157
marriage 18, 19, 24, 26, 172, 174, 179, 181–3, 185, 226
masculinity 3, 33, 34–47, 170, 179, 182
maternal 34, 35, 41, 43, 45, 47, 100, 102, 105, 109, 127
Mead, Margaret 223
media criticism 6, 223
Mercury Rising, film 4, 134, 223
Mickey Mouse, cartoons 215
minority cultures 225
mise-en-scène 3, 13, 35, 56, 60, 195, 203
Monster House, film 5, 195–208, 223
monsters 15, 17, 20, 22, 36, 40, 41, 46, 47, 56, 57, 193, 195, 196–200, 201–8
mothers 4, 11, 18, 19, 21, 23, 25, 27, 33–5, 41, 44–6, 56–8, 61, 65, 78, 83, 96, 97, 100–5, 107, 109, 110, 11, 123–8, 133, 158, 171, 177, 183, 185, 217–20, 228
Mulan, film 174, 177, 181, 183, 185, 226
multicultural children's films 224, 227, 228, 229, 230
Mulvey, Laura 52–3, 201

Nabokov, Vladimir 51, 53, 55, 60, 61, 65, 66
natural world 212, 2, 214–16, 218, 221
Newtown shooting 119, 121 *see also* Sandy Hook Elementary shooting
No-Spin Zone, The, 140, 159n. 4

O'Reilly Factor, The, 140, 159n. 4
O'Reilly Factor for Kids, The, 140, 145–9, 153, 156–8, 159n. 5, 223

Osama, film 225, 227, 228
otherness 13, 14, 15, 17, 22, 24, 54, 66, 74, 123, 126, 127, 129, 132, 133

parents 16, 20, 25, 36, 42, 76, 77, 85, 95, 96, 100–2, 105, 108, 124–8, 133, 140, 145, 148, 156, 157, 171, 175, 176, 181, 183, 184, 185, 194, 195, 197, 198, 201, 203, 205
paternal 14, 35, 41, 43, 45–7
patriarchy 21, 35, 38
peer pressure 153, 195, 197
Pixar 5, 182, 184, 185, 211, 220, 228
Playground Association 75, 78, 79, 81, 82, 84
playground movement 4, 73, 82
playgrounds 3, 4, 71–84, 223
Pocahontas, film 174, 226
polycentric multiculturalism 224
post-enlightenment philosophy 212
postmodernism 12, 34
Princess *see* Disney Princesses
Princess and the Frog, film 181, 182, 184, 226
psychoanalysis 5, 21, 34, 100, 102, 107, 228
    Erikson 198, 200–1
    Freud, Anna 100, 101, 108
    Freud, Sigmund 61, 75, 201
    Lacan 21, 114n. 53
psychoanalytic criticism 223, 228
psychosocial development 195
puberty 15, 21, 153, 195, 196, 198, 201, 202

race 5, 6, 143, 147, 224, 226, 228, 229
Rain Man, film 122–3
realism 53, 55, 171, 213, 215, 216, 217, 227
Relative Fear, film 4, 123–31, 133, 134, 135

Sandy Hook Elementary shooting 119, 121 *see also* Newtown shooting
scopophilia 201
Secret of Roan Inish, The, film 229
Sedgwick, Eve Kosofsky 158
self-esteem 140, 147, 148
self-help genre 141, 142, 143, 145, 147, 153, 223

self-help movement 144
semiotic (Kristevean concept) 1, 34, 35, 45, 47
semiotics 1
sentimental narratives 15, 26, 82, 123, 129–35, 172, 219, 221
serial killers 127, 130, 131
sex and sexuality 15, 16, 21, 34–40, 42–5, 47, 51, 53, 54, 53–63, 65, 66, 133, 140, 149, 172, 186, 195, 201, 202
Shohat, Ella 224, 229
Shyamalan, M. Night 3, 11–21, 23–7
siblings 148
Silent Fall, film 131, 132, 134
Sixth Sense, The, film 16–18, 27, 223
Snow White, film 5, 83, 170–2, 215, 216, 217
Stam, Robert 224, 229
Streatfeild, Noel 4, 95–111, 223
subjectivity 21, 34, 72, 74, 228

Tarzan, film 176, 215
television 139, 140, 141, 144, 150, 153, 156, 158, 226, 227

Thirdist cinema 224, 225, 226, 228
Time for Drunken Horses, A, film 227
Turtles Can Fly, film 227, 228

Unbreakable, film 16, 17, 26, 27

Victorian 11, 13, 14, 52, 83, 172
Village, The, film 16, 19, 20, 21, 24
violence 2, 11, 19, 21, 22, 24, 27, 77, 119, 120, 121, 127, 128
voyeurism 201

Wall-E, film 211
wildness 212, 213, 215, 218 *see also* natural world

young readers 95, 140–1, 145–7, 149, 153, 158, 169, 175

Zipes, Jack 171, 173, 224